Rising powers, global go
global ethics

Two of the dominant themes of international relations scholarship over the last decade have been global governance and rising powers. Underlying both discussions are profound ethical questions about how the world should be ordered, who is responsible for addressing global problems, how change can be managed, and how global governance can be made to work for peoples in developing as well as developed states. Yet, these are often not addressed or only briefly mentioned as ethical dilemmas by commentators.

This book seeks to ask critical and profound questions about what relative shifts in power among states might mean for the ethics and practice of global governance. Three key questions are addressed throughout the volume:

- Who is rising and how?
- How does this impact on global governance?
- What are the implications of these developments for global ethics?

Through these questions, some of the key academics in the field explore how far debates over global ethics are really between competing visions of how international society should be governed, as opposed to tensions within the same broad paradigm. By examining how governance works in practice across the Middle East, Africa, and Asia, the contributors to this volume seek to critique the way global governance discourse masks the exercise of power by elites and states, both developed and rising.

This work will be essential reading for all those with an interest in the future of international relations and global governance.

Jamie Gaskarth is Associate Professor (Senior Lecturer) in International Relations in the School of Government at Plymouth University. He is an elected Trustee of the British International Studies Association (BISA) and Convenor of BISA's Foreign Policy Working Group.

Global Institutions

Edited by Thomas G. Weiss
The CUNY Graduate Center, New York, USA
and Rorden Wilkinson
University of Sussex, Brighton, UK

About the series

The "Global Institutions Series" provides cutting-edge books about many aspects of what we know as "global governance." It emerges from our shared frustrations with the state of available knowledge—electronic and print-wise, for research and teaching—in the area. The series is designed as a resource for those interested in exploring issues of international organization and global governance. And since the first volumes appeared in 2005, we have taken significant strides toward filling conceptual gaps.

The series consists of three related "streams" distinguished by their blue, red, and green covers. The blue volumes, comprising the majority of the books in the series, provide user-friendly and short (usually no more than 50,000 words) but authoritative guides to major global and regional organizations, as well as key issues in the global governance of security, the environment, human rights, poverty, and humanitarian action among others. The books with red covers are designed to present original research and serve as extended and more specialized treatments of issues pertinent for advancing understanding about global governance. And the volumes with green covers—the most recent departure in the series—are comprehensive and accessible accounts of the major theoretical approaches to global governance and international organization.

The books in each of the streams are written by experts in the field, ranging from the most senior and respected authors to first-rate scholars at the beginning of their careers. In combination, the three components of the series—blue, red, and green—serve as key resources for faculty, students, and practitioners alike. The works in the blue and green streams have value as core and complementary readings in courses on, among other things, international organization, global governance, international law, international relations, and international political economy; the red volumes allow further reflection and investigation in these and related areas.

The books in the series also provide a segue to the foundation volume that offers the most comprehensive textbook treatment available dealing with all the major issues, approaches, institutions, and actors in contemporary global governance—our edited work *International Organization and Global Governance* (2014)—a volume to which many of the authors in the series have contributed essays.

Understanding global governance—past, present, and future—is far from a finished journey. The books in this series nonetheless represent significant steps toward a better way of conceiving contemporary problems and issues as well as, hopefully, doing something to improve world order. We value the feedback from our readers and their role in helping shape the on-going development of the series.

A complete list of titles appears at the end of this book. The most recent titles in the series are:

Wartime Origins and the Future United Nations (2015)
edited by Dan Plesch and Thomas G. Weiss

International Judicial Institutions (2nd edition, 2015)
by Richard J. Goldstone and Adam M. Smith

The NGO Challenge for International Relations Theory (2014)
edited by William E. DeMars and Dennis Dijkzeul

21st Century Democracy Promotion in the Americas (2014)
by Jorge Heine and Brigitte Weiffen

BRICS and Coexistence (2014)
edited by Cedric de Coning, Thomas Mandrup, and Liselotte Odgaard

IBSA (2014)
by Oliver Stuenkel

Making Global Institutions Work (2014)
edited by Kate Brennan

Rising powers, global governance, and global ethics

Edited by
Jamie Gaskarth

Routledge
Taylor & Francis Group

LONDON AND NEW YORK

First published 2015
by Routledge
2 Park Square, Milton Park, Abingdon, Oxon OX14 4RN

and by Routledge
711 Third Avenue, New York, NY 10017

*Routledge is an imprint of the Taylor & Francis Group, an informa
business*

British Library Cataloguing in Publication Data
A catalogue record for this book is available from the British
Library

Library of Congress Cataloging in Publication Data
Gaskarth, Jamie.
  Rising powers, global governance and global ethics / edited by
Jamie Gaskarth.
    pages cm
  Includes bibliographical references and index.
  1. Balance of power. 2. Power (Social sciences)–Moral and ethical
aspects. 3. Globalization. 4. International relations. I. Gaskarth,
Jamie, 1976- II. Title.
  JZ1313.G37 2015
  172'.4–dc23
              2014031585

ISBN: 978-1-138-82686-1 (hbk)
ISBN: 978-1-138-82687-8 (pbk)
ISBN: 978-1-315-73890-1 (ebk)

Typeset in Times New Roman
by Taylor & Francis Books

Printed and bound by CPI Group (UK) Ltd, Croydon, CR0 4Y

Contents

List of illustrations

Figure

Tables

Contributors

Mark Bevir is a Professor of Political Science at the University of California, Berkeley. He is the author or co-author of a number of books including recently *The Making of British Socialism* (2011), *Governance: A Very Short Introduction* (2012), and *A Theory of Governance* (2013).

Thomas Biersteker is Gasteyger Professor of International Security and Director of the Programme for the Study of International Governance at the Graduate Institute, Geneva. He is the author/editor/co-editor of ten books, including *State Sovereignty as Social Construct* (1996), *The Emergence of Private Authority in Global Governance* (2002), and *UN Targeted Sanctions as Instruments of Global Governance* (forthcoming), and was the principal developer of SanctionsApp, a tool for mobile devices created in 2013 to increase access to information and improve the quality of discourse about targeted sanctions at the UN Security Council. He received his PhD and MS from the Massachusetts Institute of Technology and his BA from the University of Chicago.

Shaun Breslin is Professor of Politics and International Studies at the University of Warwick, where he is also director of the Centre for the Study of Globalization and Regionalization. He is also co-editor of the *Pacific Review* and an Associate Fellow in the Chatham House Asia Programme. He is the author/editor/co-editor of *China and the Global Political Economy* (2009), *China and the World* (2014), *Comparative Regional Security Governance* (2012), *Chinese Politics and International Relations: Innovation and Invention* (2013), among other titles.

P.N. Chatterje-Doody is a doctoral candidate at the University of Manchester. Her research interests include the politics of national identity, history, narrative, and foreign and security policy, with a particular focus on Russia and the post-Soviet space. Recent publications include chapters in edited volumes and "Harnessing History: Narratives, Identity and Perceptions of Russia's Post-Soviet role" in *Politics* (2014).

Rebecca Davies is a Lecturer in the School of Government, Plymouth University, and a Research Fellow at the Centre for International and Comparative Politics, Stellenbosch University, South Africa. Her current research focuses on the role of non-state actors in development and governance in sub-Saharan Africa, with a particular focus on diasporas in the neo-patrimonial development states of Ghana and Rwanda. She has published in *Third World Quarterly*, *Review of African Political Economy*, *Progress in Development Studies*, and *African Studies*.

Louise Fawcett is Professor of International Relations and Wilfrid Knapp Fellow at St Catherine's College, Oxford. She is the author/editor/co-editor of *International Relations of the Middle East* (3rd edn 2013), *Iran and the Cold War* (2009), *Regionalism and Governance in the Americas* (2005), *The Third World Beyond the Cold War* (2000), and *Regionalism in World Politics* (1995). Louise is a member of the International Advisory Board of the Chatham House-based journal *International Affairs* and the United Nations University Centre for Regional Integration Studies (UNU-CRIS).

Yale H. Ferguson is Professorial Fellow, Division of Global Affairs, Rutgers University-Newark and Emeritus Professor of Global and International Affairs. He has published over 60 articles/book chapters and 12 books, including (with R.W. Mansbach) *Globalization: The Return of Borders to a Borderless World?*, *A World of Polities*, *Remapping Global Politics*, *The Elusive Quest Continues*, *Polities*; and *The Web of World Politics*. He has three times been a Visiting Fellow at the University of Cambridge, Senior Fellow at the Norwegian Nobel Institute, Visiting Scholar at University of Padova (Italy), and Fulbright Professor and later Honorary Professor at the University of Salzburg (Austria).

Jamie Gaskarth is Associate Professor (Senior Lecturer) in International Relations in the School of Government, Plymouth University. He is the author/co-editor of *British Foreign Policy: The New Labour Years* (2011), *British Foreign Policy* (2013), and *British Foreign Policy and the National Interest* (2014), and has published on international ethics and foreign policy in the *European Journal of*

International Relations, International Affairs, Review of International Studies, and *Foreign Policy Analysis,* among other journals.

Patrick Holden is a Lecturer in the School of Government at Plymouth University. He has published widely on European and global trade and development politics. He is the author of *In Search of Structural Power* (2009), a monograph on structural power and European aid policy, as well as *A Dictionary of International Trade Organizations and Agreements* (2011). Patrick is a member of the editorial board of *Mediterranean Politics,* an associate of Trinity College Dublin's Institute for International Integration Studies, and a former Visiting Lecturer at Tongji University, Shanghai.

Catherine Jones is a Post-Doctoral Fellow in East Asia at the Department of Politics and International Studies at the University of Warwick. Her research focuses on Asian states' interactions with meta-international institutions. To date, this work has focused on China and issues of security and development as well as the normative power of ASEAN as a collective. She completed her PhD at the University of Reading where she was funded by the Leverhulme Trust through their major research project 'The Liberal Way of War'.

Erica Moret is a Research Associate at Oxford University's 'Changing Character of War' Programme and Visiting Fellow at the Programme for the Study of International Governance at the Graduate Institute for International and Development Studies, Geneva. She currently works on the shifting role of rising powers in international security governance, with a particular focus on economic sanctions and nuclear non-proliferation. Her DPhil (PhD) (Jesus College, Oxford, 2007) explored the political economy of US sanctions on Cuba and earlier publications include a focus on the humanitarian impacts of EU sanctions, and the role of UNSC sanctions in conflict resolution, international affairs and development.

Ian Taylor is a Professor in International Relations and African Politics in the School of International Relations, University of St. Andrews and Chair Professor in the School of International Studies, Renmin University, China. He is also Professor Extraordinary in Political Science at the University of Stellenbosch, South Africa, and an Honorary Professor in the Institute of African Studies, China. He has authored eight scholarly books, edited another eight and has published over 60 peer-reviewed academic articles, over 60 book chapters and numerous working papers and reports. He holds a DPhil from the University of Stellenbosch and an MPhil from the

University of Hong Kong. He has conducted research in and/or visited 38 African countries.

Thomas G. Weiss is Presidential Professor of Political Science and Director Emeritus of the Ralph Bunche Institute for International Studies, The City University of New York's Graduate Center, and Research Professor at SOAS, University of London. Former president of the International Studies Association and chair of the Academic Council on the United Nations, he has written extensively about multilateralism, including his latest single-authored books *Governing the World? Addressing "Problems without Passports"* (2014), *Global Governance: Why? What? Whither?* (2013), *Humanitarian Business* (2013), and *What's Wrong with the United Nations and How to Fix It* (2012).

Rorden Wilkinson is Professor and Chair of the Department of International Relations at the University of Sussex and a Professorial Fellow at the Brooks World Poverty Institute at the University of Manchester. His most recent works include: *What's Wrong with the WTO and How to Fix it* (2014), *International Organization and Global Governance* (2014), *Trade, Poverty, Development: Getting beyond the WTO's Doha Deadlock* (2013), and *The Millennium Development Goals and Beyond: Global Development after 2015* (2012). Rorden co-edits the *Global Institutions* series for Routledge and is the 2014 recipient of the International Studies Association Society for Women in International Political Economy Mentoring Award.

Acknowledgments

This book emerged from an Economic and Social Research Council-funded seminar series entitled "Normative Challenges to International Society: Rising Powers and Global Responses" (ES/J021261/1). I am very grateful to the ESRC for their support for this project. Details of the seminars and a bibliography are available at: www.risingpowers globalresponses.com.

The editor would also like to thank all the participants at the three events for their lively contributions to discussion and King's College, London and the School of Government, Plymouth University for generously hosting two of the seminars. The merits of this volume owe a huge amount to the help and encouragement of Thomas Weiss and Rorden Wilkinson, who suggested contributors, offered their intellectual insights at the seminar as well as on the subsequent manuscript, and kept the momentum going with their continued interest in the project. Thank you so much. Along the way, a number of other academics have been incredibly helpful at various stages, including Ian Hall, Steve Burman, Sophie Harman, Chris Brown, James Pattison, Jason Ralph, Tim Dunne, Mark Bevir, Kim Hutchings, Mervyn Frost, David Armstrong, Cornelia Navari, and Graeme Herd. All of these people combine intellectual brilliance with a friendly and supportive countenance to make the academic world a sunnier place to inhabit.

I would finally like to thank Nicola Langdon and Ben Nutt, my doctoral students and two future academic stars, for their assistance throughout the series. This book is dedicated to them.

Abbreviations

ACFTA	China-ASEAN Free Trade Agreement (aka CAFTA)
ACUNS	Academic Council on the United Nations System
ADIZ	Air Defense Identification Zone
APEC	Asia-Pacific Economic Cooperation
ASEAN	Association of South Eastern Nations
AU	African Union
BASIC	Brazil, South Africa, India, China
BICs	Brazil, India, China
BRICs	Brazil, Russia, India, China
BRICS	Brazil, Russia, India, China, South Africa
CELAC	Community of Latin American and Caribbean States
CENTO	Central Eastern Treaty Organization
CETA	Comprehensive Economic and Trade Agreement
CIS	Commonwealth of Independent States
CIVETS	Columbia, Indonesia, Vietnam, Egypt, Turkey, and South Africa
CPI	Commodity Price Index
CSTO	Collective Security Treaty Organization
CTBT	Comprehensive Nuclear Test Ban Treaty
DAC	Development Assistance Committee
DPRK	Democratic People's Republic of Korea
DSB	Dispute Settlement Body
ECU	Eurasian Customs Union
EU	European Union
EurAsEC	Eurasian Economic Community
FDI	Foreign Direct Investment
FOCAC	Forum on China-Africa Cooperation
GCC	Gulf Cooperation Council
GDP	Gross Domestic Product
GLCs	government-linked companies

GVCs	Global Value Chains
HIPC	Heavily Indebted Poor Countries Initiative
HLP	High Level Panel
IAEA	International Atomic Energy Agency
IBSA	India, Brazil, South Africa
IFIs	International Financial Institutions
IMF	International Monetary Fund
IO	International Organization
ITU	International Telecommunications Union
LAS	League of Arab States
LDCs	least developed countries
MDGs	Millennium Development Goals
MDRI	Multilateral Debt Relief Initiative
MINT	Mexico, Indonesia, Nigeria, Turkey
MIST	Mexico, Indonesia, South Korea, Turkey
MOFA	Ministry of Foreign Affairs
MOFTEC	Ministry of Foreign Trade and Economic Cooperation
NAM	Non-Aligned Movement
NEPAD	New Partnership for African Development
NGO	Non-governmental organisation
NIEO	New International Economic Order
NPT	Non-Proliferation Treaty (nuclear)
NSAs	Non-state actors
NSG	Nuclear Suppliers Group
OAPEC	Organization of Arab Petroleum Exporting Countries
OAS	Organization of American States
OAU	Organization of African Unity
OECD	Organisation for Economic Co-operation and Development
OIC	Organization of Islamic Cooperation
OPEC	Organization of the Petroleum Exporting Countries
OSCE	Organization for Security and Cooperation in Europe
PCA	Partnership and Cooperation Agreement
PLO	Palestinian Liberation Organization
PSI	Proliferation Security Initiative
R2P	Responsibility to Protect
RCEP	Regional Comprehensive Economic Partnership
RwP	Responsibility Whilst Protecting
SEZs	Special Economic Zones
SME	Small and medium enterprise
SOE	state-owned enterprises
SSA	Sub-Saharan Africa

SSM	Special Safeguard Mechanism
TNC	Transnational Corporation
TPP	Trans-Pacific Partnership
T-TIP	United States Transatlantic Trade and Investment Partnership
UNCTAD	United Nations Conference on Trade and Development
UNSC	United Nations Security Council
UNSCR	United Nations Security Council Resolution
WIPO	World Intellectual Property Organization
WTO	World Trade Organization

Introduction

Jamie Gaskarth

- **Rising power?**
- **The BRICS (and other acronyms)**
- **Global governance**
- **Global ethics**
- **The structure of this volume**

Two major themes of discussion in international relations scholarship over the last decade have been global governance and rising powers. The first is indelibly linked to globalization: the freer movement of goods, services, people, and information globally.[1] This process has reduced the salience of borders, challenged the primacy of national governments, and highlighted the existence of transnational problems that are beyond the capacity of individual states to resolve. In response, there has been a proliferation of new actors, institutions, regulatory mechanisms, and practices seeking to shape human behavior in the social, political, and economic spheres. The term governance emerged to capture this more fluid and diffuse policy environment. Governments are no longer seen as the only, or even at times the primary, actors that matter in international politics. Rather, we are said to have entered a "post-sovereign" world in which the management and control of political outcomes is shared by state and non-state, public and private actors.[2]

The second, and seemingly contradictory narrative is that certain states are rising in world politics and that this represents a profound challenge to both the structure of the international system and the normative foundation of international society. In describing these states as rising or emerging powers, the locus of power is portrayed as national, sovereign spaces, rather than transnational or sub-state groups. For all the talk of a globalizing world, commentators see international society and law as created and maintained by states (particularly Anglo-European, developed ones). With a shift in relative power towards rising states, new patterns of order underpinned by new normative ideas are expected to emerge. In the cases of China and India, their economic rise is seen as inevitably leading to political and ethical influence.[3] Meanwhile, Russia and Brazil have resisted Western norm entrepreneurship, notably in their criticism of the logic and conduct of the responsibility to protect and humanitarian intervention.

Importantly, these states place great emphasis on sovereignty and autonomy and so potentially threaten to unravel the institutions of global governance, especially those that seek to pool sovereignty and reduce the freedom of action of individual states. In their place, inter-governmental groupings such as the BRICS (Brazil, Russia, India, China and South Africa), BASIC (Brazil, South Africa, India, and China) and IBSA (India, Brazil, and South Africa) are touted as potential challengers to the dominance of previous configurations such as the G7, or the P5 of the UN Security Council (UNSC). In a reversal of the trend towards global norm convergence, scholars and commentators see a more fragmented future for international society, in which regional and national forms of governance will hold sway.

Underlying both discussions are profound ethical questions about how the world should be ordered, who is responsible for addressing global problems, how change can be managed, and how global governance can be made to work for peoples in developing as well as developed states. Yet, these are often not addressed as ethical dilemmas in the literature. Global governance is sometimes conveyed as a process where agency is all but lost because of the complexity of the decision-making environment and the myriad range of actors who contribute to outcomes. Policy-making becomes a matter of finding fixes to problems and so is depicted as a technical and managerial exercise rather than a moral one. According to Antonio Franceschet, the liberal assumption that transnational cooperation is inherently good threatens to mask the "existing power hierarchies in world politics and the distributive effects of the political economy of global governance."[4] In other words, there are losers as well as winners from the spread of global governance.[5]

At the same time, the rising powers literature often presents a structuralist interpretation of history and then from this extrapolates predictions about future behavior. These accounts assume that, regardless of variations in the domestic politics of states, states behave in like ways given the common condition of international anarchy. They take the desire for power maximization for granted, and see international norms and societal practices as the manifestation of underlying material power; the corollary of this being that when material power changes, so will global norms. Newly powerful states will want to shape a world that fits their material interests and declining powers will no longer be able to impose their own values or resist those of other rising states. In other words, global ethics are merely the epiphenomena of material structures.

This volume seeks to address this gap in the literature by asking critical and profound questions about what relative shifts in power among states might mean for the ethics and practice of global governance. Three key questions are addressed throughout the volume, namely: Who is rising and how? How does this impact on global governance? What are the implications of these developments for global ethics?

The first question concerns whether grouping supposedly rising states together under acronyms such as BRICs (Brazil, Russia India, China), BRICS, CIVETS (Columbia, Indonesia, Vietnam, Egypt, Turkey and South Africa), MIST (Mexico, Indonesia, South Korea, Turkey), and MINT (Mexico, Indonesia, Nigeria and Turkey) is appropriate. Some states are rising within their region, whereas others are having an impact outside, on other continents. Beyond the BRICS, a host of states are seeing a rise in their economic capacity. These states may have contradictory or separate goals, distinct cultural ideas and norms, and differing resources which resist simple comparisons. There is also a question mark over how far it is really the state that is rising (implying the whole of the community within its borders) rather than simply a select stratum of society. In other words, should we be discussing rising elites rather than rising states or powers? Linked to this debate is the problem of identifying the economic and ideological roots of the discourse on rising powers.

This leads us to the second theme: how does the relative increase in power of some states impact on global governance? Does this mean that state agency is being reasserted and global governance arrangements undermined and fragmented? Many rising powers have resisted efforts to solidify common global values through the coercive use of force. The way in which governance arrangements are often weighted towards developed states has come under scrutiny and existing institutions have, at times, been challenged and subverted by new groups of rising states. Dominant Western ideas about how governance should be practiced, from the liberalization of markets and privatization of state industries to the regulation of trade, reach of civil society, pooling of sovereignty, and proliferation of networks are not universally accepted. Therefore, it is important to consider what new forms of social knowledge (if any), or adaptations of existing ideas, are being advanced by the rising powers. Does governance mean the same to them as it does to elites and commentators in the established developed states? What kind of governance arrangements do they favor and how are they advancing them? Do these assumptions change depending on *where* governance is occurring, geographically and politically?

Thirdly, the book seeks to examine how these developments impact on global ethics. There is an often implied assumption in the rising powers discussion that economic power naturally translates into normative power. However, this has not been the case historically. Not only have rising states in the past struggled to change global norms and promote their own ethics, but declining states have continued to exert social and normative influence despite a relative weakening of their material strength. Moreover, it is questionable how far rising powers really seek to overturn or challenge global normative frameworks. The case could be made that it is the United States and European states that have most dramatically questioned global ethics in recent years, with other states seeking to uphold prior and longstanding assumptions about sovereignty and responsibility.[6]

Thus, the authors critically examine how far debates over global ethics are really between competing visions of how international society should be governed, as opposed to tensions within the same broad paradigm. Within this discussion, many of the chapters also seek to problematize the assumption that global governance itself represents some form of public good. The liberal notion that cooperation is itself desirable tends to downplay the coercive elements of governance and makes efforts to resist such arrangements seem unreasonable. By examining how governance works in practice across the Middle East, Africa, and Asia, the contributors to this volume often seek to critique the way global governance discourse masks the exercise of power by elites and states, both developed and rising.

In sum, the book's major contribution is not only the way its authors synthesize a range of diverse literatures to highlight important connections between them, but also how they challenge and critique the assumptions made about governance, power, and ethics in contemporary global politics. There have been occasional studies of ethics and global governance[7], rising powers and global governance[8]; and a number of texts on rising powers in recent years[9]; but none combines in one volume an examination of the ethics of global governance with a critique of the conceptual and practical discussion on the impact of rising powers.

For the rest of this introduction I intend to sketch out in more detail some of the major debates and assumptions in the literature on rising powers and global governance. This will provide a context to the particular contributions of the chapters that follow. Although the authors in this volume examine a range of different case studies and theories, they share a desire to highlight and critique the conceptual framework currently in use to understand global order and governance.

Rising power?

Surveying the literature on rising powers, it becomes apparent how dominated it is by consideration of China's rise; specifically, there is much concern over how this is likely to affect the United States' position in world politics and the forms of global order that it supports. A vocal group of commentators has put forward the view, based on power transition theories, that this will be a destabilizing influence on world order and that great power competition—and hence conflict—will likely be the result. Power transition theory incorporates a range of scholars, using different case studies and coming from a variety of theoretical backgrounds. However, there is broad agreement among them that if a state rises in the international structure such that it begins to challenge or even overtake the economic and military capacity of the dominant power or powers within the existing order, this will give rise to global insecurity. As the rising state's capabilities expand, so will their policy goals, meaning they will want a greater say in international decision-making. To achieve this, existing patterns of organization will usually have to be rearranged to accommodate them, and new rules and practices instituted.

These changes introduce greater insecurity into the system as a whole by unsettling existing normative assumptions and providing a more heterogeneous set of "interests, concerns, values and historical memories."[10] Most importantly, they may lead to declining states fearing a "loss of control," insecurity about their status in world politics, and worries about their capacity to defend themselves from the potential threat from emerging states.[11] The risk of conflict is seen as not just deriving from the rising state seeking to bring about change by force, but also from established states wishing to preempt challengers and defend the status quo. Thus, the United States' National Security Strategy of 2002 promised that "America will act to prevent any other state from building up military capabilities in the hope of 'surpassing, or even equaling, the power of the United States.'"[12]

Although most often associated with the structuralist analysis of neorealists like John J. Mearsheimer,[13] the perception of China's rise threatening international order has also been supported by liberal,

Marxist, and constructivist scholars. Aaron Friedberg notes that liberal beliefs about the virtues of the democratic peace thesis—the view that liberal democracies do not go to war with each other—can lead to the obverse perception that authoritarian non-democratic states are inherently threatening.[14] Constructivist scholars have drawn attention to Chinese nationalism as a powerful influence on how that state frames its relations with others.[15] Tow and Rigby have identified a recurring nationalist strain of Chinese thought which argues that "the decline of US power is inevitable, and...their country should stand up to Washington more directly and exert global leadership."[16] These arguments can be linked in that the illegitimacy of China's government (in liberals' eyes at least), with its lack of civil liberties, means that it has to appeal to nationalist sentiments to justify its existence. Meanwhile, for Marxists "economic expansion means imperialist competition for resources and markets that leads to wars."[17]

To reinforce this sense of China as a threat or challenger to both the United States and the current configuration of world order it upholds, scholars have questioned Chinese government narratives about their peaceful history and current intentions. Ja Ian Chong has recently critiqued a number of myths of Chinese history that are pervasive in much of the discussion of China's rise, namely: that China was historically unified and internally stable; that its regional hegemony was peaceful; and that Chinese elites had a proud tradition of resisting foreign intervention.[18] Chong concludes that "Closer readings of history suggest that an ascendant China presents more a variation on major power behaviour than an exception."[19] The former Australian Prime Minister, Kevin Rudd, describes China as having a "hard-line, realist view of international relations," which he partly attributes to their absorption of Western IR theorists such as Clausewitz, Carr, and Morgenthau who are "mandatory reading in military academies."[20] In this analysis, the transference of social knowledge is actually undermining efforts at cooperation and creating more conflictual international relations.

The China threat thesis is also supported by a particular interpretation of the recent record of Chinese engagement with the liberal world order. Ronald Tammen notes that although China may have joined the World Trade Organization (WTO) in 2001, this is contrasted with "the Chinese refusal to cooperate fully with international treaties and organizations dealing with proliferation of weapons of mass destruction and associated delivery systems. Libya, Pakistan, Iran, and North Korea have all benefited from covert Chinese proliferation," activities which he sees as signaling "a degree of dissatisfaction with prevailing international norms under US leadership."[21] China has faced allegations that they are behind cyber attacks on Western firms and government agencies. When combined with a number of high profile territorial disputes, commentators see this as evidence of an increasingly aggressive Chinese foreign policy. According to Minxin Pei, "China's current acquiescence in this order does not add up to an endorsement of it."[22] Rather, it is merely a reflection of their relative weakness vis-à-vis the United States. Fundamental differences between the openness of the liberal international order and the closed domestic political system of China mean that "it is doubtful that Chinese elites will ever view the Western order as legitimate, even if they concede its practical usefulness."[23]

There are a number of problems with power transition theory and associated arguments framing China as a threat to global order (and hence governance). The historical basis of assertions about what happens when new powers emerge is very narrow, largely focusing on the European experience, with a particular emphasis on Germany prior to each of the World Wars. That one state failed twice to be accommodated peacefully by international society is hardly compelling evidence that China, a non-European state with a very different history and culture, will encounter the same problems. Important social ideas that have bred aggressive behavior in the past, such as feelings of racial superiority, the notion that military power is evidence of moral strength, and the colonialist project to spread civilization to barbarians and savages via conquest, have been comprehensively marginalized in international society. These unit-level changes in social beliefs make historical comparisons problematic because the world has changed in ways that have had an impact on behavior. Narratives of power transition sometimes seem to imply that states are rising in a political vacuum; whereas in reality they are subject to considerable pressures of socialization from international society.[24]

In addition, contemporary international relations are now far more institutionalized than they were in the past. Rather than a state's rise leading to conflict, liberals argue that they become increasingly enmeshed in these frameworks and as a result are drawn towards "more cooperative patterns of behaviour."[25] Perhaps the most optimistic adherent to this view is G. John Ikenberry, who has authored a series of essays suggesting that the liberal world order will continue to thrive despite the rise of an authoritarian state such as China. Ikenberry asserts that "compared to past international orders that rising states have confronted, this order is easier to join and harder to overturn."[26] The global public goods that the liberal order produces, such as a rule-based system of relatively open markets, mechanisms to resolve disputes, and recognition of sovereignty and non-interference (allowing for national differences in political and social cultures), are ones to which all states broadly subscribe. The main sources of tension, according to Ikenberry, are over "rights and privileges in the global political hierarchy"[27] rather than ideology, and China is "increasingly working within, rather than outside of, the Western order."[28] This is supported by Alastair Iain Johnston who asserts that studies of China's involvement in the World Bank and International Monetary Fund (IMF) suggest they are a constructive member of these organizations which follows the rules and does not try and subvert them in their own favor.[29] Having been able to rise to a position of immense importance in the current order, the question as Miles Kahler puts it is "why should governments endanger the institutional formula that has brought them success?"[30]

It is not surprising that these two major factors in global politics, ideas and institutions, are not considered by structuralist analyses as they are outside the scope of their theories. However, if we move away from a language of threats, competition, and conflict, a fundamental question of global governance in the coming decades will be how to manage change and facilitate peaceful interaction between emerging and developed states. This will involve the exchange of ideas and ethical assumptions, as well as relying heavily on the institutions of global politics to provide forums and mechanisms to do so amicably. Scholarship too can fulfill a useful function by avoiding simplistic historical analogies and instead promoting a deeper understanding of how policymakers are influenced by the past—and how entrenched attitudes might be transformed in the future.

A number of the chapters in this volume set out to do just that. For instance, Jones and Breslin see Chinese foreign policy-making as much more complex than any rational actor model would suggest. China's relations with its neighbors are influenced by local, national, and regional politics and these can have important effects on the pursuance of policy goals. Interpreting Chinese behavior as part of some grand struggle for power or resistance to global norms may ignore the reality of China's fragmented policy-making apparatus. In their section on China, Bevir and Gaskarth find deep cultural fears over disorder that make comparisons between China and other rising states of the past, such as Nazi Germany, wide of the mark. Yale Ferguson critiques the sense of China's inexorable rise and problematizes the narrow interpretation of what it takes to be a hegemon in world order. Meanwhile, Weiss and Wilkinson challenge scholars to theorize changes *of* and *in* global governance in a far more rigorous fashion to understand how change can be brought about without conflict—in contrast to much of the literature on power transitions.

In other words, this volume makes an explicit effort to move beyond the narrow parameters of the China rising debate by incorporating ideas, institutions, and ethical assumptions. Its major contribution is the range of case studies offered which provide a more nuanced understanding of change, the configuration and practice of global governance, and the influence of rising states on world politics.

The BRICS (and other acronyms)

Linked to, but distinct from the debate over China's individual rise, has been the considerable commentary in recent years on the growth in the Russian, Indian, and Brazilian economies and the effect this might have on global governance. On one level, Jim O'Neill's original selection of Brazil, Russia, India, and China (the original BRICs) as emerging markets has proved remarkably prescient. All four countries are now among the top 10 largest national economies in terms of GDP. They have even moved from being disconnected markets with little beyond growth to unite them to a cooperative intergovernmental group, holding summits, advocating South-South cooperation, criticizing inequalities in the institutions of global governance, and proposing to create a development bank in accordance with their economic interests. The addition of South Africa to the group increased the sense of the BRICS as advancing a different agenda to the existing pattern of global governance.

Yet, despite the considerable amount of discussion the BRICS have generated, their actual impact on global governance has been limited. There are a number of reasons for this. The overestimation of the BRICS' rates of growth and their likely continuation is an important factor. Far too many seminars on the BRICS in recent years have included graphs with lines of economic growth proceeding ever higher in a neat diagonal line upwards. In reality, growth levels fluctuated during the financial crisis— although these states did initially seem to ride out the crisis better than European ones. Brazil and India have both seen their economic wealth suffer from high inflation and faltering growth in the last two years. Focusing on economic growth is symptomatic of what Hans Morgenthau once called the "fallacy of the single factor."[31] In reality, power is made up of far more than just economic output in any brief period of time.

Globally, the record of cooperation among the rising powers is mixed to say the least. Instead of a consistent and coherent group advocating a shared agenda in world politics, we actually find ad hoc coalitions and groups that unite on individual issues but can often contain a diverse range of opinions and interests. Thus, the BASIC countries briefly acted in concert to shape the outcome of the Copenhagen summit in 2009.[32] Brazil, India, and China (BICs) have sought increased quota shares and/or voting rights in the WTO, World Bank, and IMF and represented themselves as leaders of South-South cooperation and a more developmental paradigm. In the NAMA-11 coalition, Brazil and India have worked together to safeguard the industrial parts of their economy from trade liberalization.[33] The BRICS grouping has formalized its meetings and jointly agreed some common positions, as in the July 2012 decision to contribute to the IMF's bailout fund designed to tackle the European financial crisis.[34] Their agreement in July 2014 to form a new development bank, based in Shanghai with an Indian President, is also an important signal of their shared attitudes to development.

Yet, these countries have also exhibited some marked differences of opinion at times. Brazil and India have disagreed about the liberalization of trade and lowering of tariffs in the agricultural sector.[35] The 2013 Durban summit revealed divisions over the BASIC countries' preferences for the governance of climate change. Territorial disputes between China and India have led to a military show of force by China and the blocking of investment from the Asian Development Bank in a contested region.[36] India in turn is said to have exploited Chinese compliance with oil sanctions on Iran to increase its own purchases from the country.[37] Although the BRICS did issue a joint statement on the Ukraine situation, condemning Western interference, behind the scenes there were internal rumblings over Russia's behavior towards Ukrainian sovereignty. Its recognition of the breakaway regions of Georgia, and annexation of Crimea, caused particular discomfort for China, which has strong views about legitimizing separatists.

To explore these differences, Bevir and Gaskarth here analyze each original BRIC country and highlight the distinct national experiences that shape each state's interpretation of governance locally and globally. These accounts are important to understanding how social knowledge about governance is shared, reinterpreted in local and national contexts, and projected and received abroad. Efforts to generalize the experience and attitudes of the BRICs towards global governance as somehow amounting to a shared resistance to Western ideas and institutions are not sustainable when we go deeper into each case study. Rather we find a more complex range of divergences among the BRICs, as well as problems of central government authority and policy efficiency that are common to developed states.

Another aspect affecting how far the rising powers might challenge existing configurations of order and governance is the way their rise is shaped by elite interests at home and in wider international society. As noted, the acronym derives from a Goldman Sachs report designed to attract investment in new markets and so has its origins in a social milieu of transnational capital transfer and global capitalist elites looking for opportunities to enrich themselves. Eulogizing developing markets has had the correlative effect of implying that developed states are somehow less virile, and their higher regulatory standards and social welfare spending are delegitimized as hampering their competitiveness. Therefore, while the BRICS may have domestic governance traditions associated with developmentalism and state interference in the economy, their new elites often buy into and reproduce neoliberal ideas about deregulation, privatization, and reduced social security spending. When combined with their emphasis on sovereignty and non-intervention, these states could potentially create a more fertile environment for rampant capitalism, unfettered by state interference, than the Anglo-European powers.

In this vein, Patrick Holden in his contribution to this volume notes that the BRICS rhetoric does not fundamentally challenge the WTO system, the interests they promote are often divergent with least developed countries, and the emphasis on infrastructure aid without good governance conditions reflects the BRICS' national interests rather than any common group or global public good. Similarly, Rebecca Davies and Ian Taylor here argue that the short-term economic interests of African elites and rising powers may be having a deleterious effect on the long-term governance reforms that are needed if ordinary Africans are to achieve sustainable prosperity. Overall, elite interests among rising powers are more likely to steer these states towards greater integration with the global order rather than in the direction of fragmentation. The same old problems of exploitation and inequality are likely to persist in any reconfigured global order incorporating the rising powers, regardless of the rhetoric of solidarity and South-South relations.

As noted above, a host of other groups (CIVETS, MIST, MINT) have been identified in global governance debates since the BRIC acronym was coined. At times, it is hard to see what they represent beyond an advertising tool for investment fund managers. Some of these states are rising within their region, whereas others are having an impact outside, on other continents. They are a useful reminder that beyond the BRICS, a host of states are seeing a rise in their economic capacity. However, these states often have contradictory or separate goals, distinct cultural ideas and norms, and differing resources which resist simple comparisons.

In his chapter, Ferguson notes that identifying supposedly rising powers on the basis of single economic measures makes little sense, especially when stock market rises and high growth can often figure in countries that have continuing economic problems. Meanwhile, Fawcett highlights the difficulties that arise if we wrench countries such as Egypt and Turkey out of their regional context and try and imply some global connection with countries on other continents. The idea of a state rising is often imbued with the sense that they will achieve a leadership position—something the various contenders for leadership in the Middle East have failed to do for any length of time because of the spoiler tactics of rival states. However, Biersteker and Moret's focus on four "pivotal emerging powers" (India, Brazil, Indonesia, and Turkey) is a reminder that it can be fruitful to identify categories of states with similar positions in the global hierarchy, provided this is done to say something profound about how global governance works and how different regional powers interact with this structure, rather than reducing such complexity to simple blocs of states with little to unite them.

Overall, by providing a range of case studies from a variety of countries and regions, this volume aims to offer a wider and deeper understanding of how global governance operates, and the potential challenges to its prevailing norms, than is afforded by the dominant focus on the BRICS. In the process, we get a more nuanced understanding of configurations of power across the globe, can identify a greater diversity of ideas about global governance, and appreciate the kinds of reform that are needed to accommodate the desire for change.

Global governance

As suggested above, the notion of rising powers seems to present a challenge to the idea of globally coordinated modes of governance. Global governance often includes a wider range of actors than just states, and addresses transnational problems such as climate change, terrorism, migration, crime, and economic crises that transcend national sovereign borders. The last two decades have seen a rapid expansion of global governance mechanisms and institutions that seek to regulate, steer, and control these processes. States have agreed to abide by common rules and pool sovereignty in the hope of achieving a more real influence on outcomes than afforded by national sovereignty. The reassertion of state agency that the rising powers discourse implies seems at odds with these developments. Realist predictions of security competition between great powers in the Asia-Pacific resurrect the state as the sole security provider, with the major security threat being inter-state war (rather than the more global security problems outlined above). In this narrative, change is brought about and managed via war—as it has been throughout history.

In a sense, both positions caricature the reality of global politics. Decision-making is still primarily conducted by state governments, as Weiss and Wilkinson note here in their chapter. To simplify and make sense of a diffuse and complex policy environment, officials now divide issues up into manageable and discreet agenda items, which Stewart Patrick describes as "global governance in pieces."[38] This is a more fragmented process than the sense of inevitable convergence that accompanied much writing about global governance in the 1990s. Moreover, not all states view global governance as a universal good, or even something that should promote global public goods. In her chapter, P.N. Chatterje-Doody suggests that Russia sees the BRICS grouping as a means to counter Western dominance of global governance, creating alternative avenues for influence even while it craves equal status in established forums.

However, there is a sense that there is more to global governance practices than just intergovernmental bargaining. As Matthew Stephen puts it in a recent article, the rising powers must be understood not just as states but also as "social formations embedded in a global political economy."[39] Signs of norm convergence are identifiable among elites and the middle classes of the emerging and the developed world.[40] Furthermore, in a nuclear age, change has to be managed peacefully between the nuclear powers or the human species itself will be threatened. A focus on war and predictions of imminent conflict tell us nothing about how to prepare for more effective global governance in peacetime.

It is here that Weiss and Wilkinson's chapter makes a series of important contributions to the debate. Rather than focus on war as the catalyst for change, they suggest that the challenge is to understand how change has been managed peacefully in the past and could be in the future. This entails an acknowledgement that forms of global governance have been apparent in many different historical periods, but that our current historical moment has brought forth new challenges which are different to those humans faced in the past. Theorists need to consider how incremental as well as transformative changes are governed as these can have profound normative implications.

Biersteker and Moret take up this challenge in their chapter by considering how and why international organizations and institutions might adapt to the rising powers. Rather than a monolithic set of governance mechanisms that would resist change, Biersteker and Moret note that many of the existing organs of global governance might welcome the rising powers and the opportunities they bring for greater funding, legitimacy, and policy scope. Change can occur at the ideational and the structural levels of organizational practice and could invigorate as well as threaten governance practices. Nevertheless, tensions will arise over the distribution of the costs and benefits of change and countries' future status in any reconfigured order. Managing this process and resolving these disputes are fundamentally ethical questions.

Global ethics

The definition of ethics I find most useful sees them as the consideration of the question "how ought we to live?" As we formulate a response to this dilemma, we have to think about what sort of characteristics we would see as admirable when applied to ourselves, or our group, how we ought to behave towards others, what kinds of principles we think we should be governed by, and what institutions we should establish to foster the good life as we define it. Who gets to decide the answers to these questions is an ethical and political question in itself. Clearly, all human societies have coercive aspects and the actors that are able to manipulate any instruments of coercion most efficiently will likely dominate. The importance of economic strength to state power is undeniable. It is significant both in determining access to markets and terms of trade, as well as a means to acquire the latest military technology for offensive or defensive purposes. For this reason, it is often assumed that economic power naturally translates into normative power. However, this has not always been the case. An important aspect of the exercise of power, especially normative power, is recognition of the actor's status and legitimacy in acting.[41] States that have built up reputations as positive contributors to global public goods may continue to have influence even as their relative material power wanes. Obversely, rising powers that cannot package their qualities in a way that might attract other states and provide positive benefits to the common weal will struggle to have a systemic impact.

Moreover, it is questionable how far rising powers really seek to overturn or challenge global normative frameworks. Three of the key ethical problems that have arisen when it comes to global governance and emerging powers concern human rights, distributive justice, and authority. When it comes to human rights, it is European countries like the United Kingdom and France, as well as Canada, Australia, and the United States that have arguably been most revisionist about the norms of international society, seeking to change norms of sovereignty and non-interference to a unified concept of sovereignty as responsibility. The unequal distribution of rights and privileges under current structures of global governance is something that a number of rising powers have spoken against. However, this has for the most part been expressed in terms of an increased national stake in each institution rather than a transformation of the entire system of trade, or security provision. As Neera Chandhoke points out, many rising powers loudly bemoan global inequalities while remaining quiet about domestic inequality within their borders.[42]

As for authority, this goes to the heart of much of the discussion of global governance, rising powers, and global ethics: who gets to decide on how governance operates?[43] The geographical and demographic size of the original BRICs affords them some legitimacy as interlocutors in global governance forums, even if their domestic governance credentials are not always admirable. Yet, there are tensions among the rising powers over whether each should be afforded a permanent seat at the higher echelon of the UNSC. Whether the expansion of membership at the top tier of the international hierarchy would benefit or further marginalize less developed states is an important ethical problem. Holden, and Davies and Taylor do not seem optimistic that widening the scope of authority at the top will have positive outcomes for the poorest people, especially in Africa.

In this way, the volume speaks to current debates over global ethics by exploring how far international society really is being pulled apart by competing normative beliefs. Ferguson argues that Western states blow hot and cold over human rights and so can hardly criticize other states for doing the same at times, according to their interests. Rising powers show a remarkable divergence of opinion on a host of ethical questions, from countering proliferation to protecting human rights and preserving sovereignty. Things are more complicated than simply binary divisions between North and South, rising and developed, East and West, or BRICS versus the rest. It is also important to highlight, as many of the contributors do in this volume, the coercive elements of global governance. Even if on balance cooperative governance arrangements amount to a public good, that should not blind us to their possible negative side-effects, nor should we be unaware of the political economy and ideological aspects to these institutions. Thus, P.N. Chatterje-Doody in her chapter notes how Russian efforts to utilize the BRICS and other groups as alternatives to Western modes of governance are often criticized as motivated by self-interest. But are they simply more naked examples of what Western states do all the time?

The structure of this volume

To summarize, this volume contributes to a series of key debates on global governance and rising powers, from the implications of China's rise, to the shifting coalitions and groups of rising powers, the nature of global governance, and the extent to which global norms are converging or fragmenting. It is structured in two sections. The first looks at theoretical insights into the literature on global governance and the rising powers. The second section explores the governance practices of rising powers in the World Trade Organization (WTO), East Asia, the Middle East, Africa, and internationally.

We begin with Yale Ferguson's critique of the notion of rising powers, the conceptual terrain of global governance, and how they intersect. The author is skeptical of the utility of rising powers as a label without a corresponding theory of power to go along with it. Although optimistic about the chances of increased cooperation in the economic aspects of global governance, Ferguson is concerned about the lack of an effective or united response from Western countries to what he sees as direct challenges to the sovereignty of their neighbors from Russia and China. Thomas G. Weiss and Rorden Wilkinson then examine possible explanations for changes *in* and changes *of* global governance. They argue that only by understanding what holds governance formations together, and what encourages their transformation, can we understand changes of world order. Although the international system remains anarchic, the authors note a series of changes in its structure and within the practices of governance it contains. They also examine changes *of* global governance and ask whether this can be brought about without a cataclysmic event. The normative quest they set themselves is to understand how significant change can be brought about peacefully to address the complex problems of contemporary global governance.

Keeping a focus on governing change, Biersteker and Moret advocate a shift away from thinking about system maintenance to thinking about system adaptability. They consider why rising powers are important to international organizations (IOs) and how IOs might adapt in anticipation of the emergence of new powers. Their chapter then moves on to an analysis of how four pivotal powers, India, Brazil, Indonesia, and Turkey, view and interact with international security organizations when it comes to countering nuclear proliferation. The book's theoretical section is rounded off with an analysis of how the four original BRIC countries have approached governance, domestically and internationally, in recent decades. Changes of governance have been interpreted and managed in very different ways in each national context. However, there is also evidence of knowledge transfer across borders and similar dilemmas over how to make government more effective and efficient to those identified in developed states. In the practical section that follows, Patrick Holden's chapter analyses the attitudes of rising powers towards trade and development. Through an exploration of their negotiating stances in the Doha Development Round and Aid for Trade initiative, Holden finds little evidence of a coherent alternative ethical stance on these policy issues. Contradictions in the self-identity of some of the rising powers are seen as inhibiting their ability to formulate a viable alternative to current global governance arrangements in these areas. This theme is apparent in Jones' and Breslin's consideration of how China interacts with its neighbors across a number of regions. The authors assert that China at present is speaking to a number of audiences in these regions without clear coherence between them, presenting not only the opportunity for confusion but also the danger of political tensions and potential conflict because of it.

Louise Fawcett then provides an innovative analysis of the idea of rising powers by considering the various attempts of states in the Middle East to assume a leadership position in the region. In the process, Fawcett asserts that the absence of recognized and effective regional leaders has had a negative impact on institutional and normative developments, and therefore regional and ultimately global order. This serves as a reminder of how important leading states can be in forging cooperative governance arrangements—and how destructive competition between rival leaders can be in turn.

In their chapter, Rebecca Davies and Ian Taylor argue that the actions of the rising powers are helping to reify Africa's place in the global division of labor as a primary commodity exporter. They offer evidence of de-industrialization and growing dependency despite the rhetoric of rising powers, who assert that their interaction with Africa is built on equality and mutual advantage rather than exploitation. P.N. Chatterje-Doody then examines Russia's involvement in various regional governance initiatives. Perhaps the most strident rising power when it comes to challenging Western dominance of global governance, Russia has sought to utilize these organizations as a political and normative counter-weight to United States and European influence. This underlines the extent to which potential challengers to norm convergence exist in global politics and have attracted some support in the last decade in response to dissatisfaction with the perceived revisionism of developed states. We conclude with a series of continuing dilemmas and questions concerning the role rising powers will have in future global governance arrangements. Throughout the text, theoretical insights are applied to practical examples to give a grounded analysis of how rising powers are shaping the governance of global politics, and the ethical implications that flow from this.

Notes

1 Useful primers on globalization and the link to global governance include: Rorden Wilkinson, ed., *The Global Governance Reader* (London: Routledge, 2005); David Held and Anthony McGrew, eds, *The Global Transformations Reader* (Cambridge: Polity Press, 2000); David Held and Anthony McGrew, *Globalization/Anti-Globalization: Beyond the Great Divide*, 2nd Edition (Cambridge: Polity Press, 2007); Jan Aarte Scholte, *Globalization: A Critical Introduction*, 2nd Edition (Basingstoke: Palgrave, 2005); Yale H. Ferguson and Richard W. Mansbach, *Globalization: The Return of Borders to a Borderless World?* (London: Routledge 2012).
2 See James N. Rosenau and Ernst-Otto Czempiel, *Governance Without Government: Order and Change in World Politics* (Cambridge: Cambridge University Press, 1992); James N. Rosenau, *Along the Domestic-Foreign Frontier: Exploring Governance in a Turbulent World* (Cambridge: Cambridge University Press, 1997); Margaret E. Keck and Kathryn Sikkink, *Activists Beyond Borders: Advocacy Networks in International Politics* (New York: Cornell University Press, 1998); Ole Wæver, "Resisting the temptation of post foreign policy analysis" in Walter Carlsnaes and Steve Smith, *European Foreign Policy: the EC and Changing Foreign Policy Perspectives in Europe* (London: SAGE, 1994).
3 Bill Emmott, *The Rivals: How the Power Struggle Between China, India, and Japan Will Shape Our Next Decade* (Boston, Mass.: Mariner Books, 2009).
4 Antonio Franceschet, "Ethics, Politics, and Global Governance," in *The Ethics of Global Governance*, 3. A notable exception is Thomas G. Weiss, *Thinking about Global Governance* (Abingdon: Routledge, 2011).
5 This point is well made in Craig N. Murphy, "The Emergence of Global Governance," in *International Organization and Global Governance*, Thomas G. Weiss and Rorden Wilkinson, eds, (London: Routledge, 2014), 32–33.
6 Peter Ferdinand, "Rising powers at the UN: an analysis of the voting behaviour of BRICS in the General Assembly," *Third World Quarterly* 35 no. 3 (2014): 380.
7 Ibid.
8 Alan S. Alexandroff and Andrew F. Cooper, eds, *Rising States, Rising Institutions: Challenges for Global Governance* (Washington, DC: Brookings Institution Press, 2010); Kevin Gray and Craig N. Murphy, *Rising Powers and the Future of Global Governance* (London: Routledge, 2013); Michael Barnett and Raymond Duvall, *Power in Global Governance* (Cambridge: Cambridge University Press, 2004); and Andrew F. Cooper,

and Agata Antkiewicz, eds, *Emerging Powers and Global Governance* (Waterloo, ON: Wilfrid Laurier University Press, 2010).

9 Christophe Jaffrelot, ed., *The Emerging States: The Wellspring of a New World Order* (London: Hurst & Company, 2008); Emmott, *The Rivals*; Vidya Nadkarni and Norma C. Noonan, eds, *Emerging Powers in a Comparative Perspective* (London: Bloomsbury, 2013); Uwe Becker, *The BRICs and Emerging Economies in Comparative Perspective: Political Economy, Liberalisation and Institutional Change* (London: Routledge, 2013); and Amrita Narlikar, *New Powers: How to Become One and How to Manage Them* (London: Hurst & Company, 2010).

10 Andrew Hurrell and Sandeep Sengupta, "Emerging powers, North–South relations and global climate politics," *International Affairs* 88, no. 3 (2012): 464.

11 G. John Ikenberry, "The Rise of China and the Future of the West; Can the Liberal System Survive?" *Foreign Affairs*; 87, no. 1 (Jan/Feb 2008): 23–37, http://search.proquest.com/indexingvolumeissuelinkhandler/40670/Foreign +Affairs/02008Y01Y01$23Jan$2fFeb+2008$3b++Vol.+87+$281$29/87/1? accountid=14711.

12 Christopher Layne, "China's Challenge to US Hegemony," *Current History* (January 2008): 15.

13 John J. Mearsheimer, "The Gathering Storm: China's Challenge to US Power in Asia," *The Chinese Journal of International Politics* 3 (2010): 381–396; John J. Mearsheimer, *The Tragedy of Great Power Politics* (New York: Norton, 2003).

14 Aaron L. Friedberg, "The Future of U.S.-China Relations: Is Conflict Inevitable?" *International Security* 30, no. 2 (Fall, 2005): 7–45.

15 Ibid., 37–38.

16 William Tow and Richard Rigby, "China's Pragmatic Security Policy: The Middle-Power Factor," *The China Journal* no. 65 (January 2011): 160.

17 Guoguang Wu, "The Peaceful Emergence of a Great Power?" *Social Research* 73, no. 1 (Spring 2006): 325.

18 Ja Ian Chong "Popular Narratives versus Chinese History: Implications for Understanding an Emergent China," *European Journal of International Relations*, published online 27 November 2013.

19 Ibid.: 19.

20 Kevin Rudd, "Beyond the Pivot," *Foreign Affairs* 92, no. 2 (2013): 9–15.

21 Ronald L. Tammen, "The Impact of Asia on World Politics: China and India Options for the United States," *International Studies Review* 8, no. 4 (Dec 2006): 573.

22 Minxin Pei, "How China and America See Each Other," *Foreign Affairs* 93, no. 2 (2014): 143–147.

23 Ja Ian Chong, "Popular Narratives versus Chinese History: Implications for Understanding an Emergent China."

24 David Armstrong, *Revolution and World Order: The Revolutionary State in International Society* (Oxford: Oxford University Press, 1993).

25 Andrew Hurrell, "Hegemony, liberalism and global order: what space for would-be great powers?", *International Affairs* 82, no. 1 (2006): 6.

26 G. John Ikenberry, "The Rise of China and the Future of Liberal World Order," The C Douglas Dillon Lecture, 7 May 2014.

27 Ikenberry, "The Rise of China and the Future of Liberal World Order," 4.

28 Ikenberry, "The Rise of China and the Future of the West; Can the Liberal System Survive?"

29 Alastair Iain Johnston, "Is China a Status Quo Power?" *International Security* 27, no. 4 (Spring, 2003): 23.

30 Miles Kahler, "Rising powers and global governance: negotiating change in a resilient status quo," *International Affairs* 89, no. 3 (2013): 711.

31 Hans Morgenthau, *Politics Among Nations: the Struggle for Power and Peace* (New York: McGraw Hill, 1993), 174–179.

32 Xinran Qi, "The rise of BASIC in UN climate change negotiations," *South African Journal of International Relations* 18, no. 3 (2011): 295–318.

33 Eugénia da Conceição-Heldt, "Emerging Powers in WTO Negotiations: The Domestic Sources of Trade Policy Preferences," *The International Trade Journal* 27, no. 5 (2013): 443.

34 Stephan Keukeleire and Bas Hooijmaaijers, "The BRICS and Other Emerging Power Alliances and Multilateral Organizations in the Asia-Pacific and the Global South: Challenges for the European Union and Its View on Multilateralism," *Journal of Common Market Studies* 52, no. 3 (2014): 586.

35 Eugénia da Conceição-Heldt, "Emerging Powers in WTO Negotiations," 445.

36 Suisheng Zhao, "China: A Reluctant Global Power in the Search for its Rightful Place," in *Emerging Powers in a Comparative Perspective*, Vidya Nadkarni and Norma C. Noonan, eds (London: Bloomsbury, 2013), 105–106.

37 George Gilboy and Eric Heginbotham, "Double Trouble: A Realist View of Chinese and Indian Power," *The Washington Quarterly* 36, no. 3 (2013): 132.

38 Stewart Patrick, "The Unruled World," *Foreign Affairs* 93, no. 1 (2014): 58–73.

39 Matthew D. Stephen, "Rising powers, global capitalism and liberal global governance: A historical materialist account of the BRICs challenge," *European Journal of International Relations*, published online 21 May 2014.

40 Ikenberry, "The Future of the Liberal World Order"; Stephen, "Rising powers, global capitalism and liberal global governance," 14.

41 Ian Clark, *Legitimacy in International Society* (Oxford: Oxford University Press, 2005); and Yannis Stivachtis, "Power in the Contemporary International Society: International Relations Meets Political and Social Theory—A Critical Appraisal of US Foreign Policy," *Journal of Political and Military Sociology* 36, no. 1 (2008): 96–97.

42 Neera Chandhoke, "Realising Justice," *Third World Quarterly* 34, no. 2 (2013): 305–20.

43 David Held, "The Diffusion of Authority," in *International Organization and Global Governance*, Weiss and Wilkinson, eds, 60–72.

1 Rising powers and global governance

Theoretical perspectives

Yale H. Ferguson

- **Rising powers**
- **Global governance**
- **Rising states and global governance**
- **Conclusion**

This chapter focuses on several important but controversial concepts and explores what different international relations (IR) theoretical perspectives would each likely highlight and possibly contribute to our understanding of rising powers, global governance, and the relationship between the two.

Rising powers

"Rising powers" evokes memories of the late nineteenth- and twentieth-century German and Japanese challenges to the established European "order" and the grief that ultimately ensued. Both countries rapidly increased their economic and military capabilities, suffered ignominious defeat in the First World War (Germany) and the Second World War (Germany and Japan), and then began to "rise again." For a time some analysts predicted that the twenty-first century would be "the Japanese century," but in fact that country remained militarily weak and soon entered a lingering period of economic stagnation. Germany eschewed another military build-up, but steadily worked its way back to an economically pre-eminent position in the European Union (EU). If there are any lessons in all of this, they must be that everyone's crystal ball is cloudy. What looks like a trend is often only a phase or cycle, and we need to examine any claims about rising powers with a critical eye.

Start with the term "rising." Rising in what respects, from what level, compared with what, how measured, how inexorably rising, and so what anyway? In mid-December 2013 the four best performing stock markets were—who would have expected it?—Venezuela (452 percent), Iceland (38 percent), Greece (35 percent), and Ireland (35 percent).[1] Thus, are these four countries rising powers? Venezuela's stellar performance was apparently caused by fears of a national currency crisis. As one analyst explained it: "Domestic investors [sought] to protect their bolivars from devaluation and inflation by buying the few stocks available on the local exchange—pushing up prices."[2] Iceland and Ireland have been in recovery mode, and Ireland paid back its bailout loans, but does anyone expect Greece to be a financial (or any sort of) powerhouse anytime soon? Well, perhaps tourism, because Greece has enduring assets in that area. Meanwhile, China was the worst performing stock market in Asia in 2013. The Shanghai Composite Index declined by 6.75 percent.[3] Is China therefore a declining power?

Having adequate and reliable information to make a proper judgment is always a concern, and even more important is what we make of whatever "facts" we do have. A modern classic case is the "superpower" status of the former Soviet Union, which was true enough with respect to its nuclear capability, rather less true with regard to its overall military establishment, and definitely not true in terms of its economy. The Soviet regime fed the world funny numbers, and those gathered by foreign intelligence agencies also proved wildly unreliable.

Contemporary China is another case in point. Although there is wide consensus that China has been experiencing impressive economic growth, measuring and ranking the size of China's economy has proved to be a daunting task. China-watchers rightly worry about the accuracy of statistics from that country's bureaucratic agencies, but that is only part of the problem. By 2013, according to *The Economist* and estimated in traditional "nominal" terms, China's GDP was \$5,927bn, compared with the United States' \$14,587bn, or (for instance) Bulgaria's \$47.7bn.[4] *The Economist* in 2014 listed GDP per capita of the same three countries as \$7,740, \$54,920, and \$7,530, respectively.[5] Using nominal GNP as a baseline, numerous analysts concluded that China's economy had recently overtaken Japan's as the world's second largest and might well pass that of the United States no later than 2030. However, the World Bank in late April 2014 switched to purchasing power parity (PPP) as a means of calculating GNP, which measure suggested that China's economy is already poised to become the world's largest in 2014.[6] For its own reasons,[7] even the Chinese government campaigned against the PPP standard and ultimately refused to endorse the World Bank's report.[8] Many leading

Western experts have also criticized the PPP referent as potentially misleading. Martin Wolf and David Pilling write: "It is possible to debate whether the newly revised numbers are right. The answer is they are reasonable. A more important question is what do they mean. What they do not mean is that China is already the world's greatest economic power." Wolf and Pilling go on to observe—among several other important things—that China is still in many respects a poor country, China's purchasing power per head continues to be relatively low, and that as China invests close to half of its output, per capita consumption is inevitably lower than macro statistics might otherwise suggest.[9] Michael Levi goes further:

> [PPP] measures national incomes in terms of what they can buy at home. Because domestic spending is dominated by items such as food and housing that aren't traded internationally, and because most goods and services are cheaper in China than in the United States, this comparison boosts China's apparent economic strength. Yet compared using market exchange rates, which measures national incomes in terms of what they can buy on international markets (where every country pays the same price), the United States' economy remains nearly twice as big as China's. Indeed it is this latter measure that matters most when comparing economic power.[10]

Turning to security, can we say with any degree of certainty where on the ladder of nuclear military powers Iran and North Korea stand today? Why should we even care, absent a perception that nuclear weapons in the hands of either regime might be somewhat more likely to be used? Moreover, whether or not one credits official statements, both governments have blown hot and cold at intervals about limiting or abandoning their nuclear weapon programs entirely. It might also be observed that until Russia recently began to use its military forces to seize Crimea and intimidate Ukraine, few noticed that the Putin government for some years has been quietly improving the quality of its regional strike forces. More important, such improvements seem all the more significant because of heightened fears that Moscow intends to use its military to threaten other neighboring countries and perhaps to bolster its claims in the Arctic. If that is the case, does this indicate that Russia is rising or only beginning a period of self-inflicted isolation and economic reversals?

There is no doubt that the notion of "rising powers" in recent years has been closely connected in analysts' minds with that of "emerging markets," even though rising powers has inherently broader connotations than simply the economic realm. Nevertheless, early in 2014 there was a substantial sell-off under way in emerging-market stocks, precipitated by a sharp drop in the Argentine peso coupled with reports of a slowdown in Chinese manufacturing, but also reflecting wider concerns about the possible effects of Federal Reserve "tapering" of its quantitative easing policies in constricting the flow of investment to emerging market countries.

IR social constructivists persuasively argue that despite the existence of an "objective" reality, much of our current understanding of the world is "subjective"—a matter of perceptions. And how quickly and radically perceptions often change. As Rachir Sharma observes, about halfway through the last decade the average emerging-market-country growth rate was over 7 percent and the "hype" began. "China would soon surpass the United States as an economic power...and India, with its vast population, or Vietnam, with its own spin on authoritarian capitalism, would be the next China." "Beijing would soon lead the new and rising bloc of the BRICs—Brazil, Russia, India, and China—to ultimate supremacy over the fading powers of the West. Suddenly the race to coin the next hot acronym was on, and CIVETS (Columbia, Indonesia, Vietnam, Egypt, Turkey, and South Africa) emerged from the MIST (Mexico, Indonesia, South Korea, and Turkey)." Now, "that euphoria and all those acronyms have come to seem woefully out of date." The average growth rate slowed to 4 percent in 2013, and even the BRICs seem to have been greatly overrated.[11]

Brazil has harbored great power ambitions for generations, but these have yet to be fulfilled. The country's Gini coefficient that measures inequality is at a 50-year low, but a 7.5 percent growth rate in 2010 raised expectations that soon fizzled.[12] The economy remained sluggish in 2011 through 2013, and only a 2.5 percent growth rate is expected in 2014.[13] Despite all the publicity surrounding Brazil's welcoming the World Cup, the *Financial Times* described the country's economic outlook as "go-go to so-so" and "teetering on the brink of a technical recession."[14]

Of late, initially, Russia's Putin raised his country's profile by sheltering Edward Snowden, achieving a shaky chemical weapons deal for Syria, contesting Ukraine's trajectory toward the EU, and hosting the Winter Olympics. Even before Russia's military seizure and annexation of Crimea, outside analysts frequently observed that Russia's level of official corruption remained alarmingly high and the country's economy was close to recession (growth rate about 1 percent), almost wholly dependent on oil and gas, and generally unattractive to foreign investors.[15] Now, after Putin's blatant aggression against Ukraine, all bets are off, although most forecasts suggest a full-fledged recession and an extended period of diplomatic tensions and relative isolation. Over the longer term, Russia will need to decide the degree to which it will pursue visions of autarky, closer ties with Beijing (as its May 2014 major gas deal with China might suggest), and/or fence-mending with the EU and global trade partners.[16]

India experienced a grave economic crisis in mid-2013 and no longer seems to be in any position to compete with China. Indeed, its present GDP per capita is now less than a quarter of China's.[17] David Pilling sums up India's problems well:

> India's economic model looks shakier than before. Not only has it failed to turn GDP into social justice, the basis of growth itself looks less certain. India has not turned itself into a serious manufacturing center. Investment has stalled... The state has no legitimacy ... The biggest beneficiaries of the status quo are the crony capitalists who have been permitted to extract rent to no one's obvious interest but their own.[18]

Whether the recent sweeping electoral victory by the Bharatiya Janata Party and its leader, Narenda Modi, will eventually lead to significant reforms remains to be seen.

China weathered the global financial crisis well and has currently established—and so far maintained[19]—an annual growth rate target of 7.5 percent. However, Beijing's aging bureaucratic authoritarian regime is having to manage a difficult transition to a somewhat slower growth model that is less dependent on exports, a debt-fueled credit boom, competitive wages, and undervalued currency, and based more on increasing domestic consumer demand—all this while attempting to rein in endemic corruption at all levels, appease a "wired" attentive public insisting on greater political freedom and transparency, orchestrate unprecedented mass migration from the countryside, improve social welfare and services, and address quality of life issues such as horrific pollution in major cities. Meanwhile, China has been increasing its military budget and adopting a much more assertive strategic posture in the South and East China Seas.

Landon Thomas comments that "[r]ecent turmoil in [the BRICs and other emerging] markets has produced a rival expression: the 'Fragile Five': Turkey, Brazil, India, South Africa, and Indonesia."[20] Turkey offers another quick rise and fall story, inspiring Paul Krugman to coin a new term "Istanbearish."[21] Tim Arango observes: "To some extent,

Turkey and [Prime Minister Recep Tayyip] Erdogan are victims of their own success, having created an attractive investment climate that brought in billions in dollar-denominated lending, particularly after the financial crisis of 2008." Western officials looked to him as a "prime example of a leader who could meld democratic values, Islam and economic prosperity." "But much of the money was funneled to a group of insiders who made fortunes while building malls and other developments that increasingly lacked sound underpinnings." The result was a host of "bad loans," "accusations of cronyism," and eventually "bond investors fleeing" and emergency increases in interest rates to help stem a complete collapse of the Turkish lira.[22] Erdogan reacted in heavy-handed fashion to huge public protests and a sweeping corruption inquiry that he insisted was inspired by his former Gulenist allies. Authoritarian creep has become more like a trot, with broad political purges, as well as curbs of the judiciary, press, and even social media. It now appears that Erdogan was elected President in August 2014 and (with or without a change in the constitution) will likely rule until 2023.[23] Otherwise, Erdogan's ambitions to play a pivotal role in a rapidly changing Middle East have been frustrated. His support for the opposition in Syria and the Morsi Muslim Brotherhood government in Egypt have all come to naught.

Sharma notes that forecasters are currently trying to discern why they have been mostly wrong about rising states and emerging markets generally. Although mistakes were "legion," he highlights several key ones: first, forecasters "stopped looking at individual stories and started lumping them into faceless packs with mindless acronyms." They credited optimistic speeches of emerging-market politicians and tended to ignore the impact on growth of "easy money" emanating from the United States and Europe. They also placed "far too much predictive weight on a single factor" like demographics or even globalization itself. Finally, and perhaps most important, they made "the cardinal error of extrapolation," simply assuming that "recent trends would continue indefinitely."[24]

James Kynge, *Financial Times* Emerging Markets Editor, underscores the point that the countries in this supposed group are quite varied in their susceptibility to a crisis similar to the 1997 one in Asia—a cautionary note also relevant to rising powers. Those in the worst trouble are those suffering both from domestic economic mismanagement and unusual exposure to external forces. Kynge cites the work of Capital Economics analyst Neil Shearing, who divides emerging markets into five groups: The "most vulnerable" include "serial economic mismanagement" countries Argentina, Ukraine, and

Venezuela. Ukraine, of course, is now trying to hold the remains of the country together after the loss of Crimea. Venezuela is roiled by an uneasy post-Chávez political transition. A second grouping is countries that have "lived beyond their means," characterized by credit booms and increased current account deficits. These include Turkey, South Africa, Indonesia, Thailand, Chile, and Peru. Shearing views this second group as being especially susceptible to United States tampering. A third group is Eastern European countries like Hungary and Romania that are similarly vulnerable, but to actions of the European Central Bank. The fourth group is the BRICs, all of which "face domestic policy challenges" and significant political ones as well. Finally, a fifth group contains countries—South Korea, Philippines, and Mexico—that should actually benefit from rising export demand.[25]

Contrast the sort of diversity we have been describing with the kind of world an IR classical realist or neorealist would have us envision. After all, the concept of "rising powers" has a distinct realist/neorealist flavor to it. Realists of both types see a world mainly of states that is essentially anarchic. Certain "power factors," primarily but not exclusively military in classical realism, together constitute the "power" of a state, which each state inevitably seeks to increase. States pursue their (objectively defined) "national interests" that ultimately translate into maximizing power. Rules, norms, and morality have very little place. Whatever "order" exists derives from a prevailing "balance of power" and what realists hope will be a measure of "prudence" exercised by individual state actors and their allies. Neorealists of both the Waltzian and Wallersteinian varieties go a step further, to suggest that the overall "structure" of the "system" determines most of the important things that happen therein. Rising powers fit neatly into either a realist or neorealist framework. States have different capabilities, some are powerful and others less so or much less so (weak), some are advancing and others declining in a perennial struggle for power, shifting alliances are to be expected, and the overall distribution of power/capabilities establishes the nature of the international system as a whole. At this point, however, some of the internal theoretical consensus in realism/neorealism breaks down. There is debate, for example, about the degree of stability likely to be achieved in bipolar versus multipolar systems, and (among power transition theorists) as to whether the most dangerous stage is when one or more rising powers are conspicuously moving up or when they are drawing even with previously dominant powers.

The problems with traditional realist/neorealist worldviews are fairly well-known. "Power" is an almost meaningless concept except insofar as it is regarded as being influence in a particular context. As one of my Columbia graduate school professors, W.T.R. Fox (who claimed to have invented the term "superpower"), was fond of putting it, power is not like money in the bank, a fund that you can spend at any time to get almost anything and diminishes proportionately as you draw the balance down. Power is *always* a *relative* matter, and Fox offered his students his "Complete Power Statement," which he insisted was the only way to speak or write meaningfully about power: A has power over B with respect to issue C under specified conditions D. Even superpowers, hegemons, and very great powers (or so they seem) are practically powerless to achieve many of the things they would like to achieve.

Moreover, there are different sources of power, including (as Joseph Nye has reminded us) various forms of "soft power." Countries may enhance their influence simply by being admired, and in this regard (contrary to realism) values and behavior widely perceived as "moral" can themselves be sources of power. The reverse is also true. Turkey's main (albeit not only) problem with its longstanding application to enter the EU is that (rightly or wrongly) some member governments do not believe that Turkey is sufficiently "European/Western" in culture, and increasing Islamic influences in public policy and Erdogan's authoritarian proclivities are certainly not helping Turkey's image in the EU. China is broadly credited with remarkable economic accomplishments but finds its soft power undermined in some quarters by less-positive features of its development (e.g., human rights, environment) and especially its sweeping and legally shaky territorial claims and saber-rattling in the South and East China seas. Furthermore, as critics of realism/neorealism observe, there is nearly always a strong subjective dimension to any determination of a country's "national interests," with choices made all the more difficult as perceived national interests are so often in conflict. China regularly refers to its vigorous pressing of its China Sea ambitions as part of its "core national interest," but logic might suggest that equally or more important are avoiding dangerous military confrontations and cultivating better relations with Asian neighbors. Or is stoking nationalist emotions to distract from problems at home the principal aim behind blustering behavior?

David Shambaugh's recent assessment of China's power and global role is worth examining in some detail because it is revealing, balanced, and highly relevant to our subject. He concludes that China today is only a "partial power" and "has a very long way to go before it becomes—if it *ever* becomes—a true global power." Yes, China does look good in at least some of the usual realist power categories: the world's largest population exporter and foreign exchange reserves, second largest (arguably largest) economy with a rapid growth rate, a vast continental territory, and so on. But China has grave domestic problems, most of which we have already mentioned. Overall, Shambaugh (in my opinion rightly) concludes that China is significantly deficient in the most important bottom-line measurement of power—*influence*. Its global influence is largely limited to its impact on trade, commodity and energy markets, finance, real estate purchases, and tourism—and its negativity on such issues as climate[26] and Syria. Militarily, except for ballistic missiles, a small space program, and cyber mischief-making, China is not (yet) able to "project power outside of its Asian neighborhood" and only in a limited way there. The country has "little soft power, if any, and is not a model for other nations to emulate." Its vigorous pursuit of "narrow self-interests" with regard to the South and East China Seas, Taiwan, Tibet, Xinjiang, and human rights does not inspire widespread admiration. "China is a lonely power, lacking close friends and possessing no allies." Its relations with Russia, Pakistan, and North Korea involve a strong measure of "distrust." (*The Economist* lately described China and Russia as "best frenemies.") However, ironically—more social constructivism here—Shambaugh does acknowledge that "global publics" *perceive* China's global standing much more positively. He cites a 2011 Pew poll in 22 countries, wherein the opinions of the public in 15 of these countries was "that China will—or *already has*—replaced the United States as the world's leading power."[27] In that regard China has to be respected or possibly feared.

Global governance

Next we turn to another contested concept: global governance. Only a few dreamers believe world government that governs broadly like a sovereign state is either remotely possible or desirable. However, must global governance be genuinely global in scope and/or limited only, as some would have it, to international organizations that are the product of agreements among states? Does governance, of necessity, rest on formal authority, or can it also be informal? What is the relationship between authority and legitimacy? Is effective control or significant influence over particular outcomes at least as important as anything else?

In general, liberal theorists tend to focus on international institutions and regimes. English School Hedley Bull, liberal institutionalist Robert Keohane, and even constructivist Alexander Wendt all acknowledged a clear debt to classical realism.[28] States remain central to analyses, but liberals stress that, in the larger scheme of things, cooperation often serves the national interest of states as well as competition and conflict.

Thus, in Wendt's felicitous phrase—albeit neglecting other actors—"anarchy is what states make of it." Existing international institutions, international law, less-formal rules, practices, and expectations as to acceptable behavior do "matter." Involvement with international organizations and regimes can be a socializing experience for states, and positive "unintended consequences" may flow from initial experiments in international institution-building.

In recent decades, much more expansive—and, I believe, "realistic" in the dictionary sense—conceptions of global governance have come to the fore. Bull had the foresight to ruminate about global trends that might possibly herald a "new medievalism." Self-styled "structural realists" Buzan and Little wrote about "deep structure" and "governing" within the "international system" that involves a greater variety of actors and levels.[29] Rosenau and Czempiel coined the phrase "governance without government,"[30] and Rosenau elaborated his own theoretical perspective of "post-international politics" in a highly "complex" and "turbulent world." To Rosenau "governance" could best be understood as countless "spheres of authority" (SOAs) that exercised control or significant influence over outcomes.[31] Ferguson and Mansbach similarly extolled the virtues of "postinternational theory" over a state-centric view of IR and conceived of a world of "polities" (some "nested") engaging a wide range of actor types in multiple and often overlapping domains. In their view, whatever degree of "order" results is the "real world order."[32] Such broader understanding of global governance, not coincidentally, has evolved in conjunction with increasing awareness of "globalization" in academic work and media generally. As examples of contemporary nesting, it is important that China, Turkey, and Russia are keenly aware of their former status as great powers and empires—and that their neighbors, for better or worse, have certainly not forgotten that history either. China, in particular, also continues to find itself challenged domestically by longstanding regional identities, problems with minorities, and the pattern of cycles of centralization and decentralization that have characterized Chinese rule since ancient times.

Today, a more expansive conception of global governance has gradually established itself in the academic and policy mainstream. By way of illustration, consider first a recent collection of essays edited by Guzzini and Neumann. Guzzini titles his contribution "The Ambivalent Diffusion of Power in Global Governance." He identifies two "takes" on global governance, one which "alerts us to the different players" beyond sovereign state governments, and the other, that "takes the multitude of actors for granted and explores the ensuing rules of the game." The latter approach, which Guzzini obviously favors and regards as "Foucauldian," sees "international political order or power ... reaching into, and using the lever of, market actors and global civil society." He comments: "It is probably not accidental that the English School in IR has been particularly sensitive to this because it is based upon the idea that there is an international society, though not one akin to the national one."[33] Kolodziej similarly concludes: "Three key properties define the world society: the increasing connectedness of its members; the multiplying mutual dependencies of global actors across all major areas of human concern; and the multiplicity and growing number of empowered actors engaged in defining the scope and impact of global governance."[34]

A second recent analysis by Stewart Patrick (Director of the International Institutions and Global Governance Program at the Council on Foreign Relations) makes a number of important related points. He observes that, despite the persistent "creaking and crumbling" of the "postwar order," the "demand for international cooperation is greater than ever, thanks to deepening economic interdependence, worsening environmental degradation, proliferating transnational threats, and accelerating technological change." Yet effective responses are "increasingly occurring outside formal institutions, as frustrated actors turn to more convenient, ad hoc venues." Most multilateral institutions, even those that supposedly operate under binding international law "lack real power to enforce compliance with collective decisions." So, in addition to "long-standing universal membership bodies, there are various regional institutions, multilateral alliances and security groups, standing consultative mechanisms, self-selecting clubs, ad hoc coalitions, issue-specific arrangements, transnational professional networks, technical standard-setting bodies, global action networks, and more." In Patrick's view, states "are still the dominant actors, but nonstate actors increasingly help shape the global agenda, define new rules, and monitor compliance with international obligations."[35]

Rising states and global governance

Realists have traditionally regarded international institutions and international law and norms generally with a mixture of cynicism and skepticism. In this perspective, institutions and rule either directly serve the interests of powerful states or are widely ignored by them. Much more likely than cooperation is competition and conflict, and rising states should be expected to challenge any aspects of the existing "order" that they perceive to be hindering their advance. China's defiant language about defending its core national interests in the South and East China Sea, as well as military build-up and feisty naval patrols, would appear to be right out of the realist playbook. Beijing spurns serious negotiations about territorial settlements or "codes of conduct" in the area as well as calls for testing claims in any legal forum, court, or arbitral tribunal. Similarly *realpolitik* is Russia's cynical insistence on its "right" to "defend its interests" by committing aggression against Ukraine and annexing its sovereign territory in Crimea. Moreover, China and Russia have expressed no support for making such important countries as India and Brazil permanent members of the UN Security, nor, of course, for abolishing permanent-member status entirely. The BRICs and most other emerging market countries have been stalwart strict constructionists with regard to traditional state sovereignty (although China gave Putin a pass on Ukraine), have repeatedly opposed Western intervention and the use of force for "regime change," and remained unconvinced of any consistent "obligation to protect." Shambaugh speaks of China's "teaming up" "with other authoritarian regimes" to constitute "coalitions of the unwilling."[36] Otherwise, there has always been among the BRICs what Patrick describes as a lack of "common vision."[37] Meanwhile, the United States' Congress has stalled ratification of agreed reforms to the International Monetary Fund (IMF) and the World Bank that would allow emerging economies a greater role in governance of those institutions.

Liberal, English School (ES), and normative theorists are eager to see progress in global governance—including, but not strictly limited to, international institutions, law, and more informal norm-building. Some such analysts have expressed nagging fears that certain desirable Western norms—especially with regard to human rights, democracy, and humanitarian intervention—may be constrained or "diluted" with the addition and amplification of non-Western voices. This is a contemporary reflection of an old debate about the effects of rising "multiculturalism" on the "international order" established after two world wars.[38] I believe there is increasing reason for concern. Authoritarian regimes do form alliances of convenience and encourage extreme right-wing political elements in the EU states and elsewhere. The authoritarians' targets are not only human rights, democracy, and humanitarianism but also, in the case of Russia and China, formal and informal prohibitions against the use of military force for territorial gain that seemed to have gained general acceptance after WWII—and were convincingly reaffirmed when UN-authorized forces turned back Saddam Hussein's invasion of Kuwait. In contrast, China and Russia currently evince a peculiar combination of hyper-defense of their own absolute sovereignty coupled with contemptuous disregard for the territorial sovereignty or reasonable territorial claims (East and South China seas) of others.

That said, it is important to keep things in perspective. As postcolonial theorists would remind us, any Western-order consensus on human rights, democracy, and humanitarian intervention has been half-hearted at best. Most of the European empires were hardly exemplary supporters of human rights and political participation in their domains. The UN regime for human rights, including the covenants and UN Human Rights Council, lacked meaningful enforcement mechanisms from the beginning and the Council is structured almost to guarantee having some of the worst offenders as members. Even such a horrific case as the genocide in Rwanda failed to elicit any international reaction until it was effectively over. The four BRICs did abstain on UN Security Council Resolution 1973 that helped to legitimize the North Atlantic Treaty Organization (NATO)'s Operation Unified Protector in Libya, but so did Germany. South Africa initially backed the resolution and only later complained that NATO was exceeding its mandate for the purpose of regime change. Would the feeble global response to the carnage in Syria likely be substantially different were rising powers out of the picture? Turkey has been a strong advocate of multilateral intervention to depose President Assad. In the last analysis (realism again), Western countries continue to blow hot and cold on human rights, as their respective perceived "interests" dictate. Case in point: UK Prime Minister Cameron—whose 2012 public meeting with the Dalai Lama enraged Beijing—in November 2013 was conspicuously silent about human rights violations when he went hat-in-hand to China soliciting business deals.

International law "realists" have long insisted that international law evolves by a process of assertion and response, that norms are continually tested and interpreted through practice. As for normative rules against aggressive territorial expansion, the Western "response" to Putin's earlier moves into Georgia and most recently Ukraine has been starkly revealing. Western leaders immediately expressed their consternation and condemnation, but governments imposed only limited/targeted individual and economic sanctions. It was abundantly clear that business concerns came first, not least in Germany, which has the closest economic ties with Russia and thus simultaneously the most leverage and the most to lose. *Russlandversteher* spokespersons soon surfaced, including two former Social Democratic chancellors, Helmut Schmidt and Gerhard Schröder, and various members of Chancellor

Merkel's own inner circle of advisers. Schmidt described Russia's actions in Ukraine as "understandable," while Schröder celebrated his own 70th birthday literally embracing Putin in St. Petersburg.[39] Meanwhile, in the EU, Bulgaria, and Hungary strongly opposed strong sanctions,[40] and at the height of the crisis France pressed ahead with its sale of two helicopter assault ships to Russia.[41] Perhaps still more unsettling was the strong showing of right-wing populist parties in the May 2014 European Parliament elections that are intent on curbing if not dismantling the EU, and openly express their admiration for Putin's Russia as a counterweight to liberals in the EU and US influence.[42]

However, in other normative realms—especially that of global capitalism—there is ample evidence that rising powers are far less eager to challenge whatever degree of Western global order may exist than to join and have a more effective voice within it. "New" global governance theory, we have noted, points up the wide range of actors at all levels engaged in increasingly diverse and complex governance arrangements. Setting aside for a moment the mega-international organizations/treaties/conferences—which appear to be losing steam and favor anyway—rising powers are increasingly making their presence felt in regional, bilateral, and public-private venues. This is a very complicated and important story that deserves far more exposition than I can give it here. But just for recent example, consider—with respect to global finance—the more flexible trading range allowed for China's renminbi and its gradual progress towards probably becoming one of the world's few reserve currencies.[43] Beijing has repeatedly argued that dollar hegemony should be replaced by a basket of reserve currencies. London has sought to become a leading offshore hub for trading in renminbi, following a bilateral agreement late in 2013 opening direct renminbi-sterling trading and permitting Chinese banks to establish UK branches. UK-based Standard Chartered and Agricultural Bank of China have now inaugurated renminbi clearing services.[44] Also, in November, the EU and China agreed to start talks on a new mutual investment treaty that, if eventually concluded, would be the first such Europe-wide agreement negotiated by the EU[45]—thus further linking China and the EU into global finance. Yet another multifaceted case is Turkey: As Erdogan's rather forlorn and tense visit to Brussels in January 2014 underscored, through thick and thin—even the dangerous financial crisis in the Eurozone and grave domestic political problems—Turkey has persisted in pursuing its application for full membership in the EU. Few today give that application much chance of success, but, in fact, who ultimately knows, given rapidly shifting conditions on both sides.[46] All along, however, Turkey's accession has been far less urgent because of its customs union with the EU that has been in place since 1995. Additionally, in December 2013 the EU also agreed to consider lifting visa requirements for Turkish citizens in exchange for a better procedure to return illegal immigrants.

The global governance of trade is, of course, central to the world economy, and for many years now, the most important institution in this area has been the WTO. Over time, that organization, and its predecessor the General Agreement on Tariffs and Trade (GATT), have been phenomenally successful in reducing average tariffs and non-tariff barriers to trade, and defining and combating "unfair" trading practices. Recently, however, the WTO has been seen as virtually "moribund" because negotiations to implement the goals established in the 2001 Doha Round remained largely deadlocked and there was some rise in protectionism during the post-2008 financial crisis. Late in 2013 the 159 WTO member states did reach a modest agreement[47] on reducing bureaucratic red tape in customs procedures, but the era of sweeping global trade pacts currently does appear to have ended or at least has come to a dramatic pause. Such a pessimistic view gives inadequate credit to the WTO's continuing and remarkably active Dispute Settlement Body (DSB). For comparison, to date (May 2014) the United States has been complainant (C) in 107 cases, respondent (R) in 121, and a third-party (P) in 114; and Japan C in 19, R in 15, and P in 144. China was admitted to the WTO in 2001, and Russia (after 18 years of negotiations) in 2012. China became especially active in WTO policy circles[48] after 2008 and has acted in the DSB as C in 12 cases, R in 31, P in 110. Russia's record (so far) is C in two cases, R in four, and P in 17. Brazil has been C in 26, R in 15, and P in 85. India has been C in 21, R in 22, and P in 99. Turkey has been C in two, R in nine, and P in 63.[49]

Now that further significant progress on the WTO's larger global trade goals appears to be stalled, attention has shifted to the regional level, with three or possibly even four major agreements potentially in view. The first, now successfully concluded, is a Comprehensive Economic and Trade Agreement (CETA) between the EU and Canada. The second is an EU–United States Transatlantic Trade and Investment Partnership (T-TIP). All new trade agreements involving the United States are currently imperiled by the US Senate's reluctance to allow for a "fast track" procedure during the ratification process that would limit amendments and debate. With regard to the T-TIP, the EU fears that proposed new investment rules could allow US corporations to challenge environmental or health laws that restrict their operations.

There are several other serious issues, including the US insistence that financial services regulation be excluded, as well as agricultural subsidies, and genetically modified foods. France has partially secured a "cultural" exception, limiting importation of foreign movies, television programs, and other media. Europeans have also been arguing for privacy safeguards against snooping by US security agencies.[50]

More directly relevant to rising powers is a Trans-Pacific Partnership (TPP) that would involve the United States and at least 11 other countries, including Australia, Brunei, Canada, Chile, Japan, Malaysia, Mexico, New Zealand, Peru, Singapore, and Vietnam[51]—together accounting for two-fifths of the world economy and one-third of all trade.[52] The TPP faces perhaps even greater obstacles than the T-TIP. Malaysia, in particular, has had its frictions with global capitalism since the earlier Asian Financial Crisis. The United States will have to reduce tariffs and quotas for sugar, dairy products, catfish, footwear, and textiles. Japan is determined to continue protecting rice, beef, pork, sugar, and dairy products. Vietnam does not like rules restricting its capacity to buy yarn for textiles from non-member states like China. Australia is troubled by dispute settlement procedures that would limit its control of multinational investment. And so on. A fourth suggested agreement, less ambitious than the other two and still at a very early stage, is the Regional Comprehensive Economic Partnership (RCEP) that would group the 10 Association of Southeast Asian Nations (ASEAN) countries with Australia, China, India, Japan, New Zealand, and South Korea.

As one commentator observed, China's "involvement in the RCEP makes the two pacts look like rivals." The United States "is trying to design a trade regime which China will eventually have to join—rather than getting to set its own rules as its clout increases."[53] Interestingly, China has itself signaled a major shift in its own conception of global governance relating to trade. China has long taken the position that the WTO should remain the principal venue for all international trade matters. However, at the December 2013 WTO meeting in Bali, China's commerce minister surprised other delegates by stating: "We're also open-minded towards other multilateral—and plurilateral—negotiations."[54]

In other respects China, the United States, and other states have lately been more cooperative than confrontational in addressing issues of global importance. China's participation in efforts to curb threatened SARS and successive bird-flu pandemics has been crucial to global health. Post-Kyoto Protocol UN climate talks have been about as unproductive as the WTO Doha trade negotiations, but Beijing and

Washington have at least been agreeing bilaterally on a few policies like phasing out the use of hydrofluorocarbons. On another climate related front, the Arctic Council—current members Canada, Denmark, Finland, Iceland, Norway, Russia, Sweden, and the United States—in May 2013 granted observer status to China, India, Italy, Japan and Singapore. The EU has also applied for observer status, but its application awaits resolution of a dispute with Canada over trade in seal products. Patrick also highlights the multinational antipiracy armada in the Indian Ocean that has involved naval ships from "not only the United States and its NATO allies but also China, India, Indonesia, Iran, Japan, Malaysia, Russia, Saudi Arabia, South Korea, and Yemen."[55]

Conclusion

This chapter began with a close examination of the key concepts of rising, power, and global governance, and found all of them to require careful definition by anyone wishing to use them meaningfully. Particular countries may be said to be rising and powerful only in particular respects, relative to other actors, and only when both issue and temporal contexts are specified. As we have explained, various schools of IR theory have their own perspectives on the behavior and prospects of purported rising powers, but constructivists are certainly correct that perceptions are often more important than "objective" factors in making assessments.

We reached a mixed verdict on the likely effect of rising powers on global norms and governance. China's authoritarianism and authoritarian trends in Russia, Turkey, and elsewhere shadow the global future of democracy, human rights, and humanitarian intervention. Even more disturbing is the lack of an effective or even united response from Western countries to direct challenges from Russia and China to prohibitions against the use of force for territorial gain. However, much more optimistic is the outlook for rising powers supporting the existing norms and institutions ordering the global economy.

Shambaugh notes that China began to use the term global governance— and then only in an economic context—in 2009 and since then has not evidenced "full assimilation of the values that reflect the norms and regulations of the Western liberal system." Much of China's compliance thus far appears to be the result of a "conscious, instrumental calculation." However, although he is not highly optimistic, he is clear that the "world should expect more from Beijing."[56] I emphatically believe the same should be said of my own country, the United States, whose attitude toward global governance over the years has been strained at best and often curiously contrary to (what I at least perceive to be) its own best interests, e.g., Congress' reluctance to accept more inclusive governance structures in the IMF and World Bank, unprecedented opportunities for expanded trade agreements, the Law of the Sea Treaty that would give Washington more leverage in maritime disputes, and tighter regulations to mitigate climate change. At the end of the day, I would argue, the surest way to address any challenge from rising powers is for established powers to act responsibly.

Notes

1 Kyle Caldwell, "The 10 Best Performing Stock Markets of 2013," *The Telegraph*, 19 December 2013.
2 Ibid.
3 Neil Gough, "China Ends Year as Asia's Weakest Market," *New York Times*, 31 December 2013.
4 *The Economist: Pocket World in Figures 2013 Edition* (London: Profile Books, 2012).
5 *The Economist: The World in 2014*.
6 See, Chris Giles, "China Poised to Pass US as World's Leading Economic Power This Year," *Financial Times*, 30 April 2014.
7 Some have suggested that China is neither anxious to alarm the United States nor to be pressured to assume larger international obligations as a consequence of its increased prosperity.
8 Jamil Anderlini, "China Tried to Undermine Economic Report Showing Its Ascendency," *Financial Times*, 1 May 2014.
9 Martin Wolf and David Pilling, "China: On Top of the World," *Financial Times*, 2 May 2014.
10 Michael A. Levi, "China Isn't Overtaking America," *New York Times*, 13 May 2014.
11 Ruchir Sharma, "The Ever-Emerging Markets: Why Economic Forecasts Fail," *Foreign Affairs* 93, no. 1 (2014): 52.
12 "Grounded: Special Report Brazil," *The Economist*, 28 September 2013, 4.
13 *The Economist: The World in 2014*, 107.
14 "Brazil's Economy: Go-Go to So-So," *Financial Times*, 25 February 2014.
15 Vladimir Isachenkov, "Putin Triumphs in 2013 Yet Tough Challenges Remain," *The Associated Press*, 31 December 2013.
16 Andrew Kramer, "Competing Visions for Russia's Economic Future," *New York Times*, 22 May 2014.
17 "India's Strongman," *The Economist*, 24 May 2014, 11.
18 David Pilling, "India Is Out of the Woods But a Long Way from Safe," *Financial Times*, 4 December 2013.
19 Lucy Hornby, "China Factory Outputs Points to Q1 Lull," *Financial Times*, 1 February 2014; and Keith Bradsher, "As China Economy Slows, the Pain Hits Home," *New York Times*, 29 January 2014.
20 Thomas Landon Jr., "'Fragile Five' Is the Latest Club of Emerging Nations in Turmoil," *New York Times*, 28 January 2014.

21 Paul Krugman, "Istanbearish," *New York Times*, 30 January 2014, krugm an.blogs.nytimes.com/2014/01/30/istanbearish.

22 Tim Arango, "A Leader Shows Vulnerability in Turkey's Cash Crisis," *New York Times*, 31 January 2014.

23 "Erdogan to Seek Turkish Presidency, Reign Till 2023, Aide Says," *New York Times*, 31 May 2014.

24 Sharma, "The Ever-Emerging Markets," 52.

25 James Kynge, "Similarities with 1997 Emerging Market Crash Only Go So Far," *Financial Times*, 24 January 2014.

26 There are some signs that China may be increasingly amenable to more constructive environmental policies at home and abroad.

27 David Shambaugh, *China Goes Global: The Partial Power* (New York: Oxford University Press, 2013), argument and quotations in this paragraph drawn from pp. 6–10.

28 Hedley Bull, *The Anarchical Society* (London: Macmillan, 1977); Robert Keohane, *After Hegemony: Cooperation and Discord in the World Political Economy* (Princeton N.J.: Princeton University Press, 1984); Alexander Wendt, *Social Theory of International Politics* (Cambridge: Cambridge University Press, 1999).

29 Barry Buzan, Charles Jones, and Richard Little, *The Logic of Anarchy: Neorealism to Structural Realism* (New York: Columbia University Press, 1993).

30 James N. Rosenau and Ernst-Otto Czempiel, eds, *Governance Without Government: Order and Change in World Politics* (Cambridge: Cambridge University Press, 1992).

31 James N. Rosenau, *Along the Domestic-Foreign Frontier: Exploring Governance in a Turbulent World* (Cambridge: Cambridge University Press, 1997).

32 Yale H. Ferguson and Richard W. Mansbach, *Remapping Global Politics: History's Revenge and Future Shock* (Cambridge: Cambridge University Press, 2004).

33 Stefano Guzzini, "The Ambivalent 'Diffusion of Power' in Global Governance," in *The Diffusion of Power in Global Governance: International Political Economy Meets Foucault*, Stefano Guzzini and Iver Neumann, eds (New York: Palgrave Macmillan, 2012), pp. 4, 2, 6.

34 Edward A. Kolodziej, "Global Governance and World Order," in *Encyclopedia of Global Studies*, vol. 2, Helmut K. Anheir and Mark Juergensmeyer, eds (Los Angeles, Calif.: Sage, 2012), 270. See also John Gerard Ruggie, "Global Governance and 'New Governance Theory': Lessons from Business and Human Rights," *Global Governance* 20 (2014): 5–17.

35 Stewart Patrick, "The Unruled World: The Case for Good Enough Global Governance," *Foreign Affairs* 93, no. 1 (2014): 58–59.

36 Shambaugh, *China Goes Global*, 9.

37 Patrick, "The Unruled World," 61.

38 Adda Bozeman, "The International Order in a Multicultural World," in *The Expansion of International Society*, Hedley Bull and Adam Watson, eds (Oxford: Oxford University Press, 1984), 387–406.

39 "How Very Understanding," *The Economist*, 10 May 2014, 51.

40 "Charlemagne: The Eastern Blockage," *The Economist*, 17 May 2014, 53.

41 Hugh Carnegy, "France Resists Pressure to Scrap Euro 1.2bn Russian Ships Deal," *Financial Times*, 12 May 2014.

42 Tony Barber, "Putin's Rightist Fellow Travellers Are a Menace to Europe," *Financial Times*, 27 May 2014.

43 See Yale H. Ferguson, "The Politics and Economics of the Renminbi-Dollar Relationship," in Mingjiang Li, *China Joins Global Governance: Cooperation and Contentions* (Lanham, Mass.: Lexington Books, 2012), pp. 95–113; and Yale H. Ferguson, "The Renminbi-US Dollar Relationship: Politics and Economics of a Diminishing Issue," in *Handbook of International Political Economy of Monetary Relations*, Thomas Oatley and W. Kindred Winecoff, eds (Northampton, Mass.: Edward Elgar, 2014), 123–43.

44 Paul J. Davies, "Clearing Deal Fuels London Ambition to Become Renminbi Hub," *Financial Times*, 2 December 2013.

45 Jamil Anderlini, "China and EU Agree to Talks on Bilateral Investment Treaty," *Financial Times*, 21 November 2013.

46 See Yale H. Ferguson, "Turkey and the EU: A Changed Context," *European Review* 21 (2013): 362–71.

47 India did succeed in extracting a five-year "peace clause" to allow more time to reconsider WTO rules affecting national programs that provide food to the poor.

48 See especially Henry Gao, "China's Participation in Global Trade Negotiations," 57–74; Xiaojun Li, "Learning and Socialization in International Institutions: China's Experience with the WTO Dispute Mechanism System," in *China Joins Global Governance*, 75–93.

49 These DSB statistics and others can be found at: www.wto.org/english/tra top_e/dispu_e/dispu_by_country_e.htm.

50 See James Politi, "US Trade Chief Vows to Fight for Farmers," *Financial Times*, 19 March 2013; and James Politi, "White House Set for Wall Street Clash over Trade Talks," *Financial Times*, 7 July 2013.

51 See Executive Office of the President, Office of the United States Trade Representative, "The United States in the Trans-Pacific Partnership," www.ustr.gov/about-us/press-office/fact-sheets/2011/november/united-states-trans-pacific-partnership.

52 "Banyan: Trade, Partnership, and Politics," *The Economist*, 24 August 2012, 40.

53 Ibid.

54 Shawn Donnan, "China Signals Shift Towards Plurilateral Trade Deals," *Financial Times*, 5 December 2013, www.ft.com/intl/cms/s/0/cd4e632a-5da f-11e3-95bd-00144feabdc0.html?siteedition=intl#axzz2sXtbhORk.

55 Patrick, "The Unruled World," 62.

56 Shambaugh, *China Goes Global*, 131, 9. See also *China Joins Global Governance*.

2 Continuity and change in global governance

A normative quest

Thomas G. Weiss and Rorden Wilkinson

- **Global governance**
- **Continuity, changes *in* global governance**
- **Changes *of* global governance**
- **Continuity or change?**
- **Conclusion**

We are hardly the first to indicate how ubiquitous "global governance" is, or how it is used and abused by academics, pundits, and policy-makers. While two decades ago it was almost unknown, Michael Barnett and Raymond Duvall quipped that already a decade ago it had "attained near-celebrity status ... [having] gone from the ranks of the unknown to one of the central orienting themes in the practice and study of international affairs."[1] Its omnipresence and marquee status means that global governance has become an alternative moniker for international organizations, a descriptor for a world stage packed with ever more actors, a call to arms for a better world, an attempt to control the pernicious aspects of accelerating economic and social change, and a synonym for world government. This imprecision has undermined its utility as an academic endeavor, which more recent work has sought to overcome.[2]

The pursuit of a more analytically useful engagement with questions of global governance has an appeal in itself not least because it may help us understand better how world orders are held together by refocusing and refreshing international relations as a field of study.[3] It also encourages the deployment of greater analytical precision for more normative purposes—the aim of this chapter. Our purpose here is to embark on a more explicitly normative quest by exploring what we have ignored to date in many analyses of global governance, namely explanations for what we judge to be continuity versus change in global governance—or perhaps better said, possible explanations for changes *in* and changes *of* global governance—with a view to encouraging change or even transformation that is progressive and not regressive. As a first step we are seeking better answers about the ultimate drivers of change in order to better prescribe future actions to address not only what former UN secretary-general Kofi Annan called "problems without passports,"[4] but also grander questions of order and organization.

Why is a better understanding of consequence for our normative pursuits? One straightforward answer is, as *The Human Development Report 2013* summarizes:

> The changing global economy is creating unprecedented challenges and opportunities for continued progress in human development. Global economic and political structures are in flux at a time when the world faces recurrent financial crises, worsening climate change and growing social unrest. Global institutions appear unable to accommodate changing power relations, ensure adequate provision of global public goods to meet global and regional challenges and respond to the growing need for greater equity and sustainability.[5]

Understanding how to move international society away from cobbling together feasible, but ultimately inadequate, responses to life-threatening global challenges and toward adequate solutions is our ambition. It is commonplace to state that many of the most intractable contemporary problems are transnational, ranging from climate change, migration, and pandemics to terrorism, financial instability, and proliferation of weapons of mass destruction; and that addressing them successfully requires actions that are not unilateral, bilateral, or even multilateral but rather global. Yet, while everything else is globalized (or at least globalizing) our politics is not. The policy authority and resources necessary for tackling such problems remain vested in individual states rather than collectively in universal institutions. The fundamental disconnect between the nature of a growing number of global problems and the current inadequate structures for international problem-solving and decision-making goes a long way toward explaining the fitful, tactical, and short-term local responses to challenges that require sustained, strategic, and longer-run global perspectives and action. We are seeking a better roadmap—and perhaps someday a GPS—for that unfinished journey.

So that we can better understand processes of change, we must first establish the current state of thinking, the task of the next section. Thereafter we draw a distinction between changes *in* and changes *of* global governance; here we distinguish between those facets of world order that encourage basic continuity in systems of global governance as well as those that encourage fundamental ruptures. Our claim is that only by understanding what holds grand formations of governance together, and what encourages their transformation—what might be thought of as centripetal and centrifugal tendencies—are we able to understand both changes in and of world order as well as how positive alternations and transformations can be brought about.

Global governance

Mainstream thinking has shifted decidedly away from the study of intergovernmental organization and public international law toward global governance. The term itself was born from a marriage between academic theory and practical policy in the 1990s and became entwined with that other meta-phenomenon of the last two decades, globalization. James Rosenau and Ernst Czempiel's theoretical *Governance without Government* was published in 1992,[6] just about the same time that the Swedish government launched the policy-oriented Commission on Global Governance under the chairmanship of Sonny Ramphal and Ingmar Carlsson. Both set in motion explorations of what was dubbed "global governance." The 1995 publication of the commission's report, *Our Global Neighbourhood*,[7] coincided with the first issue of the Academic Council on the United Nations System (ACUNS) journal *Global Governance*. This newly minted quarterly sought to return to the global problem-solving origins of the leading journal in the field, which seemed to have lost its way. As Timothy Sinclair reminds us, "From the late 1960s, the idea of international organization fell into disuse ... *International Organization*, the journal which carried this name founded in the 1940s, increasingly drew back from matters of international policy and instead became a vehicle for the development of rigorous academic theorizing."[8]

These developments paved the way for a raft of works about growing global complexity, the management of globalization, and the challenges confronting international institutions.[9] In part, global governance replaced an immediate predecessor as a normative endeavor, "world order studies," which was viewed as overly top-down and static. Having grown from the World Peace through World Law movement, world order failed to capture the variety of actors, networks, and relationships that characterized contemporary international relations.[10] It did, however, force us to think about how—as John Ruggie puts it—the world "hangs together,"[11] even if we forgot to learn the lessons world order studies taught us about patterns of continuity and change, and of coherence and interconnectivity.

When the perspectives from world-order scholars started to look a trifle old-fashioned, the stage was set for a new analytical cottage industry. After his archival labors to write a two-volume history of world federalism, Joseph Barrata aptly observed that in the 1990s "the new expression, 'global governance,' emerged as an acceptable term in debate on international organization for the desired and practical goal of progressive efforts, in place of 'world government.'" He continued, scholars "wished to avoid using a term that would harken back to the thinking about world government in the 1940s, which was largely based on fear of atomic bombs and too often had no practical proposals for the transition short of a revolutionary act of the united peoples of the world."[12]

Yet, the emergence of the term—and alterations in the way that aspirations for insights from it were expressed—did not empty global governance of the normative content stemming from preoccupations that had motivated numerous previous generations of international relations and international organization scholars. We are speaking not only of those who studied and advocated for the League of Nations and the United Nations, but a long genealogy whose family tree sprouted with Dante's *Monarchia* at the beginning of the fourteenth century, which initiated a tradition of criticizing the existing order and replacing it with a universal government. Others in this normative quest include: Hugo Grotius, the Dutch jurist whose *On the Laws of War and Peace* (1625) usually qualifies him as the "father" of international law; Émeric Crucé, the French monk who died in 1648, the same year as the treaties of Westphalia, and dreamed of a world court where nations could meet and work out disputes and agree to disarm; and of course Immanuel Kant, whose *Perpetual Peace* (1795) envisioned a confederation of pacific, republican states.

Global governance can be seen as the latest entry in a distinguished normative genealogy and one that for many is concerned with our collective efforts to identify, understand, and address worldwide problems and processes that reach beyond the capacities of individual states. In this formulation it reflects a capacity of the international system at any moment in time to provide government-like services in the absence of world government and encompasses a wide variety of cooperative problem-solving arrangements that were visible but informal (e.g., practices or guidelines) or were temporary formations (e.g., coalitions of the willing). Such arrangements could also be more formal, taking the shape of hard rules (laws and treaties) or else institutions with administrative structures and established practices to manage collective affairs by a variety of actors—including state authorities, intergovernmental organizations, nongovernmental organizations, private sector entities, and other civil society actors.[13]

Yet global governance need not take this form; and our ready association between the term and the way that we understand it is as much part of the problem as it is a pointer towards the solution. Formulated as a pluralistic—that is, multi-actor, sometimes acting in concert or constellation, sometimes not—response to the problems of world order (insecurity, climate change, financial crises, human rights abuses, and so on), global governance fixes in time how we understand the organization of the world around us. It does not allow us to imagine different forms of global governance—which include but are not limited to singular global systems or functional but nonetheless atomized wholes—that may help generate thinking about our preferences when moving from one world order to another; nor does it allow us to see that other forms of world organization immediately and distantly past are also forms of global governance: imperialism and tributary systems included. However, it is in understanding that global governance is distinguishable by form that we are better able to mark out what constitutes a change *in*—as opposed to a change *of*—the way that the world is governed.

Continuity, changes *in* global governance

Most contemporary observers would point to significant, perhaps even dramatic, alterations currently taking place in world politics: new challenges to international peace and security and human survival have arisen; new non-state actors have appeared on the world stage, and older ones have occasionally been transformed; new conventions and norms have proliferated; new intergovernmental initiatives and institutions have been established; new powers have "risen"; and new challenges have emerged (or older ones exacerbated to such an extent that they are qualitatively different) confronting the planet. Yet the dominant reality in world politics (whether within or outside international organizations) remains decision-making by states. Nothing has altered the validity of an evaluation two decades ago by Adam Roberts and Benedict Kingsbury: "international society has been modified, but not totally transformed."[14]

The world thus still reflects what Hedley Bull and virtually all political scientists call "anarchy,"[15] or the absence of a central global authority. In spite of the construction of a seemingly ever-denser web of international institutions, there is nothing approaching a world government or overarching global authority in the offing. Although it would be inaccurate to ignore the extremes—ranging from fractious political authority in states of varying degrees of collapse to a kind of supranational integration of the European Union—it still is accurate to point to an overwhelming and fundamental continuity: state sovereignty remains the core tenet of our conception of international relations, and the basis on which contemporary global governance unfolds.[16]

Nonetheless, within this fundamental continuity there have been changes in global governance arising from the perceived character of global problems, nature of actors, and limitations of international measures to govern the planet. Indeed, these are why global governance as a concept emerged and has thrived. Beginning in the 1970s, interdependence and rapid technological advances fostered the growing recognition that many problems defied the problem-solving capacities of a single state. Prior to this time, and the evidence of world wars and the Great Depression notwithstanding, most observers would have argued that powerful states could usually solve problems on their own, or at least could insulate themselves from their worst effects. Efforts to eradicate malaria within a geographic area and to prevent those with the disease from entering a territory should be seen as qualitatively different from halting terrorist money-laundering, avian flu, or acid rain. Today no state, no matter how powerful, can labor under the illusion that it can protect its population from such threats. Rich states earlier could insulate themselves by erecting effective barriers, whereas a growing number of contemporary challenges to world order simply cannot be prevented by erecting walls. The development of a consciousness about the global environment and the consequences of human interactions, and especially the 1972 UN conference in Stockholm, is usually seen as a game-changer in the evolution of thinking in this regard.[17]

The second development underpinning growing interest in global governance was the sheer expansion in numbers and importance of non-state actors, particularly civil society and for-profit corporations, and more especially those with transnational reach.[18] Although analysts of international relations and international organization had become aware and included them in their thinking and concepts, they are still seen by many purely as appendages to the state system and as peripheral to problem-solving.[19] Such growth has been facilitated by the so-called third wave of democratization,[20] including institutional networks similar enough to facilitate greater transnational and transgovernmental interactions described by Anne-Marie Slaughter and David Grewal,[21] a growing disillusionment with state capacity *and* state willingness to deal with social issues, and the onset of a more pernicious global economic environment, including mushrooming inequalities.

A third driving force lay in concerns to upgrade the UN system for the post-Cold War period. Combining worries about the increasingly transborder nature of problems and state incapacity to address them with a desire to draw from the untapped potential of "new" global actors, scholars and practitioners sought to shore-up the world body by encouraging it not only to reform but also to partner with others to address pressing issues. One aspect of this movement pushed the world organization to recognize the comparative advantage of other actors that were better able to fulfill key tasks, including roping nongovernmental organizations and transnational corporations more closely into the work of the United Nations through the Global Compact. Another explored the capacity for a "complex multilateralism" to emerge designed to capture the capacity of global social movements to fill a legitimacy gap in global governance.[22] Another still sought to address the "crisis of multilateralism" through root and branch reform of UN institutions.[23]

Whatever the exact explanatory weight of these driving forces—and they are not an exhaustive list—the emergence and widespread recognition of transnational issues that circumscribed state capacity along with the proliferation of non-state actors (NSAs) responding to perceived shortfalls in national capabilities and a willingness to address them in the context of a perceived crisis of multilateralism combined to stimulate new thinking. Scholars of international relations, organization, and law began to ask questions about the precise role of other actors that were to varying degrees already global agents. Multinational corporations and philanthropic institutions, for instance, had been obscured from the sight of analysts who focused on states as the only or at least the most consequential actors.[24] As a consensus about the pace and extent of global change grew, so did the impulse to understand the significance of an even greater range of players, extending later to faith actors and financial rating agencies as well as such less salubrious agents as transnational criminal networks and terrorist movements.[25] At the same time, scholars began to ask what kind of governance was exerted by mechanisms such as markets that had previously been the sole purview of international political economists.[26] The result was the deployment of a new moniker—global governance—to describe how this pluralist world was constituted.

At one level this new term was liberating. Whereas states and the intergovernmental organizations that they had created had once monopolized the attention of students of international organization, the closing decades of the twentieth century encouraged an analytical shift from state-centric structures to a far wider range of actors and mechanisms. At another level, however, it has proven to be problematic. Instead of encouraging us to use the increasing pluralism of the late twentieth and early twenty-first centuries as a platform for enquiring how the world was, is, and should be governed, analysts simply accepted global governance as a descriptor of a particular historical moment and set about attempting to realize the possibilities for cooperation that lay therein. In our rush to realize the progress that the post-Cold War moment generated, we cast in concrete a term whose utility for understanding change and encouraging much grander moments of advancement had yet to be realized.

Changes *of* global governance

In pursuing a more predictable, stable, and just world order, we are concerned with significant changes *of* global governance, or what might better be termed "transformations" rather than mere changes *in* global governance—which we equate to be adjustments that leave the fundamental shape and form of a system largely intact. Kalevi Holsti's *Taming the Sovereigns* probes the concept of change and ways of measuring it. As he puts it, "These include change as novelty or replacement, change as addition or subtraction, increased complexity, transformation, reversion, and obsolescence."[27] Change thus can be analyzed in quantitative and qualitative ways. If we think simply in terms of the growing scale and scope of international organizations and staff or their budgets, or of similar increases by non-governmental organizations (NGOs) and transnational corporations (TNCs), there would be no debate. If change can be additive or subtractive and thus measured quantitatively, on any conceivable measure, the contemporary system of global governance has expanded exponentially; but the system's essential character remains intact. Our concern is, however, with *qualitative* change, or a difference in kind. The presumption is of a clear break between what once was and what currently is.[28] To that extent, we are looking for discontinuities, when new forms replace old ones.

In *The Structure of Scientific Revolutions*, Thomas Kuhn famously outlined how a dominant paradigm—or "way of seeing the world"—is replaced. Shortcomings in a worldview become clear when puzzling anomalies (or things that make no sense) require alternative explanations. If too many anomalies and auxiliary hypotheses result, a new paradigm is required because "the anomalous has become the expected."[29] Kuhn's classic example was the shift from Ptolemy's model of planets rotating around a fixed Earth when that orthodoxy simply could no longer explain observations made with new instruments (the telescope especially) or predict what was going to happen.

We have not arrived in a comparable place for state sovereignty and the contemporary global governance system. That is, the Copernican moment is not yet upon us. If anarchy is understood as the absence of central authority for the world, that definition still holds. Nonetheless, other elements of the classic definition have far less explanatory value than even a few decades ago, and certainly it makes no sense, despite the resilience of great power politics, to analyze international relations through the lens of a unitary state acting alone and with autonomy. Hence, we should emulate a young Copernicus; we should stare at the sun and planets at which others have been gazing for three-and-a-half centuries but articulate alternative views for the relations among them. We can point to the obvious reality that sovereign states remain the foundation of the contemporary world order, but that they no longer are unquestioned authorities, too rarely provide public goods, and increasingly are unable to solve global problems crying out for solutions.

In exploring change and ways of measuring it, Holsti points out that change is quite different for someone playing the stock market and for those of us trying to understand international relations, where recent events are not of interest unless they have a demonstrable effect on how diplomatic, military, economic, political, or humanitarian work is actually done. He notes, "This is the Hegelian and Marxist problem: at what point does quantitative change lead to qualitative consequences?"[30] In other words, we can also characterize as "new" a tipping point at which quantitative change is so substantial that it constitutes something qualitatively "new"—or, that "more is different."[31]

Our feeble understanding of what drives change in the way that our world is organized renders the discipline of international relations, as a broad intellectual undertaking, ahistorical.[32] An exception is Craig Murphy's *International Organization and Industrial Change*, which illuminates the role played by international organizations as modes of governance in advancing forms of economic accumulation.[33] His work with JoAnne Yates on what might be called "creeping global governance" shows how minute, functionalist developments that standardize economic behavior and social norms lock in place systems of command and control that give rise to particular economic outcomes and social goods (some beneficial, some not). Murphy and Yates are exceptions in a field that has consistently failed to account for change. Our claim here is not that first rate historically sensitive worlds are wholly absent, but that the mainstream of the field has chosen to eschew them,[34] especially in systems of governance.[35] However, even they only peer back into the relatively recent past and not into past epochs of what can only be described as "global governance."

If that term is appropriately deployed as an analytical lens, we are forced to explain change not just today or in the post-Cold War era or in the nineteenth century, but in other times and under other circumstances. In looking for explanations for radical change in the institutionalized ways that human beings deal with such transboundary problems as war and economic uncertainties, international order has been built, destroyed, and rebuilt on numerous occasions, particularly when yesterday's institutions have been exposed as ill-equipped to tackle today's problems.

The clearest driver of dramatic changes of global governance without a doubt is cataclysm. As students of international organizations and of history, a burning question is whether a third generation of multilateral organizations will arise quickly and as a result of unnecessary and unspeakable tragedies—just as crisis innovations such as the League of Nations or the United Nations arose phoenix-like from the ashes of the twentieth century's world wars and the Congress of Vienna from the Napoleonic wars—or more deliberately based on the evolutionary potential of constructing an edifice on the basis of more modest functional bases. Contemplating the former option is not soothing even if history informs us that such tragedies are the customary currency for global institutional transformations. As inveterate optimists, we are betting on the human capacity for learning and adapting to prevent suffering on a scale that could well dwarf the twentieth century's wars. "Whether our accumulated connectivity and experience has created fresh perspectives on global governance and an ability to transcend national orders," Ian Goldin cautions, "remains the most critical question of our time."[36] The pressing question here is "does catastrophe—war, plague and so on—have to be the major driver of changing systems of global governance?" Historical precedent does not constitute causal certainty. Thus, confecting change that is not first preceded by cataclysm but that nonetheless results in better global governance ought now to be the task ahead.

Continuity or change?

For all of the interest that growing complexity has engendered, and the novel scholarly thinking about global governance that has emerged as a result, old ways have persisted. Three-quarters of a century of distinguishing the study of international relations from political science as a focus on states as the primary units of analysis continues to condition thinking and inhibit normative pursuits. Although disavowing path dependency, the past nonetheless weighs heavily on the way that scholars understand the contemporary world, even a dramatically altered one. Similarly, students of international organization and law have continued to emphasize the role of major powers in intergovernmental organizations as the central lens through which to view human progress.

Thinking outside of these boxes is not really—nor should it be understood as being—that new. The late Harold Jacobson observed that the march by states toward a world government was woven into the tapestries decorating the walls of the *Palais des Nations* in Geneva— now the UN's European Office but once the headquarters of the defunct League of Nations. They "picture the process of humanity combining into ever larger and more stable units for the purpose of governance— first the family, then the tribe, then the city-state, and then the nation— a process which presumably would eventually culminate in the entire world being combined in one political unit."[37] The post-Enlightenment period was fruitful in blending science and thinking about how to link individuals in ever-larger communities. "As man advances in civilization, and small tribes are united into larger communities," was how Charles Darwin put it, "there is only an artificial barrier to prevent his sympathies extending to the men of all nations and races."[38]

However, other than a few surviving members of an almost extinct species, the world federalists, virtually no one believes that is where we are headed. Mark Mazower, for one, sees the disappearance of this noble but megalomaniacal, visionary but delusional idea.[39] Thus, while we have labeled the complex, contemporary world where authority is commonly agreed to be exercised differently as "global governance," we have maintained familiar state-centric ways for identifying what counts, and how we frame normative pursuits as a result. We speak of "variable geometries" but essentially view other actors and activities as appendages to the international system that analysts have observed since the Peace of Westphalia. The ups and downs of global changes, to be sure, have injected elements of curiosity and new questions, which revolve around how the world is organized and authority and power are exercised. Whilst making room for the knowledge and insights missing when merely peering at states, we stop short of providing real answers to questions that push us beyond comfort levels with older modes of thinking.

In the end, it is a fool's errand to expect to settle grand debates about continuity and change. There are always and invariably elements of both. That said, we may be approaching a transitional moment, an interlude signaling a possible tectonic shift in the way that we can govern the world. Can human beings organize themselves to address and attenuate the global problems that we and our ancestors have created? The image of a "global village" is hackneyed, and not all problems are global. Yet for those that are—and an increasing number are no longer abstract specters but actually staring us in the face—we actually do inhabit a global village. If we are to respond affirmatively to the question, transformative institutional developments should be integral to our thinking and not far beyond the pale.

Conclusion

Without a concerted effort to press forward our understandings of the complexities of global governance, the way that authority and power are exercised, and the ideational and material aspects of the way that the world is governed, we risk not only misunderstanding the current world order but also underestimating our capacity to make meaningful adjustments to that order. In short, we can no longer ignore global governance's capacity to understand change—past and future as well as present.

Our unfinished normative journey involves a potentially fruitful way of thinking about global governance, one that removes some of the blinders of its association with the post-Cold War moment. We understand global governance as the sum of the informal and formal ideas, values, norms, procedures, and institutions that help all actors—states, intergovernmental organizations, civil society, and TNCs—identify, understand, and address transboundary problems. If so, we ought to pursue this topic not merely on the basis of its *contemporary* manifestations, which emerged from a specific and recent historical moment, which responded to a perceived need to better understand what was going on, and which sought to capture global change as a positive phenomenon. Pursuing better answers to "How is the world governed?" across time should also give us a better idea of whence we have come, why change has happened, and where we are as well as could and should be going.

In comparison with international organization, peering through the lens of global governance opens the analyst's eyes to viewing a host of actors and informal processes of norm and policy formulation as well as options for action. The crucial normative challenge in the near term is, as we have challenged ourselves and others, to push the study of global governance beyond the notion of "add actors and processes into the international organization mix and stir."[40]

We analysts of global governance have failed as agents of change— that is, we have fallen short as purveyors of opinion and proposals about a better and fairer world order. As such, we do not serve our students and those practitioners who seek our advice; and for those of us who take on policy briefs, we no longer push out the envelope of what is considered acceptable. We too seldom offer a set of tools for understanding how the world works, a grounding on which socially beneficial policy can be created, and most importantly a framework for thinking about substantial changes of global governance.

Chief among a host of thorny problems resulting from the widespread confusion about that term's meaning is our failure to recognize that the global governance of the 1990s and early 2000s is different from the kind of global governance that existed in the nineteenth century, the first millennium CE, or today. We should recognize that global governance is not merely a descriptor for a post-Cold War pluralistic moment but rather a legitimate set of questions about how the world is governed, ordered, and organized in every historical period.

Historical change is perhaps our best point of departure. If we apply the same kinds of questions that led to understanding global governance as a pluralization of world politics at the end of the last century, we should also be able to determine what kinds of systems of world order existed before the current one, and how power and authority were exercised therein. We should have insights about all drivers of change and their impact. A more profound investigation of contemporary global governance can potentially capture accurately how power is exercised across the globe, how a multiplicity of actors relate to one another generally as well as on specific issues, how to make better sense of global complexity, and how to account for alterations in the way that the world is and has been organized (or governed) over time—both within and between historical periods.

However, wrenching global governance from the contemporary moment and applying it historically is half the conceptual battle and none of the normative one. The move backward would have limited salience if it also was not valuable for understanding tomorrow. The future-oriented value lies in treating global governance as a set of questions that enable us to work out how the world was, is, and could be governed as well as how changes in grand and not-so-grand patterns of governance occurred, are occurring, and ought to occur.

Notes

1 Michael Barnett and Raymond Duvall, eds, *Power in Global Governance* (Cambridge: Cambridge University Press, 2005), 1.

2 See Thomas G. Weiss and Rorden Wilkinson, eds, *International Organization and Global Governance* (London: Routledge, 2014).

3 Thomas G. Weiss and Rorden Wilkinson, "Global Governance to the Rescue: Saving International Relations?" *Global Governance* 20, no. 1 (2014): 19–36.

4 Kofi A. Annan, "What Is the International Community? Problems without Passports," *Foreign Policy*, no. 132 (September–October 2002): 30–1. See also, Thomas G. Weiss, *Governing the World? Addressing "Problems without Passports"* (Boulder, Colo.: Paradigm Publishers, 2014).

5 United Nations Development Programme, *Human Development Report 2013: The Rise of the South, Human Progress in a Diverse World* (New York: UNDP, 2013), 2.

6 James N. Rosenau and Ernst Czempiel, eds, *Governance without Government: Order and Change in World Politics* (Cambridge: Cambridge University Press, 1992).

7 Commission on Global Governance, *Our Global Neighbourhood* (Oxford: Oxford University Press, 1995).

8 Timothy J. Sinclair, *Global Governance* (Cambridge: Polity Press, 2012), 16.

9 See, for example, Robert W. Cox, "The Crisis of World Order and the Challenge to International Organization," *Cooperation and Conflict* 29, no. 2 (1994): 99–113; Aseem Prakash and Jeffrey A. Hart, eds, *Globalization and Governance* (London: Routledge, 1999); and David Held and Anthony McGrew, eds, *Governing Globalization* (Cambridge: Polity Press, 2002).

10 Richard B. Falk and Saul H. Mendlovitz, eds, *A Strategy of World Order*, volumes I-IV (New York: World Law Fund, 1966–67); and Grenville Clark and Louis B. Sohn, *World Peace through World Law* (Cambridge, Mass.: Harvard University Press, 1958).

11 John Gerard Ruggie, *Constructing the World Polity: Essays in International Institutionalization* (London: Routledge, 1998), 1.

12 Joseph Preston Barrata, *The Politics of World Federation*, 2 volumes (Westport, Conn.: Praeger Publishers, 2004). Quote from vol. 2, 534–535.

13 Thomas G. Weiss and Ramesh Thakur, *Global Governance and the UN: An Unfinished Journey* (Bloomington: Indiana University Press, 2010).

14 Adam Roberts and Benedict Kingsbury, "Introduction: The UN's Roles in International Society since 1945," in *United Nations: Divided World*, 2nd edn, Adam Roberts and Benedict Kingsbury, eds (Oxford: Oxford University Press, 1993), 1.

15 Hedley Bull, *The Anarchical Society: A Study* (New York: Columbia University Press, 1977). A more recent treatment is Robert Jackson, *The Global Covenant: Human Conduct in a World of States* (Oxford: Oxford University Press, 2000).

16 Thomas G. Weiss and Rorden Wilkinson, "After Sovereignty: Global Governance beyond IR?" in *International Relations Theory Today*, Toni Erskine and Ken Booth, eds (Cambridge: Polity, forthcoming).

17 Peter Newell, *Globalization and the Environment* (Cambridge: Polity Press, 2012).

18 Peter Willetts, *Non-Governmental Organizations in World Politics: The Construction of Global Governance* (London: Routledge, 2011).

19 Robert O. Keohane and Joseph P. Nye, eds, *Transnational Relations and World Politics*, a special issue of *International Organization* 25, no. 3 (1971).

20 Samuel P. Huntington, *Third Wave: Democratization in the Late Twentieth Century* (Norman, Okla.: University of Oklahoma Press, 1991).

21 Anne-Marie Slaughter, *A New World Order* (Princeton, N.J.: Princeton University Press, 2004); and David Singh Grewal, *Network Power: The Social Dynamics of Globalization* (New Haven, Conn.: Yale University Press, 2008).

22 Robert O'Brien, Anne Marie Geotz, Jan Aart Scholte and Marc Williams, *Contesting Global Governance: Multilateral Economic Institutions and Global Social Movements* (Cambridge: Cambridge University Press, 2000), 3.

23 Edward Newman, *A Crisis of Global Institutions? Multilateralism and International Security* (London: Routledge, 2007).

24 See, for instance, Michael Moran, *Private Foundations and Development Partnerships* (London: Routledge, 2014); Jonathan J. Makuwira, *Non-Governmental Development Organizations and the Poverty Reduction Agenda* (London: Routledge, 2014); and David Hulme and Michael Edwards, *NGOs, States and Donors: Too Close for Comfort?* (Basingstoke: Macmillan, 1997).

25 Timothy J. Sinclair, *The New Masters of Capital: American Bond Rating Agencies and the Politics of Creditworthiness* (Ithaca, N.Y.: Cornell University Press, 2005); Katherine Marshall, *Global Institutions of Religion: Ancient Masters, Modern Shakers* (London: Routledge, 2013); and Frank Madsen, *Transnational Organized Crime* (London: Routledge, 2009).

26 Robert W. Cox, "An Alternative Approach to Multilateralism for the Twenty-first Century," *Global Governance* 3, no. 1 (1997): 103–116.

27 Kalevi J. Holsti, *Taming the Sovereigns: Institutional Change in International Politics* (Cambridge: Cambridge University Press, 2004), 12–13.

28 The related distinction between evolutionary and revolutionary change also is germane, as is the analytical distinction between punctuated equilibrium and evolution. See John Campbell, *Institutional Change and Globalization* (Princeton, N.J.: Princeton University Press, 2004), 34.

29 Thomas S. Kuhn, *The Structure of Scientific Revolutions*, 2nd edn (Chicago, Ill.: University of Chicago Press, 1970), 4, 53.

30 Holsti, *Taming the Sovereigns*, 8.

31 P.W. Anderson, "More is Different: Broken Symmetry and the Nature of the Hierarchical Structure of Science," *Science* 177, no. 4047 (1972): 393–6.

32 Andrew J. Williams, Amelia Hadfield, and Simon J. Rofe, *International History and International Relations* (London: Routledge, 2012).

33 Craig N. Murphy, *International Organization and Industrial Change: Global Governance since 1850* (Cambridge: Polity Press, 1994).

34 For exceptions, see Justin Rosenberg, *The Empire of Civil Society: A critique of the Realist theory of International Relations* (London: Verso, 1994); Barry K. Gills and William R. Thompson, eds, *Globalization and Global History* (London: Routledge, 2006); and Stephen Hobden and John M. Hobson, eds, *Historical Sociology of International Relations* (Cambridge: Cambridge University Press, 2002).

35 Craig Murphy and JoAnne Yates, *The International Organization for Standardization (ISO)* (London: Routledge, 2009).

36 Ian Goldin, *Divided Nations: Why Global Governance Is Failing and What We Can Do about It* (Oxford: Oxford University Press, 2013), 166–7.
37 Harold K. Jacobson, *Networks of Interdependence: International Organizations and the Global Political System*, 2nd edn (New York: Knopf, 1984), 84.
38 Charles Darwin, *The Descent of Man and Selection in Relation to Sex* (New York: Appleton and Co., 1897), 122.
39 Mark Mazower, *Governing the World: The History of an Idea* (New York: Penguin, 2012).
40 Thomas G. Weiss and Rorden Wilkinson, "Rethinking Global Governance: Complexity, Authority, Power, Change," *International Studies Quarterly* 58, no. 2 (2014): 207–215.

3 Rising powers and reform of the practices of international security institutions

Thomas Biersteker and Erica Moret

- **Emerging powers and security governance institutions**
- **How can pivotal rising powers influence non-proliferation sanctions?**
- **Ambivalence in behavior**
- **Conclusion**

Emerging powers appear to be fundamentally ambivalent about their situation and place in the world. They find themselves located in a space between, on the one hand, an aspiration for respect, a desire for a genuine role in global governance, and readiness for a serious place at the table in global institutions as emerging or rising regional and global powers. At the same time, they consider themselves still remaining on the outside of established institutions, as representatives of the developing world, facing real problems of development of their own. They continue to identify themselves as profoundly part of the Third World, the non-aligned world, and the Global South, and they are strongly opposed to most forms of external intervention, particularly from great powers. Their non-aligned status remains a very important part of their identity.

It is not a contradiction for them to be in both spaces at the same time. Both characterizations are essentially accurate. It is because of their fundamental ambivalence that it is difficult to predict their behavior in international institutions, to estimate their stance on any given issue, and to assess their likely impact on existing international organizations. They also differ considerably among themselves and are hardly of one mind on most issues. There is also the unique situation of China compared with the rest of the so-called emerging powers, because in so many ways China is in a class by itself, rather than just another member (or even the leader) of a group of emerging powers.

Much of the discussion about emerging powers and global governance or emerging powers and contemporary international organizations focuses on what emerging powers want and on whether they will
be "responsible" institutional players and/or contributors to resolving
the challenges and collective action problems of contemporary global
governance.[1] Being "responsible" tends to be highly correlated with
maintaining the institutions already established by the traditional
North, developed world, European and North American powers, or
under United States hegemony. Although there is good reason to
expect that emerging powers will reinforce the institutions from which
they benefit,[2] this tends to lead to a rather condescending approach
overall.

We recommend that the emphasis should be changed from thinking
in terms of the concerns of system maintenance to thinking about
system adaptability. Indeed, adaptability is an important criterion for
the evaluation of the quality of global governance.[3] International
organizations themselves have to adapt in order to survive, to maintain
themselves, and to remain relevant to the ever changing problems and
challenges they face.

Thus we should begin with a different approach, and by asking some
different kinds of questions. First, how do emerging powers view or
define the issue domain addressed by different international organizations? What do they see as the principal challenges, collective action
problems, and priorities for global action? What norms would they like
to see advanced in the issue domain? What do they see as the scope for
action? Second, how do emerging powers assess the nature of the
existing regimes, regime complexes, and international organizations?
Who do they view as the principals, the major players, and/or the
essential participants in contemporary governance of the issue domain?
Third, only after considering the first two sets of questions should we
turn our attention to the kinds of governance changes emerging powers
would like to see. This is not the first question we should ask, but follows from assessments of the prior two questions. That is, what kinds
of changes would emerging powers like to see in formal international
organizations operating in an issue domain, within regimes or regime
complexes concerned with the issue?[4] Whether these changes are consistent with existing institutional designs is an interesting and important
question.

Even with this change in orientation away from the question of what
do they want and whether they will be responsible, it is important to
recognize that this is only one aspect of the larger issue at hand. We
need also to think about emerging powers and international

organizations in relational terms. It is not just the interests of states applied to international organizations that we should be looking at—this is a rather traditional way to think about international organizations, one that emphasizes principal/agent relationships. Rather, we should also consider, as appropriate, the reciprocal actions taken by international organizations to anticipate and prepare for the emergence of new locations of power, influence, and authority in the international system.

International organizations are not passive players, or agents solely reflective of the interests of principals (states) utilizing them to maximize national interests. Once created, international organizations can also become principals themselves, attempting to steer debates, direct resources, and shape agendas. They have a productive role and power, as Barnett and Duvall have argued,[5] and they should be conceptualized as such.

Although they are by no means fully autonomous agents at all times, most international organizations are constantly adapting themselves in search of resources and in anticipation of future locations of global power. They are doing so in their self-interest (and here we take a rather public choice view of institutions). The first priority of most institutions is survival. Success or effectiveness is evaluated not only in terms of policy outcomes or stated institutional goals (or their ability to address collective goods problems), but also in terms of their ability to grow, to expand their mandates, their budgets, their personnel, and the spaces they occupy, both physical and normative. If one reads carefully the annual report of any institution, there will be references to all of the above. To be sure, their achievements are always legitimated in terms of some larger notable goals or objectives, but internal reports to boards are full of other, internal indicators of growth (like staff, budget, and space). Thus, when we think about international organizations and emerging powers, we need to look at both sides of the relationship between them, from vantage points on both sides of the issue. Emerging powers have reasons to care about international organizations, and international organizations have reasons to be interested in emerging powers.

Why might international organizations care about emerging powers? First, international organizations have an interest in maintaining their relevance to new issue domains identified by emerging powers. New state actors are likely to bring new priorities or concerns to existing issue domains, and in order to maintain their central role in the domain, international organizations have an interest in demonstrating their adaptability. Second, international organizations have an interest in maximizing their impact in a given issue domain. They might choose to rely on emerging powers for the dissemination of existing or novel ideas and approaches. For example, in the sanctions issue domain (discussed in more detail below), emerging powers outside the sanctions regime could potentially provide the greatest source of evasion (or trade diversion) for targeted entities and are therefore of particular significance to the maintenance of the global regime. Third, international organizations have a self interest in securing access to financial resources.[6] Emerging powers are inherently attractive to international organizations because they increasingly have resources to invest in new initiatives, unlike the prevailing or existing great powers that originally initiated many of the institutions and have recently been cutting back on their annual contributions to them.

There are at least two different ways international organizations could adapt themselves in anticipation of emergence of new powers: through ideational adaptation and/or through substantive, structural reform. In ideational terms, international organizations might adjust their mandates, allow emerging powers to play a greater role in agenda setting, or engage them more directly in institutional strategic planning. They might also adapt existing monitoring and enforcement mechanisms to suit emerging power sensitivities and concerns about sovereign non-intervention. International organizations could also encourage or participate in processes or reviewing contested norms, as evidenced by UN institutional support for Brazil's recent diplomatic initiatives on "responsibility while protecting," and, more recently, Brazil's initiative on internet governance in 2014. Altering public discourse through thematic annual reports, organizing special sessions, or embarking on new substantive initiatives of particular interest to emerging powers are other ways in which international organizations could adapt themselves in ideational terms.

When it comes to structural or more material adjustments, international organizations could adapt their institutional structure to accommodate emerging powers. Replacing senior leadership with representatives from emerging powers is one way to accomplish this objective. The appointment of a Brazilian national to head the World Trade Organization in 2013 is indicative of this type of institutional adaptation. Changing an organization's governance structure or decision-making procedures is another way of altering institutional structure. The international financial institutions brought representatives of the Arab world into their governing and decision-making bodies following the dramatic rise in petroleum revenues in the 1970s and 1980s (and the substantial increases in contributions to the financial institutions from OAPEC member states). Altering membership criteria is another way of adaptation, as seen in the expansion of the informal club of the G7 and G8 to the G20 in recent years, particularly in the wake of the global financial crisis of 2007–8.

Anticipatory forms of adaptation are visible in both long-established international organizations and in newly created ones. Recently established international organizations such as the UN Peacebuilding Commission, its Human Rights Council, and UN Women have shown both ideational and structural accommodation of emerging power concerns, leading to an increase in institutional power on the part of both developing countries and emerging powers from the developing world.[7] The picture is somewhat different for longstanding international organizations, such as the WTO, International Telecommunications Union (ITU) and World Intellectual Property Organization (WIPO). Generally speaking, reform efforts in these countries tend to remain at the ideational level, not the institutional structural level (with the exception noted above of the recent appointment of a Brazilian to head the WTO).[8]

Emerging powers and security governance institutions

Much of the analysis of emerging powers and international organizations has been focused on international economic issues, organizations, regimes, and institutions. In this chapter, we propose to broaden the discussion and explore the attitudes of emerging powers toward the current practices of global security institutions, organizations operating in an issue domain that is typically more resistant to institutional change than economic ones.

Our focus is on one key aspect of security governance: the imposition of targeted sanctions by the United Nations Security Council (UNSC) to support non-proliferation goals. The UNSC has the responsibility to define what constitutes a threat to international peace and security on a global basis, and it can employ a variety of different measures—from formal statements of condemnation of specific actions to the application of sanctions, and ultimately the authorization of the use of force. When the Security Council imposes targeted sanctions on a member state in support of non-proliferation norms, it does so under Chapter VII of the UN Charter, and therefore its actions are legally binding on all member states of the organization.

There have been 25 different country sanctions regimes imposed by the UN in the last 24 years. Most UN sanctions, or nearly 60 percent of country case episodes, have been imposed in situations of armed conflict, primarily in situations of internationalized, intra-state conflicts in Africa. The Council has also been active in imposing sanctions to counter-terrorism (in approximately 15 percent of the cases), to oppose non-constitutional changes of government or support democracy (in about 10 percent of the cases), and in support of the contested norm of the responsibility to protect (in only one case, Libya in 2011).[9] The UN has acted in support of non-proliferation norms and imposed targeted sanctions on two countries since 2006: Iran and North Korea (the DPRK), constituting about 10 percent of the total case episodes of targeted sanctions since 1990. Non-proliferation is an issue domain of high visibility, and one with a high potential threat (both regionally and globally).

The UNSC is typically considered to be an institution highly resistant to change, and the fact that two of the most frequently mentioned emerging powers—China and Russia—are already permanent members of the Council, might suggest that emerging powers are already well-represented on the body. There was a major effort to extend the membership of the UNSC 10 years ago during the lead up to the World Summit in 2005, but the effort to expand the membership to include other emerging powers like India and Brazil came to naught. Beyond the inherent conservatism of the Permanent Five members of the Security Council, there was strong regional opposition to each of the major candidate countries—from Pakistan to India, Argentina to Brazil, Italy to Germany, and China to Japan. Emerging powers have sought, and have been elected to, two-year terms on the UNSC with increasing frequency in recent years, however, along with major financial contributors to the UN like Germany and Japan.

Whilst it has not altered its size or changed its permanent members, the Council has shown an ability to adapt in another dimension. It has exhibited a great deal of institutional innovation by expanding its mandate through the use of Chapter VII collective security instruments since the end of the Cold War. It has moved far beyond the condemnation of inter-state war, and in addition to the objectives identified above (counter-terrorism, non-constitutional change of government, responsibility to protect, and nuclear non-proliferation), it has defined as threats to international peace and security: transnational crime, massive human rights abuses, global climate change, and violence against women and children.

We are interested in exploring in this chapter the attitudes of four pivotal emerging powers—India, Brazil, Indonesia, and Turkey—on the use of UN sanctions in support of non-proliferation goals. These are countries that have worked hard to support the nuclear order in many areas, while simultaneously frustrating non-proliferation sanctions in some others. They have argued forcefully against intervention and the use of coercive measures, particularly unilateral sanctions imposed by the United States and the European Union, while occasionally employing sanctions themselves in pursuit of their own foreign policy objectives. Although they do not seek an outright elimination of sanctions, they generally favor multilateral approaches and prefer UN multilateral sanctions to unilateral sanctions of the sort imposed by the United States and the EU on Iran and North Korea that go considerably beyond the measures approved by the UN.

The four emerging powers we are examining have different regional vantage points, worldviews, and strategic interests, but have found some common ground in the domain of international security affairs. They have generally opposed interference in the domestic affairs of other states on the grounds that they undermine the authority of multilateral institutions. They tend also to agree on measures in support of counter-terrorism, but they have voiced reservations about over-reliance on and the use of military power to combat it. Although they all supported the 2005 World Summit Outcome General Assembly resolution, they have each expressed subsequent reservations about the idea of "Responsibility to Protect," (R2P) in particular that it could lead to an interventionist foreign policy. This is particularly strong in the case of Brazil, which has embarked on an important post-Libya initiative to explore the idea of "being responsible while protecting." It is one of the more significant new ideational initiatives undertaken by an emerging power in the security domain in recent years, an initiative that could have far reaching implications for the development and application of the norm in the future.

The four employ diverse approaches to global security policy, have been unable to reach consensus on some areas of security governance, and do not tend to agree with one another on important UN decisions. Despite this fact, they have all taken stands on the global nuclear order and non-proliferation regime complex that have been critical of the existing order's ability to accommodate the interests and concerns of emerging/rising powers. All pivotal emerging powers, alongside Russia and China and most developing countries, raised concerns over the use of unilateral coercive measures (including targeted sanctions), voting in favor of a UN Human Rights Council resolution in March 2012 arguing that "unilateral coercive measures in the form of economic sanctions can have far reaching implications for the human rights of the general population of targeted states, disproportionately affecting the poor and most vulnerable classes."[10]

This criticism of sanctions is indicative of the ambivalence, ambiguousness, and one might say inconsistency of the position taken by some of the emerging powers that voted in favor of the resolution. India, for example, has a long history of using sanctions for its own foreign policy purposes against "recalcitrant entities"—from maintaining its territorial integrity (against Hyderabad) to pursuing decolonization (against Portuguese Goa), to imposing unilateral sanctions of its own and using them as a foreign policy instrument against South Africa, Rhodesia, Israel, Fiji, Nepal, and Pakistan.[11] China, despite its criticisms of unilateral measures, has also employed its own unilateral sanctions against North Korea, as recently as 2013, following the detonation of another nuclear device by the DPRK.

The UN has used targeted sanctions to support non-proliferation goals against Iran and North Korea since 2006. For its part, the United States has successfully lobbied other major entities, including the European Union, Japan, Canada, Australia and South Korea to "exercise vigilance" with regard to finance, insurance, and shipping, measures that have significantly expanded the scope of the targeted UN measures against both countries. Some emerging powers, including India, have supported these efforts, at least to a limited degree. This is significant, as pivotal rising powers with their growing importance in the global economy, could otherwise play an important role in undercutting the more extensive non-UN measures.

Brazil and India are particularly interesting with regard to their respective roles in the global non-proliferation regime. Brazil voluntarily ceased activity on its advanced nuclear weapons program in 1990 following political rapprochement with Argentina, although it continues to retain civilian nuclear capabilities. The Brazilian government has agreed reluctantly to most legal dimensions of the non-proliferation order. It has entered the Missile Technology Control Regime, signed the Non-Proliferation Treaty (NPT) and ratified the Comprehensive Nuclear Test Ban Treaty (CTBT). Nevertheless, it has expressed opposition to new non-proliferation regulations, and, like all other pivotal rising powers other than Turkey, has refused to sign the United States-led Proliferation Security Initiative (PSI),[12] citing sovereignty concerns.[13] Brazilian officials have criticized the legitimacy of the Non-Proliferation Treaty (NPT), given what they see as bias in the treaty and a failure on the part of nuclear states to fulfill their commitments. Brazil has not signed the International Atomic Energy Agency (IAEA) Additional Protocol and has refused certain IAEA inspections.[14] Brazil has had a problematic relationship with sanctions historically, particularly regarding the non-proliferation sanctions against Iran. In 2008, then Brazilian Foreign Minister Celso Amorim said "Brazil does not recognize unilateral sanctions imposed on Iran, whether by the United States or the European Union."[15]

India's acquisition of nuclear weapons—culminating in the detonation of its first nuclear device in 1974 and underground nuclear tests in 1998—renders it a highly unusual actor in the global non-proliferation community. Since the 1970s it has produced some 100 nuclear warheads and developed functioning long-range missile delivery systems, while refusing to join the NPT, sign the CTBT, or join the PSI.[16] Indian views on non-proliferation have been framed in past decades in what it termed the "nuclear apartheid" embodied by the NPT, rather than in relation to strategic concerns over problematic neighbors.[17] India has not transferred nuclear weapon technology or fissile material to third parties[18] and has been a strong supporter of nuclear disarmament and arms control. It has a good record regarding the Chemical Weapons Convention and the Biological Weapons Convention, having signed and ratified both.[19] The country seeks membership to the Nuclear Suppliers Group (NSG) and other major multilateral export control regimes and is also a supporter of the multilateral negotiation of a Fissile Material Cutoff Treaty.[20] As such, and despite its history, India is now widely, albeit problematically, described as a "responsible" nuclear power.[21]

Like Brazil, Indian officials have also voiced widespread opposition to unilateral sanctions on Iran, and they have expressed doubts in public fora over the efficacy of sanctions in general.[22] They have cited the "extra-territorial nature" of sanctions, arguing that the IAEA serves as the most suitable framework to resolve problems over the Iranian enrichment crisis.[23] In October 2005, then Indian Foreign Minister Natwar Singh declared that India would not support United States efforts to refer Iran to the UNSC. India went on, however, to support a United States-sponsored UN motion critical of Iran at the IAEA, which saw India vote with 26 other governments in February 2006 to refer Iran to the UNSC.[24] These votes were linked by many observers to the United States-India nuclear pact, which was agreed in 2006 on condition of India's support of Iran sanctions. In 2011, during its tenure as a non-permanent member of the UNSC, New Delhi proceeded to call publicly for the "full implementation of multilateral sanctions against Tehran."[25]

Turkey has never sought to possess a nuclear weapons capability and has been a strong supporter of the legal aspects of the non-proliferation order, including being party to the NPT, a signatory of the CTBT, the PSI, a member of the NSG, and other major multilateral export control regimes. Ankara has also approved the IAEA Additional Protocol and opened its civilian nuclear facilities to international scrutiny.[26] Out of the four countries being considered in this chapter, Turkey has been the most supportive of the use of sanctions in countering nuclear proliferation,[27] although it has raised concerns on numerous occasions that such measures can also be counter-productive and can damage diplomatic efforts.[28]

Along with Brazil, Turkey sought to broker a nuclear deal with Iran in May 2010 (both countries were non-permanent members of the UNSC at the time), in which Iran would ship low-enriched uranium to Turkey in return for fuel for its research reactors.[29] These meetings took place without close coordination with the Permanent Five members of the Council and on the eve of a vote at the UNSC applying additional sanctions against Iran (after the P5 had already reached consensus on new sanctions measures). The UNSC went on to pass a new round of sanctions in June 2010, which Turkey and Brazil opposed in seeming retaliation.

Indonesia adheres to the legal aspects of the non-proliferation order and is a longstanding member of the NPT and signatory to the IAEA's Additional Protocol and CTBT (although it only signed the latter reluctantly in 2011 once Washington had signed).[30] Jakarta was an active contributor to the Nuclear Security Summit and has shown leadership in attempting to advance the ratification of various nuclear-related treaties and conventions. The country has followed international security and safety guidelines in its development of a nuclear power industry, earning the IAEA's praise.[31] Indonesia has shown more reticence regarding enforcement measures, however, including regulations on maritime activities and the use of unilateral sanctions. It has also refrained from joining the PSI, citing sovereignty and legal concerns.

Indonesia abstained from voting at the UN to bring the question of Iran's nuclear program before the Security Council in 2006, but went on to support a 2007 UNSC resolution to bring sanctions on the country. In April 2007, Indonesian President Susilo Bambang Yudhoyono called UN resolutions against Iran "illegal" and highlighted the peaceful nature of the country's nuclear program.[32] Jakarta issued a joint statement with Tehran through the Non-Aligned Movement (NAM), upholding Iran's right to peaceful nuclear technology, while stressing the importance of the safeguards of the NPT and the IAEA.[33] In 2008 when Indonesia was on the Security Council, Jakarta abstained from UNSCR 1803, citing concerns over the efficacy of additional sanctions, but voted against Iran and in favor of UNSCR 1835 later in the same year.[34] These abstentions were interesting in that they showed that Jakarta would not necessarily align its position on sanctions with Beijing—who voted in favor of the measures—as a matter of course.[35]

How can pivotal rising powers influence non-proliferation sanctions?

Pivotal rising powers can affect the weight of a given non-proliferation sanctions regime in various ways. On a political level, this can include actions at the UN, at the IAEA or in informal groupings,[36] which can provide a forum to voice views and make a bid for political support.[37] These actions might include lobbying, blocking, coalition-building, and the promotion of certain norms or views. The latter may include speeches, declarations, statements, analysis, and advice, and can lead to the eventual formation of global discourse influencing non-proliferation politics more widely.[38]

In the cases of Iran and North Korea, recent support for sanctions by states that have traditionally maintained close political or economic relations with Tehran and Pyongyang—including India, Brazil, Indonesia, and Turkey alongside Russia and China—have sent powerful signals to both regimes.[39] In the case of Iran, the support for sanctions by Brazil and India—which have historically played a leading role in the Non-Aligned Movement—or Turkey and Indonesia—as predominantly Muslim nations who have shared close relations with Tehran in the past—carry considerable symbolic weight. The type of sanction and context in which it is imposed on a target can affect the reaction they provoke in third countries, including rising powers. Although only permanent members have a veto power at the UNSC, non-permanent members can also exert influence given that nine votes of 15 are required.

Through the chairing of sanctions committees, a range of countries, including pivotal rising powers, also have scope for exerting influence over how sanctions are implemented. These committees are usually chaired by elected (E10) members of the UN Security Council, but because sanctions committees on non-proliferation are so high profile, they are often chaired by a P5 country. Smaller E10 countries would struggle to carry out these roles, given the weight of expertise, resources, and personnel required, but larger countries such as India, Brazil, Indonesia, and Turkey might find themselves in a better position to assume such roles.

Ambivalence in behavior

In UNSC sanctions resolutions on Iran since 2006, India has abstained twice (UNSCR 1696 in 2006 and UNSCR 1803 in 2008) and voted favorably in one instance (UNSCR 1835 in 2008). Brazil has voted unfavorably once (UNSCR 1929 in 2010) and Turkey has voted both favorably (UNSCR 1887 in 2009) and unfavorably (UNSCR 1929 in 2010). In UNSC sanctions resolutions on North Korea in the same time period, only Turkey voted in favor of UNSCR 1874 (2009). Other pivotal rising powers were not non-permanent members at relevant times.

Despite some variation among rising powers, consensus on sanctions, including those for non-proliferation, was achieved in the majority of cases, although voting patterns do not necessarily tell the whole story. Member state behavior outside the UNSC framework has frequently been marked by discord[40] and levels of political compromise required to pass sanctions through the UNSC can often seriously limit their impact.[41]

On an economic front, rising powers can affect the efficacy of non-proliferation sanctions by filling commercial gaps left by other sanctioning powers; through either opting not to impose supplementary unilateral sanctions and/or by sanctions busting. They may help targeted regimes evade even the most stringent of sanctions through involvement in a number of methods, including trading with front companies, diverting commerce through third countries, the use of safe havens, black market contractors, alternative value sources, and the disguising of vessels.[42] Taylor suggests that "[t]hird-party support for Pyongyang and Tehran has had the biggest impact in terms of helping these countries to circumvent the worst effects of sanctions, particularly those targeting trade."[43] The extent of pre-sanctions trade between two countries can also be an important factor in determining the damage that sanctions will have on a target's economy,[44] although the level of economic pain caused will not necessarily translate into increased likelihood of reaching stated foreign policy aims.[45]

Because of the centrality of states and the existing great powers in the governance of the nuclear proliferation issue domain, there have not been very many anticipatory initiatives from existing security institutions working in the area. The Proliferation Security Initiative is largely an initiative of the United States government, and the UN sanctions committees established to oversee sanctions against Iran and North Korea have both been politicized, with individual expert panel members identifying themselves as national (P5) "representatives" on the Panels of Experts working for the committees. Their reports are also subject to much greater scrutiny and delay in publication than the reports of panels of experts reporting to other sanctions committees. Other innovative governance initiatives within the nuclear non-proliferation domain have also tended to come from individual member states, such as the Washington-led initiative to use access to United States financial markets as rather effective leverage to extend United States unilateral measures to the rest of the world (at least for the time being).

With regard to other proliferation-related security institutions, the NSG has taken up the issue of India's admission to the consensus-based grouping, but this initiative has stalled, because of opposition from another rising power: China. In its most recent annual reports, the IAEA appears to have been more focused on expanding its mandate and relevance to issues like sustainable development, than reflecting on its crucial relationship to existing multilateral sanctions regimes at the UN level.

Conclusion

In general terms, the discourse and behavior of emerging powers illustrates their ambivalence about the instrument of sanctions in general and their use in non-proliferation cases in particular. Brazil, India, Indonesia, and Turkey are not unambiguously in favor of the measures, nor are they systematically opposed to them. There are many public statements from emerging powers in opposition to the use of sanctions (including concerns that they are a precursor of military intervention), but it is noteworthy that despite their stated reservations, emerging powers are not shy about using sanctions when it suits their state interests, such as territorial consolidation or different foreign policy goals (particularly in the case of India, but also China).

Their general ambivalence is evidenced by their inconsistent voting on UNSC resolutions devoted to non-proliferation concerns in both Iran and North Korea: opposing, supporting, or abstaining in about equal numbers to date (although there is some evidence that suggests they may be moving toward more support over time). The four emerging powers surveyed above share a general aversion to external intervention in domestic affairs (the non-intervention norm), but not absolute opposition to the idea. In general terms, they have a stated preference for the use of global multilateral institutions, like the UN, rather than support for the use of regional or unilateral sanctions (even when additional measures are authorized under provisions urging member states to exercise vigilance).

In recent years, a number of member states, including three of the five permanent members of the UNSC, have argued that multilateral UN sanctions should be considered as a minimum threshold, or a "floor" upon which additional sanctions measures can be imposed, particularly when the Council resolutions call for "exercising vigilance" in a given situation. Russia and China tend to disagree with this assessment and argue rather that UN sanctions measures should be considered the "ceiling" or limit of actions taken and that any additional unilateral or autonomous measures go beyond what should be considered to be internationally legitimate. Sanctions scholars have referred to these recent debates among the P5 as the "floor versus ceiling debate" on the legitimacy of sanctions.[46] The four pivotal emerging powers explored above remain much closer to the ceiling position articulated by Russia, and to a lesser degree, by China, than they do to the positions of the United States, UK, and France.

The international sanctions against Iran over its nuclear program provide a good illustration of the phenomenon. The initial UN targeted sanctions imposed in 2006 were introduced in the wake of sanctions already imposed by the United States and the EU. Although the UN sanctions were more targeted in design and purpose, their potential scope of implementation was much broader, as they were to be applied by all member states. Subsequent episodes of the UN sanctions against Iran after 2006 expanded the sanctions and added language encouraging member states to "exercise vigilance" with regard to transactions that might facilitate the potential weaponization of Iran's nuclear program. Some states, notably the United States and the leading members of the EU, interpreted this as a basis for broadening their already more expansive measures on Iran. Others, notably Russia and China, argued that the UN sanctions constituted not the base (or floor) of legitimate international sanctions, but defined their legitimate limit (or ceiling). This debate reflects fundamentally different views among member states, particularly permanent members of the UN Security Council, about the role of the Council and sanctions, which likely foreshadows challenges to reaching agreement on difficult conflict situations in the future. This is a future issue domain in which the impact of emerging powers could tip the balance.

The four pivotal rising powers described above—Brazil, India, Indonesia, and Turkey—generally tend to view the non-proliferation regime in general, and the NPT, in particular, as unfair. Brazil called the NPT "biased," while India referred to the treaty in terms of what it called "nuclear apartheid." Yet, their fundamental ambiguity comes through when they express various degrees of support for the institutions associated with the non-proliferation regime, such as India's endorsement of the IAEA as an appropriate forum (particularly after the United States-India nuclear deal in 2006), and its current interest in joining the NSG.

The situation remains very much in process at the moment. Rising powers increasingly matter, not just in economic affairs, but also in security affairs. They remain ambivalent about the non-proliferation regime and about the use of targeted sanctions to enforce it, an ambivalence that produces what might appear to be inconsistency in their behavior. As they continue to develop, however, both through their policy actions and from the anticipatory responses of institutions associated with the regime, they will begin to influence the non-proliferation regime even further.

Notes

1 Stewart Patrick, "Irresponsible Stakeholders? The Difficulty of Integrating Rising Powers," *Foreign Affairs* 89, no. 6 (November/December 2010): 44–53.
2 G. John Ikenberry, "The Future of the Liberal World Order: Internationalism after America," *Foreign Affairs* 90, no. 3 (May/June 2011): 56–68.
3 Thomas Biersteker, "Global Governance" in *On Governance: National and International Dimensions of Measuring Governance Effectiveness*, Robert I. Rotberg, ed. (Waterloo, Ontario: CIGI Press, forthcoming).
4 Robert Keohane and David Victor differentiate regimes from regime complexes and define the latter as a "loosely coupled system of institutions ... (with) ... no clear hierarchy or core, yet many of its elements are linked in complementary ways" in "The Regime Complex for Climate Change," *Perspectives on Politics* 8, no. 1, (March 2011): 9.
5 Michael Barnett and Raymond Duvall, "Power in International Politics," *International Organization* 59, no. 1 (January 2005): 39–75.
6 Liliana Andonova, "Public-Private Partnerships for the Earth: Politics and Patterns of Hybrid Authority in the Multilateral System," *Global Environmental Politics* 10, no. 2 (May 2010): 25–53.
7 Stefan Stantejsky, *International Organizations in Times of Change: A Study on how Intergovernmental Organizations Adapt to the Emergence of a Multipolar World Order*, MA Thesis presented to the Graduate Institute for International and Development Studies, Geneva, 2013.
8 Ibid.
9 Thomas Biersteker, Sue E. Eckert, Marcos Tourinho, and Zuzana Hudáková, *The Effectiveness of United Nations Targeted Sanctions: Findings from the Targeted Sanctions Consortium (TSC)* (Geneva: Graduate Institute of International and Development, 2013), 14.
10 UN Human Rights Council resolution A/HRC/19/L.12, 15 March 2012.
11 Rishika Chauhan, "India and International Sanctions: Delhi's Role as a Sanctioner," *Observer Research Foundation Issue Brief: 58*, (ORF: New Delhi, September 2013).
12 The PSI was launched by former United States President George W. Bush in 2003, in an attempt to secure international cooperation in monitoring and intercepting naval vessels that could be transporting WMDs and related material. It calls on UN member states to inspect all cargo on their territory if thought to contain prohibited items. For more information, see Stephan Haggard and Marcus Noland, "Sanctioning North Korea: The

Political Economy of Denuclearization and Proliferation," *Asian Survey* 50, no. 3 (2010): 539–568.

13 Daniel M. Kliman and Richard Fontaine, *Global Swing States: Brazil, India, Indonesia, Turkey and the Future of the International Order*, Report prepared for the Center for a New American Security (CNAS) and the German Marshall Fund of the United States (GMF), November 2012.

14 Amrita Narlikar, *New Powers: how to become one and how to manage them* (New York: Columbia University Press, 2010).

15 "Brazil Doesn't Recognize Unilateral Sanctions on Iran," *Tehran Times*, 10 November 2008.

16 Kliman and Fontaine, *Global Swing States.*

17 Narlikar, *New Powers: how to become one and how to manage them.*

18 Kliman and Fontaine, *Global Swing States.*

19 Bernard Sitt, Masahiko Asada, Anthony Aust, Mikael Eriksson, Edward Ifft, Nicholas Kyriakopoulos, Jenifer Mackby, Bernard Massinon and Arend Meerburg, "Sanctions and Weapons of Mass Destruction in International Relations: International Group on Global Security IGGS," *GCSP Geneva Papers*, 16 (2010): 92.

20 Kliman and Fontaine, *Global Swing States.*

21 Harsh V. Pant, "A fine balance: India walks a tightrope between Iran and the United States," *Orbis* 51, no. 3 (2007): 495–509.

22 Kliman and Fontaine, *Global Swing States.*

23 Sandeep Dikshit, "Unilateral sanctions on Iran will hurt India: Nirupama Rao," *The Hindu*, 6 July 2010.

24 Pant, "A Fine Balance."

25 Kliman and Fontaine, *Global Swing States*, 21.

26 Kliman and Fontaine, *Global Swing States.*

27 Kliman and Fontaine, *Global Swing States.*

28 Kadir Üstün, "Turkey's Iran Policy: Between Diplomacy and Sanctions," *Insight Turkey* 12, no. 3 (2010): 19–26.

29 Ibid.

30 Kliman and Fontaine, *Global Swing States.*

31 Kliman and Fontaine, *Global Swing States.*

32 Mehr News Agency, 2008, quoted in Ariel Farrar-Wellman and Robert Frasco, "Indonesia-Iran Foreign Relations," *Iran Tracker*, 2010, www.ira ntracker.org/foreign-relations/indonesia-iran-foreign-relations.

33 Ibid.

34 Ibid.

35 Clara Portela, "The EU, China and the Iranian Nuclear Question" in *The EU, China and the World: Analysing the Relations with Developing and Emerging Countries*, Jan Wouters, Jean-Christophe Defraigne, and Matthieu Burnay, eds (Cheltenham: Edward Elgar, 2014).

36 Matias Spektor, "How to Read Brazil's Stance on Iran," *Council on Foreign Relations*, 4 March 2010, www.cfr.org/brazil/read-brazils-stance-iran/p21576.

37 Andrew Hurrell, "Hegemony, Liberalism and Global Order: What Space for Would-Be Great Powers?" *International Affairs* 82, no. 1 (2006): 1–19.

38 Stantejsky, *International Organizations in Times of Change.*

39 Brendan Taylor, *Sanctions as Grand Strategy*, Adelphi Series (London: Routledge, 2010). See also Mark Fitzpatrick, *The Iranian Nuclear Crisis: Avoiding Worst-Case Outcomes*, Adelphi Series (London: Routledge, 2009).
40 Portela, "The EU, China and the Iranian nuclear question."
41 Haggard and Noland, "Sanctioning North Korea."
42 Biersteker *et al.*, *The Effectiveness of United Nations Targeted Sanctions.*
43 Taylor, *Sanctions as Grand Strategy*, 105.
44 William H. Kaempfer and Anton D. Lowenberg, "The Political Economy of Economic Sanctions" in *The Handbook of Defense Economics: Defense in a Globalized World*, 2, Todd Sandler and Keith Hartley, eds (Amsterdam: Elsevier-North Holland, 2007), 868–911.
45 A. Cooper Drury, "Revisiting Economic Sanctions Reconsidered," *Journal of Peace Research* 35, no. 4 (1998): 497–509.
46 Thomas Biersteker, Sue Eckert, and Marcos Tourinho, "Conclusion," in *Understanding United Nations Targeted Sanctions* (forthcoming).

4 Global governance and the BRICs
Ideas, actors, and governance practices

Mark Bevir and Jamie Gaskarth

- **China**
- **Russia**
- **Brazil**
- **India**
- **Conclusion**

Broadly speaking, there are two narratives about what global governance means and how the concept can be used to understand global politics. One invokes new theories to understand the beliefs and behavior of global actors, the other sees new worlds emerging, with new actors and new configurations of power that require new analytical tools. They are not inherently mutually exclusive; but nor are they mutually dependent and are often contrasted.

The first sees global governance as offering a new theoretical lens to view international relations. Older theories presented international relations as an anarchical system or society of states interacting by trade, war, and diplomacy. The defining feature of this political sphere was the absence of any effective world government controlling, regulating, and coordinating the actions of different states.[1] In contrast, global governance highlights how patterns of rule can arise without hierarchic institutions let alone an international sovereign power. Actors internalize informal norms as well as have them imposed by the rules of external powers, monitor themselves as well as being supervised by others, coordinate their interactions with others through mutual adjustments as well as hierarchic organization. So, the term "global governance" draws attention to the diverse activities and processes that organize international relations. James Rosenau defines global governance as the "systems of rule" that exist "at all levels of human activity—from the family to the international organization—in which the pursuit of goals through the exercise of control has transnational repercussions."[2]

The second strand of global governance scholarship identifies the role of diverse social actors as well as states in securing patterns of rule at the transnational and global levels.[3] International organizations can shape state behavior, promote their own normative agenda and influence human beliefs and conduct beyond the confines of intergovernmental interactions. Private individuals and companies exert huge influence on the ideas and practices that underpin the organization of global society and politics. However, states, and governments acting on their behalf, remain important actors in global politics. Their bureaucratic resources and residual authority allow them to provide governance, regulate behavior, resist pressures for change and steer it in ways that favor their interests.

In short, we have two differing portraits of what global governance means. This dichotomy is apparent in the literature on the rising powers. Emphasizing the rise of states such as China, India, Brazil, and Russia is itself a reassertion of the primacy of the state as the actor in global politics. Underlying this narrative is the assumption that changes in the structure of the society of states, towards a multipolar world, will have a dramatic influence on governance outcomes. The rise of individual states is viewed as part of a wider economic and cultural shift in which Asian and/or Southern values will come to dominate global society in the future. Groupings such as IBSA, BASIC, and the BRICS are interpreted as heralding a challenge to longstanding, predominantly Western understandings of economic and political governance. The society of states may not be disappearing, but its fundamental norms will be shaped according to the values of the emerging powers, many of whom have histories of under-development, colonial exploitation, and exclusion from the global economy.

On the other hand, the rise of new centers of economic and political power is also being driven by new actors, including transnational elites, emerging religious and nationalist movements, state-owned enterprises and creative artists. These are challenging state authority both domestically and globally, leading some to question whether it is actually states that are rising or particular social strata across certain regions.

This chapter aims to bring together these disparate ideas by tracing the interplay of new theories and new worlds in the recent history of each of the original BRIC states. These accounts intend to show how transnational theories about governance have permeated borders and come to be implemented domestically by states; but also how they are reinterpreted and applied in particular national circumstances. What we find are "syncretist" elements, i.e. attitudes to governance forged by interaction with broader global actors and trends;[4] as well as more internal processes particular to the history and culture of the state in question. In analyzing each in turn, we may garner a deeper understanding of the contingent and contested nature of dominant narratives of global governance.

Rather than simply follow the BRICs order laid down by Jim O'Neill, we begin our discussion with China before exploring Russia, Brazil, and India. The similarities in authoritarian governance between China and Russia, as well as the sense they are more "resurgent" than "rising" powers, makes this progression more logical, as does the counterpoint of Brazil and India—two post-colonial powers with stronger democratic traditions.

China

China pioneered the formal, governmental aspects of governance, having had a defined territory, central executive, and bureaucracy appointed via competitive examination since the Tang dynasty (618–907). However, for nearly two centuries, central government has struggled to impose control and manage the country's myriad political, economic, and security challenges. Continual Western interventions in Chinese affairs, often with force, until the Communist takeover in 1949 are described by Chinese policy-makers as a "century of national humiliation." As a result, Chinese attitudes to external, particularly Western, powers and the international society they dominate, continue to be highly skeptical. Internationalism evokes memories of eight-nation alliances intervening to plunder Chinese resources. Conversely, national independence and sovereignty are highly prized.

Nevertheless, Chinese politics in the twentieth century have regularly been influenced by external notions of governance. European understandings of nationalism and democracy influenced the May fourth movement.[5] Marxist-Leninist political and economic ideas were adopted and translated into the Chinese context by Chinese thinkers in the inter-war period. When the Chinese communist party assumed full control of mainland China in 1949, the government embraced Soviet thinking on planning, initiating five-year plans and grand centrally conceived projects like the Great Leap Forward. In the 1950s, China made its first serious effort at modernization, importing Soviet technology and expertise to increase its manufacturing output. This was supposed to be funded by increased grain production in the agricultural sector, but when this failed to materialize, the Soviets lost interest and withdrew their support.

There then followed a period of extreme insecurity as the Chinese authorities became more erratic in their attitudes to governance. At first, communes were promoted to localize the governance of production. When the cultural revolution began in 1966, expertise and intellectualism themselves became politically suspect. The bureaucracy was blamed for governance failures and seen to promote special interests over the mass of the people, especially the rural poor. The effect was to undermine any coordinated effort at managing the country's economic and political problems.

Mao's death and the arrest of the "gang of four" who tried to assume power in his wake, heralded a dramatic shift in the Chinese leadership's attitude to both capitalism and international engagement. The government invited foreign investment to modernize its manufacturing sector, encouraged private enterprise (albeit with strong party oversight) and the new de facto leader, Deng Xiaopeng, even declared that "to make money is glorious."[6] The emphasis on communes was reversed in favor of town and village enterprises and special economic zones were created with business-friendly taxation and regulation arrangements. Interaction with the wider world also brought about changes in social outlook. As Robin Porter has noted: "it was not only the techniques of international business that were imbibed. Attitudes changed, tastes changed, and with them the expectations of young people."[7]

When these attitudes threatened to translate into calls for democracy during the Tiananmen Square protests of 1989, they were brutally suppressed by the government. However, in subsequent decades, spectacular economic growth and increasing prosperity in metropolitan areas have meant a huge number of Chinese people enjoy greater freedom and prosperity. It is tempting to see China as undergoing a gradual process of liberalization and Westernization, leading to inevitable democratic transformation. However, this would be to ignore the specific national processes that continue to influence how governance works in practice.

Although a degree of liberalization has occurred, this is not along a neoliberal model. China is not a full market economy. Few major private companies are free of governmental interference, even if this is only as a result of government investment. Senior figures in a number of supposedly independent firms have interchanged in an apparently coordinated fashion. China is described as operating a "coordinated market economy," one in which "many firms still enjoy direct support from the state or benefit from country-specific advantages where the state is a critical actor."[8] The communist party continues to exercise a strong influence on the lives of Chinese citizens, especially when it comes to formal modes of governance. In fact, the continuance of authoritarian government has itself been used to explain the success of

China's modernization. According to this argument, only an authoritarian system could have pushed through the radical changes that have occurred in the last few decades, as well as the massive infrastructure projects which have facilitated development, such as the three gorges dam.[9] That said, central government does not have it all its own way; nor are central governance practices entirely driven by national goals. Private networks of influence are also in operation. In particular, the tradition of *guanxi*—promoting the interests of friends or relations—is itself subversive, both of party control and modernization along Weberian bureaucratic lines. Such corrupt practices are seen as undermining party discipline and control. Indeed, market reforms and greater transparency are sometimes conveyed as useful in reinforcing government authority.

Promoting economic development in specific geographical areas has also had a mixed impact. Originally conceived to ensure central control over the development process, it has given rise to new power centers, where latent regional and metropolitan identities have re-emerged. Rural/urban divides have surfaced and this has caused resentment in rural communities at the perceived distance between the urban leadership and the wider community. There are estimated to be around 100,000 protests annually against local, regional, and national government, many occurring in rural areas.[10]

The existence of Chinese state-owned enterprises (SOEs) is often depicted as a challenge to the neoliberal economic model.[11] Pervasive state involvement in business and central planning of economic activity give rise to the idea that China's economic system is one of "authoritarian capitalism." Whereas Western countries have privatized and deregulated most of their largest firms, state-controlled companies are said to make up 80 percent of the market capitalization of the Chinese stock market.[12] Although the number of Chinese SOEs has declined, this process is seen as more a consolidation, with the remaining firms promoted as "national champions" in strategic industries.[13] The European Chamber of Commerce recently criticized the Chinese government for having an "overly-dominant role" in the market, arguing that "Liberalisation has stalled" due to the "partisan treatment" meted out to these enterprises.[14]

However, Chinese officials are also said to have become concerned that inefficiencies in SOEs were resulting in "deteriorating returns and accumulating debt," leading them to look to the more distanced state-private relationship of Singaporean government-linked companies (GLCs).[15] These are still amenable to state influence in strategic terms but their day-to-day running is autonomous from the state. As such, the Chinese government may embrace more private control of economic activity, not because it believes in liberalism, or neoliberalism, or because of external pressure, but because it can see this might help to overcome inefficiencies that have emerged in protected industries. In November 2013, the third plenum of the Communist Party's central committee resulted in the announcement that market competition would be given a more "decisive role" in the economy.[16] Yet, this news was seen as tempered by the affirmation that the government and state-run firms would continue to play an important part in future economic planning.[17] As Sáez and Chang put it, "China appears to want it both ways," looking to improve corporate performance through "Western management expertise" but also retaining a "controlling interest."[18]

In sum, China has an embedded authoritarian tradition of government, which has long embraced central planning as the cornerstone of its economic and political structures. Nevertheless, local governance arrangements have also existed in tandem, from communes to town and village enterprises and special enterprise zones. A fear of internal disorder (associated with foreign intervention) has led to an emphasis on strong, central management of problems to ensure political control remains with the government. Yet, the differentiated pace of economic growth in the various regions and cities could threaten to undermine the legitimacy and authority of the leadership.

The Chinese government has recently begun to use rhetoric implying it will seek to democratize but, as with the economic realm, this is usually framed as about making governance more effective. As such, it is more a technical move than a turn towards a democratic ethos along Western lines. Elizabeth Van Wie Davis sets out a picture of the Chinese government under Hu encouraging "open debate, internal leadership elections, and decision making by a diverse leadership group with disparate power centers" as a "prerequisite for good governance in the country as a whole."[19] However, this is very much an intraparty democracy that is envisaged. Tensions exist within the party over the nature and pace of economic and political reform, with some seeing a "nexus between CCP elites and business interests who have plundered the nation's assets under the cover of privatization."[20] Recent corruption clampdowns by the incoming Xi Jinping administration are viewable as an attempt to address this perception. Nevertheless, dissenting voices hint at the limits of state power and the potential existence of networks below and across government, subverting national interests.

From this brief account of governance as it relates to Chinese politics, its attitude to global governance becomes clearer. To avoid attracting foreign interest and hence interference, China has defined its entry into a dominant position in international society as a "peaceful rise."[21] Fear of internal disorder projects itself through China's global emphasis on maintaining existing patterns of order (however imperfect), upholding the sovereignty and territorial status quo of other states wherever possible. Existing international institutions are tolerable, as they have allowed China's rise, and the stability they provide in interactions is preferable to the uncertainty of radical reform.

Thus, China joined the WTO in 2001, declines to actively support reform of the UN Security Council, and is a key member of the G20. Chinese officials also boast that between 1990 and 2006, China was the biggest contributor to peacekeeping missions among the five permanent members of the UN Security Council.[22] China has normalized relations with a host of countries that it had previously had hostile relations with, including Indonesia, South Korea, and India. A Chinese official leads the Shanghai Cooperation Organization and China is also a participant in the Asia-Pacific Economic Cooperation (APEC), APEC for Pacific Rim countries, and the China–Africa Cooperation forum.

Xi's predecessor, Hu Jintao, summarized China's foreign policy goals in 2009 as seeking: profound transformation; a harmonious world; common development; shared responsibility; and active engagement.[23] At the time, the inclusion of "profound transformation" and "active engagement" seemed to imply that a more aggressive foreign policy would be forthcoming. Although the transformation envisaged was actually economic development, Chinese assertions of historical claims over the South China Sea and disputes over the Senkaku/Diaoyu islands have alienated important regional actors like Japan and India.

Yet, there is little sense that China seeks to overturn the structures of global governance. Any revolutionary sentiments have been replaced by a pragmatic attitude to governance. As the former Vice Foreign Minister, Wang Guangya put it "Our mindset today is completely different…We analyse situations in terms of real facts, reach our own conclusions—and take responsibility for them."[24] China seeks to reinforce conservative, pluralist norms such as sovereignty, non-intervention, and anti-hegemonism, to promote a more balanced multipolar international structure. As Barry Buzan has noted, it accepts the market and much of the organizational structure of global governance and merely wants to increase its own status within them, as well as resist more radical reform based on human rights, sovereignty as responsibility, democratization or, to a lesser extent, environmentalism.[25]

To summarize, China's domestic governance arrangements have involved borrowing from other cultures, from Soviet central planning initiatives to more recent efforts at economic liberalization. Its interaction with the global economy, particularly when it comes to membership of the WTO, requires regulation to coordinate its economy with other states and so offers a means of socialization to wider financial governance norms. Yet there are national cultural practices, such as the traditions of *guanxi*, authoritarian government, and state support of national firms that potentially subvert the free market. Planning at the national level predominates. For all its greater openness, China still views governance through a nationalistic lens and this hampers its embrace of global governance arrangements that compromise sovereignty. Sub-state and transnational networks, either from the private sector or civil society, are seen as subversive of national identity and the common good.

Russia

On the surface, Russia shares a number of similarities with China in its history and attitude to governance. It too perceives itself as a victim of foreign intervention. Having been invaded three times in two centuries, Russia is wary of threats from abroad. NATO enlargement and EU encroachment into previously Soviet satellite states in the post-Cold War era are viewed as threatening encirclements. Meanwhile Western-backed military interventions, particularly in Kosovo in 1999, are a humiliating sign of Western disregard for Russia's status in its near abroad. In addition, the imposition of neoliberalism in the 1990s at the behest of the United States and Europeans had a catastrophic effect on Russia's economy. Wages and living standards declined considerably—with its GDP only returning to 1991 levels in 2007.[26] The knock-on effects of the Asian financial crisis led to Russia defaulting on its international financial obligations in August 1998. This experience has led to profound skepticism in Russia over the merits of neoliberal prescriptions for economic governance.

Indeed, the problems of governance in the Yeltsin period were crucial in informing Putin and Medvedev's later reforms, and contributed to their subsequent failure. Zhuplev and Shein note that the transformation from the Soviet era to an independent Russia was one in which "administrative power, shady personal connections, or just an outright use of physical (criminal) force in business pursuits" were rife.[27] As the Russian government neared bankruptcy, it increasingly resorted to what Robinson terms "particularistic exchanges," such as bartering, granting access to resources for political favorites, and corruption.[28] Wages went unpaid to lower inflation, fuel supplies were provided in lieu of monetary subsidies to industry and local authorities, and this was funded in turn by tax concessions to energy firms.[29] Central government was increasingly weakened by a spiral of lower tax receipts and governance networks of private connections working in their own interest. A decade after the neoliberal reforms of the Russian economy, 90 percent of Russia's output was produced by private enterprises[30] and according to Shadrina and Bradshaw "state-owned companies (SOCs) produced less than 20% of Russia's oil."[31]

Under Vladimir Putin's leadership as variously prime minister and president, a concerted effort was made to wrest back control over key markets and firms from individual or foreign control and reassert central authority. Russia has a long tradition of authoritarian government and this is often interpreted as the state returning to type. Yet, if we explore these efforts to impose a more authoritarian and centralized system of governance, we find similar problems of authority and efficiency as planners in other contexts, as outlined above.

To consolidate his rule and assert central authority over the economy, Putin began by emphasizing the "vertical of power."[32] Rule from the center would be re-established and rivals to presidential power, such as the "oligarchs" (individuals who had amassed vast fortunes from the privatizations of key industries in the 1990s), would be offered a choice: Putin would afford them protection from each other and allow them to maintain their position provided they began paying their "rents" and did not openly challenge his government.[33] However, an independent line would not be tolerated. Voices criticizing the government in the media and the Duma were silenced. This was starkly illustrated in the YUKOS case—one of the largest oil producers in Russia. Its head, Mikhail Khodorkovsky, a critic of Putin's rule, was arrested, convicted, and the company forced into bankruptcy where its assets were nationalized.[34]

The vertical of power was not only asserted to neutralize criticism but also to try and eradicate bureaucratic failures. Putin was apparently misled by his own military over the sinking of the Russian submarine *Kursk* in 2000 and terrorist incidents such as the Beslan siege of 2004 were attributed to corruption and incompetence.[35] Elected regional governors were replaced with presidential appointees to impose a direct line of authority from the President downwards. Linked to this were efforts to reinvigorate central or "strategic" planning as the main mode of governance.[36] First Putin and then Medvedev set great store by grand modernization schemes. High energy prices increased tax revenues and efforts were made to diversify the economy and pay back debt to build a more robust base for growth.[37] In 2009, Medvedev announced an initiative to modernize Russia technologically, economically, and politically.[38] Again, a centralized and top-down approach was adopted.

Yet, for all the appearance of dynamic, centralized control over governance mechanisms and practice, the leadership repeatedly found itself frustrated at bureaucratic inertia and policy failure. Locating responsibility higher up the chain of command, and discouraging opposition voices that might highlight ways to innovate, mean that senior figures have had to carry much of the burden for imposing solutions to problems. This has led to the repeated spectacle of the leadership having to micro-manage complex situations and then bemoaning the fact that their instructions were not carried out. Citing a range of examples where both Putin and Medvedev's orders were not fulfilled, Andrew Monaghan notes that: "By its very nature, manual control works only when the senior official is present—the effect wears off after his departure. As a process, it is inefficient, time consuming, difficult and potentially dangerous."[39]

One problem was that Putin and Medvedev's governance reforms replaced one set of private networks influencing governance with their own. The interchange of these two individuals at the top is merely emblematic of wider continuities in relationships across the structure of governance. A tight group of individuals, who have known each other a long time, dominate key governmental and corporate positions and so shape governance networks. This arrangement has been described as a hybrid regime, a shadow state, or even a mafia state.[40] While it persists, Russia has been unable to solve its various problems of governance, from its economy's reliance on petro-dollars to political tensions over its relationships with Europe and Asia. Meanwhile, corruption continues to dog Russian economic and political life, with the country ranking 127th out of 175 in Transparency International's corruption perception index, 2013.[41]

How these processes translate into Russia's attitude to global governance is complicated. For instance, Russia's authoritarian leadership and suppression of liberal movements alienates it from the EU and hampers its modernization. Yet, its leadership sees better relations with Europe as crucial to its technological advancement. On the one hand, Russia has been fiercely critical of governance organizations like the Organization for Security and Co-operation in Europe (OSCE) and its Office for Democratic Institutions and Human Rights for seeming to follow the agenda of NGOs in being intrusive and critical about elections in the Commonwealth of Independent States (CIS). On the other hand, it used an informal meeting of the OSCE in June 2009 to try and seek a European security treaty.[42] Its corporate behavior code introduced in 2002 was apparently modeled on Organisation for Economic

Co-operation and Development (OECD) principles of corporate governance.[43] Meanwhile, Russia's process of entry into the WTO in 2012 required the introduction of new regulatory mechanisms and so, as with China, Russia has opened itself up to global norm diffusion in the economic sphere.

Yet a strong strain of authoritarianism persists in Russian attitudes to economic governance, resisting liberal influences. Russia aims to create a Eurasian Economic zone by 2015 and pressured neighbors like Ukraine to choose this arrangement over closer ties with the EU. However, this economic bloc was not intended to run along federal lines and its function seems to be as a transparent extension of Russian power rather than a liberalizing project in the EU mold. Even the pro-Russian former Ukrainian leader Viktor Yanukovych resisted joining a customs union with Russia, Belarus, and Kazakhstan. As his former foreign minister relates it:

> he had met colleagues from Kazakhstan who had warned him against joining the Russian-sponsored customs union. They said that in a meeting the Russians had explained what they wanted to do. When the Kazakhs began to put forward their own ideas, the Russians told them they were not interested because they had just made clear to them what would be done.[44]

The tone of this interaction suggests Russia sees regional and global governance as a means of constraining the actions of other states rather than promoting universal goods. Thus, it particularly favors intergovernmental institutions such as the UNSC, in which Russia can veto undesirable action, and rejects the legitimacy and authority of groups like NATO and the EU to which it does not belong.[45] Overall, Russia's nationalistic attitude has seen it characterized as "an 'anti-globalizing' actor, as she tries to retain a strong role for the state in economic activities, is averse to NGOs and works to undermine the supremacy of the United States."[46] Its relations with its neighbors are characterized by attempts to consolidate regional influence rather than spread global norms in line with Russian values. This inhibits the attractiveness of its governance activities and undermines its legitimacy in the eyes of other states and peoples.

Brazil

Unlike China and Russia, who could be described as resurgent powers as they had been significant global actors in the past, Brazil is a truly rising power. Whereas China and Russia emphasize modernization, Brazil has tended to describe their growth in terms of development, dating back to the "national-developmentalist paradigm" of the 1930s and 1940s.[47] This envisaged a strong role for the state in the economy, central planning, and protectionist measures to support key industries. For the next few decades, continuing under military rule from 1967–1985, Brazil was wary of dependency on the United States and sought to build links with the global south to promote trade on a more equal basis than could be obtained from developed states. The desire for autonomy from the United States is particularly associated with the Presidency of Ernesto Geisel in the 1970s, who outlined a policy of "responsible pragmatism."[48] In practice, this meant Brazil did not join the Non-Aligned Movement (NAM) or engage in overt obstruction of United States interests but resisted United States influence in its affairs, domestically and regionally. It was also supportive of the NAM's notion of a New International Economic Order (NIEO) and was a founder member of the G77.

After 1980, Brazil's economy experienced severe difficulties, with high inflation, crime and poverty as well as growing inequality. In the 1990s, Brazil began to embrace some neoliberal policies to try and break out of the economic stagnation it found itself in. According to a survey by the Inter-American Development Bank, from 1991 to 2001 the state "transferred the control of 119 firms and minority stakes in a number of companies to the private sector" in a privatization program described as "among the largest in the world."[49] The economy was liberalized and more foreign direct investment encouraged. However, Brazil continued to experience economic instability and in January 1999 it was forced to devalue its currency and accept an IMF loan to avoid financial collapse.[50]

Despite the partial embrace of neoliberal reforms, Brazil under Cardoso, and especially under Lula, retained an emphasis on development and equality. In contrast to the other rising powers who have seen inequality rise, Dauvergne and Farias note that: "In the 2000s, while the per capita income of the country's richest 10 per cent increased by 10 per cent, the per capita income of 50 per cent of the poorest rose by 68 per cent … Brazil is now recording its lowest GINI index (which measures inequality) since estimates began in 1960."[51] Moreover, real improvements in the condition of the poor were identified, with their number falling by 51 per cent between 2002 and 2010.[52] In response to the perceived failure of neoliberalism to overcome Brazil's economic problems, President Cardoso criticized the "asymmetrical globalization" of the global economic order and, at home, economic policy returned to using state resources to support key firms and sectors promoting development.[53] State-owned companies such as Petrobras, the largest company in the Southern hemisphere, have spearheaded Brazil's engagement with other economies and are important agents of development in their own right.[54] According to White, the result was that "Between 2003 and 2008 Brazil enjoyed its best economic performance in more than 25 years, with economic growth averaging 5% per annum."[55] In 2011, Brazil became the sixth largest economy in the world in terms of GDP and regained this position in 2013.

Yet, problems of equality and development remain. Ian Taylor has noted that 50 percent of agricultural land in Brazil is controlled by just 4 percent of landowners.[56] Hosting major sporting events like the World Cup only serves to highlight the disconnect between Brazil's increasing national power and the continued economic marginalization of sectors of its population—underlined by recent protests. Brazil has neither wholly embraced neoliberalism nor discarded it in favor of a return to developmentalism. As Joao Augusto de Castro Neves describes it, Brazil has moved from a Cold War paradigm of "autonomy through distance" to one of "autonomy through participation."[57] In other words, whilst it has embraced some of the logic of neoliberalism in reforms and privatizations designed to modernize the economy, these have only partially been adopted. Brazil has retained a belief in the benefits of state support for key sectors and firms, providing resilience and autonomy from the domination of developed countries. We can see these attitudes feeding into Brazil's engagement with global governance structures.

In the first place, Brazil has sought to avoid reliance on Western markets and governance structures, dominated as they are by the developed countries, through its promotion of South-South relations. Within its region, Brazil has privileged Mercosur, the Community of Latin American and Caribbean States (CELAC) and Unasur over the Organization of American States (OAS)—since the latter includes the United States and Canada.[58] These regional governance forums allow Brazil to adopt the role of regional leader but do not compromise national sovereignty in the way that the EU, for instance, does with its members. As Burges notes: "Both Unasur and CELAC are clear attempts to reduce United States and external influence in the region, placing Brazil in the leading position of what is effectively a coalition unimpeded by the kind of supranational framework that would allow smaller regional states to actively constrain the Portuguese-speaking giant."[59]

Globally, Brazil continues to identify with developing countries and promotes Southern interests in a range of governance groupings. With

India and South Africa, it formed the IBSA forum in 2003 that advances common aspirations for development in Africa without the conditionality and compromised sovereignty that are associated with Western development projects. These countries lack the massed ranks of NGOs and civil society activists of Europe and the United States and tend to favor an approach to development premised on economic interaction rather than normative transference.[60] It is a part of the BASIC coalition, working in the G20 with other emerging powers to balance the influence of developed countries whilst also retaining an affinity with the G77.[61] Its participation in the BRICS summits has given rise to new initiatives and proposals—such as the BRICS bank— that might establish alternative governance structures and principles to "Western" or developed country institutions. Similarly, its rejection of United States' arguments on the enforcement of patents when it came to life-saving medicines, such as for AIDS drugs, represented an important countervailing force to developed countries' previous insistence on intellectual property.[62]

This account might suggest that Brazil is a revisionist power. In reality, this is not the case. Whilst Brazil's leaders often emphasize the unequal nature of participation in current governance forums, they still participate. Brazil remains in the OAS, signed the NPT in 1998, has used funds from the IMF and World Bank, as well as the Inter-American Development Bank, and is an active member of the G20. Although it created problems, with South Africa, in the Cancun round of WTO talks in 2003, it has since been instrumental in keeping developing countries on board with the process and has been a member of the "new quad" of up to six parties (Australia, Brazil, European Union, India, Japan, United States) working to break the deadlock and secure agreement as part of the Doha round. It has also been a longstanding member of the Cairns group of states seeking liberalization of agriculture—and critical of the protectionist policies of the EU and United States. In other words, Brazil has sought to work the system of global governance rather than overturn it.

Moreover, Brazil's status as a regional leader and southern champion has not been universally accepted. Business leaders have questioned the wisdom of emphasizing South-South relations after the breakdown of talks between Mercosur and the EU in the mid-2000s.[63] Argentina resists supporting Brazil's candidature to become a permanent member of the UNSC. IBSA's condemnation of the intervention in Libya was criticized for its failure to support the victims of Gaddafi's regime. Brazil's attempt to rethink the R2P doctrine to emphasize a Responsibility Whilst Protecting (RwP) is often seen as an attempt to undermine the norm altogether by placing impractical restrictions on the use of military force.[64] In addition, Brazil's equivocal attitude to democracy promotion has led to internal tensions among Brazil's elite as well as with democracy advocates in South America and Africa. Thus, Brazil's chances of pioneering a radically different direction of governance are hampered by a lack of support domestically, globally, and regionally for it to do so. Ironically, its emphasis on sovereignty and non-intervention may prevent some of the coercive techniques that are used by the West, and required by any group of actors seeking to forge new governance structures.

Overall, Brazilian elites seek a more multipolar world—one in which Brazil is able to exercise leadership on behalf of developing countries and resist United States and European infringements on sovereignty— but not a radically altered structure of governance. Brazil has a very different negotiating style to Russia, whose belligerent attitude is noted above. In contrast, its diplomats boast that "Brazil's great skill is to be friends with everyone."[65] Despite continuing state ownership or support for key firms, Brazil is inclined to argue that global markets are not liberal enough. Its development of South-South networks does circumvent global governance mechanisms in some ways but the weak conditionality in these interactions inhibits any sense of alternative theories or worlds of governance being promoted.

India

Of all the rising powers, India is arguably the most contradictory and unpredictable in its attitude to global governance. The world's largest democracy is one of the most persistent opponents of intervention to promote democracy movements in other countries. A developing state with a space program, India is both a recipient of substantial sums in aid as well as an emerging aid donor in its own right. Whilst critical of the NPT, India has praised the IAEA and harmonized its export guidelines with the NSG. Having long championed a normative approach to foreign policy and spearheaded the NAM during the Cold War, India has since become associated with a more realist foreign policy aligned with the United States.

Domestic governance in India has historically been hugely diverse and this may provide a clue to why it supports a more pluralist international society. India is currently divided into thirty-five states and union territories but their demographic make-up varies hugely. Whilst Maharashta and Uttar Pradesh have a combined population of 320 million, some smaller states have barely 1 million.[66] Governing a country such as India, with its hugely diverse religious, cultural and economic make-up entails acceptance of different governance mechanisms. Some of its states function under communist administrations at the same time that others have extensively liberalized economies. Moreover, local governance arrangements in India centered round village life have long subverted efforts to impose authority from the center. The historical varna/jati system was in modern parlance a system of social networks based on kinship and social stratification that persists to this day in many parts of the country.[67] Efforts to impose common normative standards with regard to women's rights, for instance, or a shared Hindu religious and cultural identity are often violently resisted.

At the national level, India post-independence emphasized state planning and a command economy to promote national unity and principles of equality and social justice. This policy was described by Nehru as "democratically planned collectivism" and specifically related to "old Indian social conceptions which were all based on the idea of the group"—the group being the self-governing village.[68] However, there were tensions in these two ideas as village life in India was hugely stratified and lacked social mobility. Thus, India's leaders were promoting one form of governance (secular, centralized planning) by using language derived from a culturally distinct, and even contradictory, system of local governance based on religious principles.

Having produced many leading intellectual lights of the anti-colonialist movements of the twentieth century, India aligned itself with former colonies and developing countries after 1947, promoting the ideals of the NIEO as part of its resistance to the economic domination of developed and former colonial states. It also ostensibly distanced itself from Cold War politics through its leadership of the NAM—though in practice, it had close relations with the Soviet Union. When the Cold War came to an end in 1991, India faced severe financial pressures and in response it liberalized its economy and intensified its integration into the global economy. Its currency was devalued, tariffs and taxes were lowered and foreign investment was encouraged.[69] Over the last two decades, it has achieved remarkable growth figures and is on course to become one of the largest economies in the world in the next few decades.

Yet, this story of progress and liberalization contains internal contradictions. On the one hand, as part of its embrace of neoliberalism India created Special Economic Zones (SEZs), resulting in widening inequality at the same time that economic prosperity, at least for some, improved in absolute terms. On the other hand, India has seen a "dramatic increase in union membership" as an expression of resistance to the "hegemony of neo-liberalism."[70] While Indian conglomerates have become major global players, as demonstrated by Tata's takeover of the British firms Corus (2007) and Jaguar (2008),[71] a disproportionate number of Indian firms are still majority family-owned, with some viewing "the importance of large, family-based business groups in the Indian corporate hierarchy" as comparable with "Japanese zaibatsus"—family-based financial cliques in Imperial Japan.[72] Meanwhile, India has "the largest number of hungry people in the world, with an estimated 200 million food insecure persons."[73] Although the country has liberalized, it attracts the least foreign investment of the BRICs because of its extensive bureaucracy and fears over the effect of foreign influence on Indian society.[74]

Similar inconsistencies are apparent in India's performance in global governance forums. A longstanding critic of the UNSC's unequal distribution of voting rights and responsibilities, India sought but failed to secure a seat in the UNSC in 1997–98 before being elected in 2011 and has again put its candidacy forward for membership in 2021–22. Since 1994, it has courted permanent member status in the UNSC and is working with the G4 of Brazil, Japan, and Germany to restructure the council and increase the number of permanent members. This initiative arguably renders previous objections to the UNSC on principle as rather hollow. It is no longer inequality that India objects to, perhaps, but its own outsider status from the club.

As noted above with regard to Brazil, India is a member of IBSA, the BRICS and the BASIC groups which have often claimed to act as mediators between developing and developed states. Yet, these groups now have a distinct identity of their own, beyond their previous ties to non-aligned or developing country groupings. Moreover, the extent to which they represent a counter-hegemonic discourse to Western elites in favor of the poor is questionable. IBSA has been described as "elitist," being made up of "an agglomeration of urban-based bureaucrats, export-oriented capitalists and personally ambitious politicians."[75]

Like Brazil, India continues to promote South-South relations and offers development aid to Africa, 60 percent of which is in the form of technical assistance.[76] India's emphasis on the norms of sovereignty and non-intervention—a legacy of its struggle for independence—mean that its development aid for African states could allow undemocratic or corrupt regimes to bypass Western attempts to tie aid to good governance. In other words, in concert with other rising powers such as Brazil and China, there is the possibility that India is undermining global efforts to promote human rights and democratization norms.

However, the extent to which India could formulate a rival group of states resistant to existing forms of global governance—even if it sincerely wanted to—is limited. India lacks substantial diplomatic machinery capable of translating soft power into tangible and lasting alliances.[77] India has long had a reputation as a "moralistic, contrarian loner in the international community."[78] Its tendency to participate fully in global governance discussions but then refuse to endorse the end result due to the need for compromise—apparent in negotiations over the Rome Statute in 1998, WTO meetings in 2003 and 2008, and the implementation of R2P—alienates other states and leads to a questioning of India's commitment to these processes.

In short, the legacies of its resistance to colonialism, as well as the inherent tensions in governing its diverse population, can be seen to feed into India's confused attitude to global governance. Efforts to dilute national sovereignty to solve global governance problems are frequently greeted with Indian intransigence. At heart, India favors a pluralist international society as the best guarantee of the norms of sovereignty and non-intervention. Yet it has also paid lip service to internationalist ideals and participated extensively in global governance arrangements that entail the pooling of sovereignty and compromises over national policy goals. Although it is the world's largest democracy and has a vibrant free press, India has considerable internal governance problems related to its development and cultural divisions. To project a coherent alternative vision of governance globally, it is arguable that India would first have to demonstrate that its ideas worked at home.

Conclusion

Following these four accounts of governance as it has developed in the BRIC countries, some tentative observations can be made. Firstly, national spaces are of enduring importance in understanding the practice of governance. Cultural, political, social, and technical differences are evident between these states when it comes to the operation of governance and these can be traced to the different historical experiences of these communities. While elite interactions do exist and can be coordinated at times across borders, there are also powerful interest groups in each national setting that resist the spread of transnational ideas such as neoliberalism or developmentalism.

Although national governance spaces are important, the central governments in each state clearly struggle to steer or control political and social outcomes. New actors are emerging, or old actors reasserting themselves, but the precise nature of these differs in each national context. Thus, while corruption may be a common problem across all four states, it can take the form of *guanxi*, bribes, rent-seeking, or political favors depending on the state in question, and these may be more or less difficult to confront according to how deeply rooted they are in each culture. The governments of all four states seek more effective forms of governance but for differing reasons. Some may wish for greater equality and development, others better systems of party control and economic performance, others, consolidation of political power around themselves and key individual partners. Thus, using the term "governance" in each case may in itself be problematic as we are looking at a huge variation in the range of actors making decisions and implementing policy, and their purpose in doing so. This might lead one to question if we are really talking about government, governance, or simply patterns of behavior in a condition of anarchy. Certainly, the fact that governance operates differently in different national environments does not have to mean that national governments are necessarily the most important actors when it comes to how governance works in practice.

What comes through strongly in this analysis is that three of these states are still rising (with Russia looking at a future of long-term decline), and their policy-makers are confronting significant domestic governance challenges. As such, they are not (individually or collectively) in a position to articulate a coherent alternative to the existing normative make-up of international society—nor are they likely to be for some decades. Policy-makers in India, Brazil, and China are overwhelmingly focused on domestic politics and their attitude to international governance problems and their solutions is viewed through their respective nationalist prisms. Russia is currently asserting central control over periphery states, but this is fundamentally about projecting its domestic governance insecurities onto its near abroad. Russia sees its relations with these countries as an internal matter; essentially, an attempt to redress governance failures related to the breakup of the Soviet Union, and not as a new paradigm of how states should be established or how they should interact with one another.

Overall, if discussion of rising powers has a use when it comes to analyzing governance, it is as a reminder that for all the talk of globalization and the implied homogenization that this entails, there is still a huge variety of actors, beliefs and traditions of governance in operation across the globe. This should be seen as both a challenge to the authority and legitimacy of the governance ideas of developed states, as well as an opportunity for developed and rising powers to learn from how the problems of governance are being addressed by other peoples.

Notes

1 Hedley Bull, *The Anarchical Society: A Study of Order in World Politics* (Basingstoke: Macmillan, 1977).
2 James Rosenau, "Governance in the Twenty First Century," *Global Governance* 1, no. 1 (1995): 13.
3 Thomas G. Weiss and Rorden Wilkinson, *International Organization and Global Governance* (London: Routledge, 2014), 3–11.
4 Barry Buzan, "China in International Society: Is 'Peaceful Rise' Possible?" *Chinese Journal of International Affairs* 3, no. 1 (2010): 20.
5 Martin Sieff, *Shifting Superpowers* (Washington, DC: CATO Institute, 2010), 45.
6 Robin Porter, *From Mao to Market: China Reconfigured* (London: Hurst, 2011), 94.
7 Porter, *From Mao to Market*, 59.
8 Lawrence Sáez and Crystal Chang, "The political economy of global firms from India and China," *Contemporary Politics* 15, no. 3 (2009): 266–267.
9 Francis Fukuyama, *The Origins of Political Order* (New York: Farrar, Straus and Giroux, 2011), 186.
10 Elizabeth C. Economy, "The Game Changer: Coping with China's Foreign Policy Revolution," *Foreign Affairs* 89, no. 6 (November/December 2010): 142–153.
11 "The rise of state capitalism," *The Economist*, 21 January 2012.
12 Ibid.
13 "The state advances," *The Economist*, 6 October 2012.
14 European Chamber 2013, "Sustained Growth Requires a Fundamental Reassessment of the Government's Role in the Business Environment," Press Release, 5 September.
15 "From SOE to GLC," *The Economist*, 23 November 2013.
16 Chris Buckley, "China's Leaders Urge More Market Control of Economy," *New York Times* blog, 12 November 2013, http://sinosphere.blogs.nytimes.com/2013/11/12/chinas-leaders-urge-more-market-control-of-economy/?_php=true&_type=blogs&_r=0.
17 Ibid.
18 Sáez and Chang, "The Political Economy of Global Firms," 275.
19 Elizabeth Van Wie Davis, "Governance in China in 2010," *Asian Affairs* 35, no. 4 (2009): 195–211.
20 Van Wie Davis, "Governance in China in 2010," 199.
21 David Scott, *"The Chinese Century"? The Challenge to Global Order* (Basingstoke: Palgrave, 2008): 78.
22 Gov.cn, "China the largest."
23 Zhu Liqun, *China's Foreign Policy Debates*, EU ISS Chaillot Papers 121, September 2010, 22–3.
24 Robert Lawrence Kuhn, *How China's Leaders Think* (Singapore: John Wiley & Sons, 2010), 378.
25 Barry Buzan, "China in International Society," 17–18.
26 Richard Sakwa, "'New Cold War' or twenty years crisis? Russia and international politics," *International Affairs* 84, no. 2 (2008): 246.

27 Anatoly Zhuplev and Vladimir Shein, "Russia's Evolving Corporate Governance in the Cultural Context," *Journal of Transnational Management* 10, no. 3, (2005): 25.
28 Neil Robinson, "The global economy, reform and crisis in Russia," *Review of International Political Economy* 6, no. 4 (1999): 535.
29 Robinson, "The Global Economy, Reform and Crisis in Russia," 550.
30 Zhuplev and Shein, "Russia's Evolving Corporate Governance in the Cultural Context," 20.
31 Elena Shadrina and Michael Bradshaw, "Russia's energy governance transitions and implications for enhanced cooperation with China, Japan, and South Korea," *Post-Soviet Affairs* 29, no. 6 (2013): 465.
32 Andrew Monaghan, "The *vertikal*: power and authority in Russia," *International Affairs* 88, no. 1 (2012): 1–16.
33 Clifford G. Gaddy and Barry W. Ickes, "Russia after the Global Financial Crisis," *Eurasian Geography and Economics* 51, no. 3 (2010): 299.
34 Sergei Aleksashenko, "Russia's economic agenda to 2020," *International Affairs* 88, no. 1 (2012): 36; S. Neil Macfarlane, "The 'R' in BRICS: is Russia an emerging power?" *International Affairs* 82, no. 1 (2006): 52.
35 Monaghan, "The *vertikal*: power and authority in Russia," 9.
36 Andrew Monaghan, "Putin's Russia: Shaping a Grand Strategy," *International Affairs* 89, no. 5 (2013): 1228.
37 Sakwa, "'New Cold War' or twenty years crisis?", 246.
38 Shadrina and Bradshaw, "Russia's energy governance transitions," 467.
39 Monaghan, "The *vertikal*: power and authority in Russia," 14.
40 Nikolai Petrov, Maria Lipman, and Henry E. Hale, "Three dilemmas of hybrid regime governance: Russia from Putin to Putin," *Post-Soviet Affairs* 30, no. 1 (2014): 1–26; Luke Harding, *Mafia State* (London: Guardian Books, 2012).
41 www.transparency.org/cpi2013/results.
42 Richard Sakwa, "Russia and Europe: Whose Society?" *Journal of European Integration* 33, no. 2 (2011): 206.
43 Zhuplev and Shein, "Russia's Evolving Corporate Governance in the Cultural Context," 32.
44 Tim Judah, "Fighting for the soul of Ukraine," *New York Review of Books*, 9 January 2014, www.nybooks.com/articles/archives/2014/jan/09/fighting-soul-ukraine/?pagination=false.
45 Dmitri Trenin, "No Return to the Past for Russia," *The International Spectator* 47, no. 3 (2012): 10.
46 Filippos Proedrou and Christos A. Frangonikolopoulos, "Russia's Reemergence in the Global System: Globalizing or Anti-Globalizing Force?," *Journal of Contemporary European Studies* 18, no. 1 (2010): 79.
47 Peter Dauvergne and Déborah Farias, "The Rise of Brazil as a Global Development Power," *Third World Quarterly* 33, no. 5 (2012): 907.
48 Lyal White, "Understanding Brazil's new drive for Africa," *South African Journal of International Affairs* 17, no. 2 (2010): 223.
49 Francisco Anuatti-Neto, Milton Barossi-Filho, Antonio Gledson de Carvalho and Roberto Macedo, *Costs and Benefits of Privatization: Evidence from Brazil* (New York: Inter-American Development Bank, 2003), 3.
50 Robert Keohane, *Power and Governance in a Partially Globalized World* (London: Routledge, 2002), 200.

51 Dauvergne and Farias, "The Rise of Brazil as a Global Development Power," 908.
52 Ibid.
53 Steen Fryba Christensen, "Brazil's Foreign Policy Priorities," *Third World Quarterly* 34, no. 2 (2013): 272–3.
54 Lyal White, "Emerging powers in Africa: Is Brazil any different?" *South African Journal of International Affairs* 20, no. 1 (2013): 120.
55 White, "Understanding Brazil's new drive for Africa," 226.
56 Ian Taylor, "The South Will Rise Again"? New Alliances and Global Governance: The India–Brazil–South Africa Dialogue Forum," *Politikon* 36, no. 1 (2009): 56.
57 Joao Augusto de Castro Neves, "Brazil as an emerging power in the twentieth century," in *Emerging Powers in a Comparative Perspective*, Vidya Nadkarni and Norma C. Noonan, eds (London: Bloomsbury, 2013), 191.
58 Oliver Stuenkel, "Rising Powers and the Future of Democracy Promotion: the case of Brazil and India," *Third World Quarterly* 34, no. 2 (2013): 345.
59 Sean Burges, "Brazil as a bridge between old and new powers?" *International Affairs* 89, no. 3 (2013): 591–592.
60 Stuenkel, "Rising Powers and the Future of Democracy Promotion," 349.
61 Kathryn Hochstetler and Eduardo Viola, "Brazil and the politics of climate change: beyond the global commons," *Environmental Politics* 21, no. 5 (2012): 755.
62 Jane Galvão, "Brazil and Access to HIV/AIDS Drugs: A Question of Human Rights and Public Health," *American Journal of Public Health* 95, no. 7 (2005): 1110–1116.
63 Chris Alden and Marco Antonio Vieira, "The new diplomacy of the South: South Africa, Brazil, India and trilateralism," *Third World Quarterly* 26, no. 7 (2005): 1077–1095.
64 Sean Burges, "Brazil as a bridge between old and new powers?" 593; James Pattison, "The Ethics of 'Responsibility While Protecting': Brazil, the Responsibility To Protect, and guidelines for humanitarian intervention," University of Denver working paper no. 71, www.du.edu/korbel/hrhw/workingpapers/2013/71-pattison-2013.pdf.
65 Peter Dauvergne and Farias, "The Rise of Brazil as a Global Development Power," 906.
66 "The good of small things," *The Economist*, 30 March 2013, www.economist.com/news/asia/21574544-creating-new-smaller-states-should-be-made-easier-good-small-things.
67 Fukuyama, *The Origins of Political Order*, 171–174.
68 Jawarharlal Nehru, *The Discovery of India* (London: Penguin, 2004), 581–582.
69 Nadkarni, "India—An Aspiring Global Power," 141.
70 Michael Gillan and Robert Lambert, "Introduction: India and the Age of Crisis," *South Asia: Journal of South Asian Studies* 36, no. 2 (2013): 161.
71 Emma Mawdsley and Gerard McCann, "The Elephant in the Corner? Reviewing India-Africa Relations in the New Millennium," *Geography Compass* 4, no. 2 (2010): 85.
72 Sáez and Chang, "The political economy of global firms," 269.
73 Gillan and Lambert, "Introduction: India and the Age of Crisis," 162.
74 Amrita Narlikar, "India: Responsible to Whom?" *International Affairs* 89, no. 3 (2013): 605.

75 Taylor, "The South Will Rise Again," 56.
76 Ian Taylor, "India's Rise in Africa," *International Affairs* 88, no. 4 (2012): 788.
77 Taylor, "India's Rise in Africa," 796.
78 George Perkovitch, "Is India a Major Power," *The Washington Quarterly* 27, no. 1 (2003): 142.

5 Rising powers and the ethics of global trade and development governance

Patrick Holden

- **The rising powers and the Doha Development Round**
- **A new voice for the developing world? BRICS views on trade and development**
- **Development aid and the global Aid for Trade initiative**
- **Rising powers and the Post-2015 agenda**
- **Conclusion**

There is a wealth of literature on the impact of the rising powers on the global security, political, and economic system. However, their role in relation to the ethics of global governance is relatively under-researched. Development is an essentially qualitative, political, and ethical concept, and actors in this realm must take an explicitly ethical (if not always overtly political) approach. Global development, as a cause, implies recognition of the moral responsibility of the more developed states, regions, and classes to their poorer counterparts. This was incarnated in the global Millennium Development Goals (MDGs), agreed in 2000, which are supposed to structure and inform all international actors' approach to development. Global trade politics is not always presented as an ethical issue but trade, and especially global trade, relies on a degree of institutionalization, including normative understandings.[1] Trade disputes often involve ethical, as well as purely technical, claims and counterclaims as to fairness, trust, and good faith. The relationship of trade to development is one area where global commerce and ethical considerations fuse explicitly. Trade is increasingly viewed as key to development but there is a wide spectrum of opinion as to the relationship between both factors (from the free trade perspective to those who argue that trade must be "managed" to serve development).

The rising powers, such as India and China, might be presumed to have a special role to play here as the largest developing countries on the planet. Notwithstanding the benefits they have gleaned from the global trading system, one might expect the rising powers to be critical of existing, Eurocentric, trade and development governance structures (and concepts). Have they made use of their new prominence to formulate alternatives, ones more focused on the needs of the poor? For many decades before their rise in the global economy, both countries presented themselves as leaders of the developing world. For example, China has a longstanding relationship with the G77 developing countries, formed to promote developing country interests in global economic affairs. Is there an alternative vision, and practice, of globalization evident from their discourse and behavior? From the foregoing one might expect that to be the case but another, very popular, school of thought views the rising powers and attendant multipolarity on the global scene as a force for weakening global institutions and global norm promotion.[2] Certainly any banal assumptions as to the unity and solidarity of "the developing world" were disproven decades ago.

This chapter will make a modest contribution to answering this question by focusing on the role of rising powers in contemporary efforts to link trade and development. It will concentrate on the two largest rising powers, China and India, while also analyzing the BRICS grouping as a generator of ideas. To begin, after further clarifying the concepts at hand, it analyzes the rising powers' role in the WTO and the Doha Development Round in particular (this is necessarily quite brief and does not go into the detail and sequence of trade negotiations). Following this it considers the worldview of the rising powers (as articulated through the BRICS grouping) in this regard. The chapter then looks in detail at one very important, if challenging, global initiative to reinforce the developmental impact of trade; the WTO's global Aid for Trade (AfT) initiative. Finally, it studies the rising powers' influence on the trade-related dimensions of the UN-led proposals for Post-2015 global development objectives (the successors to the MDGs).

In this chapter, the question of "ethics" is addressed within a broader study of the ideas and norms promoted by rising powers. The focus is two-pronged. Firstly, on whether these powers may be understood as presenting resistance to "neoliberal hegemony" and globalization. Neoliberalism is understood as the theory that free markets and private individuals/companies should dominate economic life, rather than political institutions.[3] Although neoliberalism is not incompatible with nationalism,[4] insofar as it is based on reducing public power it favors a weaker state in many respects. As open markets are of primary importance to the functioning of a neoliberal brand of capitalism, neoliberalism is intrinsically globalist and advocates global free trade.[5] Apart from tariff reduction, the development of international trade law under the WTO, to include "behind the border" regulatory issues such as environmental policy,[6] has served to limit the nation state's regulatory power.[7] This can be understood as a contribution to the global "constitutionalization" of free-market capitalism.[8] With some moderation, a neoliberal understanding of the benefits of free trade and the development of the "world market" has dominated mainstream thinking. In neo-Gramscian terms it has been "hegemonic." In this case hegemony refers to a state of intellectual/ideological as well as material domination,[9] and an ideology is hegemonic if it is sufficiently dominant to be a part of the common sense assumptions of individuals and institutions. Countries such as China and India have an ambivalent relationship to neoliberalism. They have, in the aggregate, benefited from neoliberal globalization but would clearly resist some of its more transnational, universalist, implications.

The second, related, focus of this chapter is on their attitude to global governance in this sphere. The rising powers are known for being sovereignty conscious and wary of interventionist global governance in the security realm. How does this translate to areas of political economy? Do they support reformed global institutions or merely seek to limit the influence/power of those institutions? Are they rejecting global norms or reconstituting them for their own contexts? These questions can be understood in terms of the traditional pluralist versus solidarist debates of the English School,[10] the former supporting international, sovereignty-respecting governance and the latter more global norm convergence and interventionist policies. There is also an abundance of more contemporary work on "norm promotion," identity building and socialization at the international level.[11] Although the international trade regime is strongly legalized (for obvious reasons), international development policy cooperation relies much more on soft methods (voluntary policy coordination, peer pressure, and dialogue), which may be conducive to a greater role for rising powers. Given their prestige, rising powers clearly have the potential to act as "norm promoters" rather than passive recipients. However, this may involve greater engagement with global institutions and a greater willingness to make international commitments than has been the case in the past.

The rising powers and the Doha Development Round

The contemporary multilateral trading system had its roots in the aftermath of the Second World War, when the United States sought to institutionalize and therefore further embed international trade agreements. The GATT was established in 1949 and expanded on in further rounds of negotiations, culminating in the establishment of the WTO in 1995. There is a consensus that, by any measure, the GATT was skewed towards the interests of developed industrial nations.[12] Developing countries gradually got involved and increased in power, but generally had to accept what the industrialized states/regions agreed amongst themselves. India had been an original participant, because of its Commonwealth membership, but China only joined in 2001. Post-war international development policy had been mostly concerned with paternalistic aid (financial assistance) from North to South. The one major effort to radically reform the global economic and commercial system—the New International Economic Order of the 1970s/80s—failed.

In the 1990s, the era of truly global development politics had arrived with the failure of the centrally planned communist alternative. There was a new effort to link trade and development but no consensus on how this should be done. The mainstream forces (both institutional and academic) were more concerned with ensuring development policy was based on free market forces, and viewed freer trade as the key to development. A moral economy discourse emerged from Western civil society which sought to manage trade in the interests of developing countries,[13] and this had a certain agenda-setting impact but was marginalized in practice.

The round of trade liberalization talks launched in 2001 was referred to as the Doha Development Round. This was an acknowledgement that the interests of developing countries would have to be addressed and that the trade system up until then had not done so. However, in reality it was also a push for global trade liberalization, initiated by developed countries.[14] Developing countries had wanted to focus purely on remedying the inequities of global trade (fulfilling what they viewed as unfulfilled commitments from previous agreements) rather than launching a new round of liberalization. Developed countries, led by the EU and the United States, argued that they would address developing country concerns—hence the name—but were also demanding further trade liberalization all-round as a quid pro quo for this. As is well known, the Doha Round was, if not abandoned, effectively put in deep freeze from 2005 on. No universal agreement was reached. This is often viewed as a manifestation of increased developing country power, but what role did the rising powers play in this?

Developing country coalitions have grown increasingly common in multilateral trade negotiations.[15] In the initial period after Doha was launched, India, China, and Brazil (in a leading role) formed the G-20 coalition of developing countries (not to be confused with the general G20) to combat the joint United States–EU position on agriculture.[16] This was a heterogeneous group of developing countries (from pro-liberalization countries such as Brazil to more protectionist ones such as India) but they united in opposing the United States–EU agenda, which was effectively resisted, as was progress in the entire Round, at the Cancun Ministerial (2003). As negotiations developed, China, which had just joined the WTO and is known for being pro-liberalization—as a major exporter—was not one of the major countries ultimately responsible for blocking the Round. Nevertheless, it was indirectly responsible for its failure as many countries cited fear of Chinese competition as a rationale for not wanting to further open their markets.[17] India was more of a direct obstacle and produced coherent arguments against trends in trade negotiations, presenting itself as a champion of weaker countries. As the Indian trade minister at the 2005 WTO Ministerial Conference stated:

> if the content of this Round only perpetuates the inequities of global trade, then it will be no Round. To redeem the pledge we made at Doha, let us resolve to make this a Round for those who need it. Let us make this a Round that truly reflects the development dimension in its most beneficial and most effective sense.[18]

In particular, India's call for a Special Safeguard Mechanism (SSM) for poorer countries to protect their agriculture (in the interests of food security) resonated with many poorer countries.[19] This was an example of norms and national interest coinciding. India's stance was maintained and was eventually accepted by the WTO community in return for a (minor) multilateral agreement on trade facilitation in 2013.

A new voice for the developing world? BRICS views on trade and development

One of the rationales for the BRICS grouping was to provide an alternative voice for developing countries. Much has been written on the relative lack of coherence and agency of the BRICS, but even on the ideational level, what do they offer? The major "discursive" acts come from BRICS leaders' summits and some sectoral ministerial meetings. An analysis of these reveals strong support for free trade, coupled with more explicit support and flexibility for developing countries: "the Ministers reiterated the need to resist protectionist tendencies and to promote international trade as an engine of economic growth and development, while respecting the WTO consistent policy space available to developing countries to pursue their legitimate objectives of growth, development."[20] This quote shows that the BRICS are reiterating standard WTO/free trade discourse, while supplementing it with more critical ideas, namely Robert Wade's conception of "policy space".[21] This term is used as part of an argument that countries at different levels of development may need to adopt a range of different policies and regulatory models, contrary to the ideal of global regulatory harmonization.

Some skepticism is expressed in BRICS statements about the more radical transnational initiatives and concepts promoted by the WTO, such as its "Made in the World" initiative which reshapes concepts of trade flows by focusing on value added, and Global Value Chains (GVCs), rather than the flows of final products between states.[22] "Value chains" denote the global totality of activities (from suppliers to various stages of production to marketing across different countries) which go into a commercial product. The WTO seeks to highlight these to emphasize the complexity and interdependence of the global economy and to move away from a focus on bilateral trade and its winners and losers. The "Made in the World" initiative sought to promote a more transnational/aterritorial conception of economic activity; however, in 2012 the BRICS Trade Ministers voiced some skepticism about the role of GVCs as a lever of development: "In order for global value chains to serve as instruments of growth and development, it would be important to develop a deeper understanding of their developmental impact and the conditions under which they can be used to achieve long term socio-economic gains."[23]

The BRICS always cite and stress the importance of the United Nations Conference on Trade and Development (UNCTAD) as a voice for developing countries. The central role of the WTO is not questioned, however, and BRICS criticisms of the global trade system always revolve around making the WTO work: "We reaffirm our support for an open, transparent and rules-based multilateral trading system ... We will continue in our efforts for the successful conclusion of the Doha Round, based on the progress made and in keeping with its mandate, while upholding the principles of transparency, inclusiveness and multilateralism."[24]

Again this quote illustrates how the mainstream discourse is adopted by the BRICS countries, although they, of course, use it to criticize the policies of developed countries. The BRICS also strongly support multilateralism and criticize "plurilateral initiatives," moves by a limited number of countries to reach agreement on deeper trade liberalization themselves.[25] Generally, those hoping for the BRICS grouping to lead a more radical transformation of the global system to a multipolar world less dominated by capitalism have been sorely disappointed: "BRICS isn't promoting a 1970s-style New International Economic Order, North-South equality, even South-South equality. It's imitating the North in exploiting Southern natural resources."[26]

Development aid and the global Aid for Trade initiative

There is a burgeoning literature on the impact of rising powers (or "emerging donors") on the international development aid community.[27] In recent decades a Western-based international development aid regime has emerged. This is a "soft" form of international/global governance; national donors and international organizations still have authority in allocating resources but various international public institutions and civil society organizations seek to steer policy. Within the universal United Nations framework, the Millennium Development Goals set an agreed agenda and set of principles for all development donors up until 2015. There are also UN-led efforts to rally states to increase their aid levels. In regard to more specific policies the Development Assistance Committee (DAC) of the OECD has played a leading role in setting standards for state donors.[28] The DAC has set the standard methodology for classifying and measuring aid flows and also serves as a forum for policy coordination and peer pressure, as the member states publicly review each other's work. More generally, the Bretton Woods Institutions and the major aid donors have since the 1980s (at least) made aid strictly conditional on various principles: notably corruption controls and on what the donors regard as sound macroeconomic and other policies. There is also (less consistently applied) conditionality in terms of human rights and democratic practices.

The increased prominence of aid from large developing countries (such aid always existed) has challenged this "mainstream" development aid regime in several respects.[29] States such as China, in particular, and India tend to mingle their aid (government grants and cheap loans) with other forms of investment in packages which do not correspond to the OECD's definition of "aid." More fundamentally, they reject the principle of conditionality and thus many Western donors have criticized China for bank-rolling corrupt and abusive regimes in Africa (such as Angola, Sudan, and Zimbabwe), and reducing the leverage of the "international community" in the process. For their part, the emerging donors distinguish themselves from, and reject the norms of, the mainstream aid community. The term South-South cooperation has emerged to signify a new form of cooperation. It is explicitly supposed to be mutually beneficial (whereas, at least in theory, the West had evolved a purist sense of development aid as not *directly* related to the donor's economic interest). Although the West criticizes "irresponsible" giving and lending, the emerging donors explicitly reject the concept of conditionality as neocolonial,[30] although in practice there may be some conditions to aid (non-recognition of Taiwan for instance). From this perspective they are not outliers, but rather they are forging a new cooperative system. However, the fact that these states know very little about each other's policies towards developing countries[31] implies that South-South cooperation, at this stage, is more defined by what it is not (traditional aid) than what it is.

The established aid community has engaged in extensive efforts to persuade the emerging donors to support some of their practices and principles. The High Level Forums on Aid Effectiveness, led by the OECD were an effort to include donors beyond the OECD club in cooperation. The 2005 Paris Declaration on Aid Effectiveness (at the second forum) was a major agreement to harmonize management procedures and adhere to standards of transparency, but it was signed only by the mainstream donors. Efforts to include new donors such as China culminated in the Busan conference on development aid of 2011 (the fourth forum).[32] This was essentially a failure in that no, even morally, binding commitments were made by emerging donors. It was merely agreed that they might, on a voluntary basis, align themselves with the principles of the Paris Declaration. As one OECD report puts it, the Busan declaration: "strongly embraces diversity and recognizes the distinct roles these providers of South-South cooperation can play 'on the basis of common goals, shared principles and differential commitments.' It is no longer about convergence of donor practices but the emphasis is on complementarity."[33] OECD officials accept that these new donors are not coming on board. One paper on China's aid notes that cooperation between traditional and emerging aid donors is based on "interests not values,"[34] although elsewhere they reiterate common normative objectives.

Within this context of polite non-cooperation, the WTO's Aid-for-Trade (AfT) Initiative (2006) was one sector of aid policy where global cooperation was more promising. The initiative emerged from the aforementioned blockages within the WTO and the Doha Round. Developing countries, and least developed countries (LDCs), in particular, were insisting on more explicit commitments from developed nations to help them profit from trade liberalization measures (and to remedy what they saw as the inequities of the global trading system). A major issue here was that they did not just want technical assistance to negotiate and implement agreements, but substantial aid to improve their infrastructure and productive capacity. In 2005 the WTO Hong Kong Ministerial, as part of an effort to end the deadlock, launched an official "Task Force" on AfT, which reported in 2006. Thirteen states and regional organizations sat on the Task Force, including China, India, and Brazil. The major innovation of the Task Force was to make clear that AfT should involve the more substantial forms of aid mentioned previously. The following categories of AfT were defined:[35]

- Technical assistance and capacity building for trade policy (to help countries engage in trade negotiations and/or to help them implement trade agreements);
- trade development (assistance with trade promotion, market analysis, and development, and other forms of support for private sector businesses);
- assistance in dealing with trade-related adjustment costs;
- development of the productive capacities of the economy of the recipient state;
- development of trade-related infrastructure; and
- other trade related issues.

Although this expanded definition was generally welcomed, there were some concerns that this new agenda could lead to a reduced focus on human development in favor of more directly economically and commercially beneficial aid. It was agreed that AfT would be focused particularly on LDCs (those most in need, where the poverty reduction impact would be largest). Some specific commitments were given by leading donors as a part of the initiative but generally the regime was informal; peer pressure and moral suasion would be used to encourage support for AfT. The WTO Secretariat and the OECD were given the task of monitoring the adoption of AfT principles by aid donors and the major mechanism for this would be a biannual global AfT review.[36]

Thus, in the case of the AfT initiative we have one global development aid initiative in which emerging powers were centrally involved in the formulation and organization of the regime. For many, countries like China represent an example of how to benefit from trade and globalization; one Chinese government representative claimed at a review meeting that "China had developed a unique 'China model,'"[37] although what exactly this model is, or how applicable it is, is hotly debated. AfT is also particularly attractive to emerging powers as it aligns with their conception of aid and "cooperation" for mutual benefit. Accordingly China and India have been quite keen participants in the "regime," in terms of engaging in meetings and supporting the agenda. The OECD, keen to embrace any sign of cooperation, has gone out of its way to praise the role of these countries. However, when we analyze their engagement we see that it is limited, partly because they insist on sharply distinguishing themselves from developed countries. The more specific commitments to give aid are to come from the latter, who are frequently admonished by China for not living up to global commitments. Their own aid is an optional extra, as India put it, "South-South cooperation was *voluntary* and was complementary to, rather than a substitute for, North-South aid" (author's emphasis).[38] Although it is fair to state that it is complementary, it is arguable that some emerging countries (especially China with its large reserves) could make more global commitments. The rising powers can sometimes be contradictory here as China's own White Paper on aid does refer to its "international obligations,"[39] but generally they refuse to accept strict commitments on aid.

In terms of concrete contributions, China is a major AfT donor and most of its aid can be defined as AfT. In 2011 its AfT was estimated at $2.468 billion (India's AfT is less than a third of this).[40] Arguably this is not so much a response to the initiative as a continuation of ongoing bilateral aid policies. China did create a new program to help LDCs in the WTO, but the funding for this is modest, $400,000 per annum.[41] In 2013 the BRICS agreed to establish a BRICS development bank which would focus on supporting infrastructure. This has been viewed in the West as a potential rival to the World Bank and other regional development banks,[42] although there is not much evidence as to how it would be different (presumably there would be fewer political conditions attached to lending). The Bank is not yet fully operational and so cannot be judged.

In regard to their participation in the governance of AfT, China and India did not reply to the first round of donor questionnaires sent in preparation for the first global review in 2007. Only when a specific South-South questionnaire was sent around did they fully participate. They will not report their AfT statistics to the WTO/OECD, the latter simply have to estimate them.[43] In their answer to the official questionnaire on the amount of trade-related assistance China gives, the Chinese response was simply, "not sure."[44] Also, in the questionnaires, responses of both countries to more critical questions about their aid policy and how they might improve it are not answered.[45] Thus we see that even in a light-touch regime, partly designed by them, and in line with their interests the rising powers are reluctant to fully engage with the norms of participation. The AfT regime in itself can be judged a success in terms of rallying resources and thinking on this form of aid, but the share received by least developed countries/LDCs, remains relatively low.

Rising powers and the Post-2015 agenda

The Millennium Declaration and the MDGs were significant milestones in the evolution of global development policy. The Declaration was a formal collective commitment by the political leadership of the planet, in particular, of the developed world to the developing. The MDGs represented the first universal/global agreement on development priorities and targets (in previous eras this would have been unthinkable). There were eight MDGs. The first seven were standard socio-economic targets while the eighth objective for a "global partnership" strayed into potentially controversial areas as it implied various commitments on funding and reform of global economic governance. The debate on the successor to the MDGs is one of the most extensive policy processes in history. The United Nations Development Group alone has led over 50 national level post-2015 dialogues in developing countries; nine global thematic consultations; and innumerable online interactive forums for citizen and stakeholder engagement. Then there is the High Level Panel (HLP) Report (2013) and the various other global forums concerned with development issues, not to mention numerous civil society initiatives. The agenda is equally broad. The original MDGs covered education, gender, health, sustainability, and poverty. As the conception of development has continued to expand, the post-2015 agenda has widened to cover a bewildering variety of topics, from aid modalities to taxation, gender, and migration. Major themes include the need for a new global partnership between north and south, the struggle for inclusive growth, and the balance between economic and social development more broadly conceived. The link between trade and development is a major focus, partly because of the example of successful development offered by the rising powers; but have their ideas shaped the agenda in any way? The major opportunity for interventions by governments is in 2015 (via formal inter-governmental meetings) but major work in setting the parameters of the debate was done via global institutions in 2012–2013.

At the Secretary General's behest a UN Task Team (of the various UN agencies and bodies) was assembled. This prepared two reports, one on development priorities and a second on the global partnership concept. The thrust of the first Task Team report was how to "harness globalization" to transform development prospects. Four dimensions of progress were specified:[46]

- Inclusive social development (a particular focus on the poor/vulnerable, sectors of the population);
- inclusive economic development (an all-important but vague principle);
- sustainability; and
- peace and security.

Policy coherence on the part of the developed world is a key theme, which is further developed in the second report. This second report, on the concept and practice of a global partnership, cites the perceived successes of MDG 8 in consolidating donor commitments. It does note the lack of "a strong normative foundation" to the global partnership concept hitherto, which it proposes to remedy.[47] This could prove problematic for BRICS countries in that the proposed normative foundation would be based on universal human rights.[48] Trade is a major concern of the report, which also argues for much more substantial global governance (greater common but differentiated responsibilities) in a range of other areas (including commitment from the developing world to further debt relief and technology transfer). The report presses for a strong conclusion to Doha and places great hopes on the potential of an agreement to "reduce certain distortions in international trade, such as agricultural subsidies, tariff peaks and tariff escalation that still impede market access for many countries."[49] More generally, it suggests "a carefully designed conclusion of the Round would represent a step forward for the global partnership on development, enhancing coherence among trade, financial, human rights, and environmental issues and strengthening the effectiveness of the open, rules-based multilateral trading system in addressing specific development challenges."[50]

The report also reiterates the need to deal with supply side constraints, support productive capacity in particular, and provide aid for investment (very much in line with the broader AfT agenda). In regard to aid it calls for commitments beyond overseas development aid (ODA), including "targeted private investments" (based on agreed developmental needs), greater facilitation of remittances (already a massive source of finance) combined with greater domestic resource mobilization in developing countries. On the institutional procedural side it trumpets the role of multi-stakeholder sectoral partnerships and all of the different parties are intended to be involved in mutual monitoring.

To a degree this report reflects the attitude of the BRICS in terms of demanding more concessions from the developed world. In terms of economic ideas it is more radical than anything the BRICS have come up with, particularly ideas such as technology transfer. It also expounds a much stronger sense of global governance than is desired by the sovereignty-conscious BRICS, especially in stressing a normative dimension based on international human rights law. Although it advocates "differentiated responsibilities," it does demand commitments from the developing and emerging world as well. It also says much more about civil society, and the report very much supports the pluralistic, multi-stakeholder model of governance, which is not a priority of the statist-inclined rising powers.

The HLP set up represented a broader spectrum of power-brokers and national leaders beyond the UN institution. Individuals from rising powers were present on the panel.[51] Its terms of reference were to "report on key principles regarding partnership for development and strengthened accountability mechanisms, recommend on how to build consensus on the post-2015 agenda around 3 dimensions of economic growth, social equality and environmental sustainability."[52] The Panel engaged in an elaborate process of consultation before coming up with the report, and a series of background papers were also published on its website. Amongst these are several authored by experts from emerging countries, which draw on their experience and philosophy. Most notably, two Chinese economists came up with a proposal for a global "Structural Transformation Fund" to support infrastructural development and act as a form of global stimulus.[53] Infrastructure is understood as a semi-global public good, intelligent investment which could increase aggregate demand in a sustainable manner. Funding for this proposal (which was not taken up) would come from a mix of public and private sources. Much of this appears to be inspired by China's aid activities (which marshals public and private resources and focuses on infrastructure to a large degree). It is also very much in line with the AfT agenda previously described.

The final HLP report was much less radical than the UN Task Team report. It outlined five transformational shifts which the panel agreed were core to sustainable global development (followed by a series of exemplary goals and targets).[54] The first was better policies to remove absolute poverty. The second was sustainability as an overarching principle. Third was to transform economies for jobs and inclusive growth ("rapid equitable growth" facilitated by "open, fair and development-friendly trade"). This included some relatively banal points about productivity increases and an enabling environment for business (SMEs in particular). Reducing inequality is considered as a cross-cutting objective but it is not an explicit transformational priority or a specific goal, although there is a goal of equitable growth. Fourth was peace and good governance and the fifth was the global partnership itself. The report, although less trenchant than the UN Task Team report, also emphasized the importance of global economic rules and developed world reforms including stronger commitments on trade reform. Again the multi-stakeholder nature of these arrangements was emphasized. Unsurprisingly, the HLP report, although it certainly included significant challenges to developed countries, tilted more towards the free-market side of debates. Although it takes account of the emerging powers, and their economic success, there is little evidence of any input there and the report very much reflects Western globalist capitalist norms (including a focus on governance). In brief, while the rising powers will undoubtedly make their influence felt in the final shaping of the Post-2015 agreement, their influence during the agenda-setting phase on global institutions is not notable. There are a number of reasons for this. For one, the evidence suggests that they do not have radically distinctive views on global development. Also, in China's case, despite the leadership potential its economic success gives it, the government's wariness towards its own civil society, and global civil society more generally, weakens its role in this kind of process.

Conclusion

On the basis of the evidence thus far, there is little to suggest that rising powers have offered a coherent ethical or ideological challenge to the global governance of trade and development. There are examples of challenges in specific areas, notably India in the WTO, which combines support for its own interests with a more universally framed argument about policy space and food security for developing countries. In other instances, however, while the rising powers align with developing countries, their own interests are quite divergent from least developed countries (who have gained little from trade liberalization to date). Generally, rather than any kind of radical support for systemic transformation, the rising powers tend to base their arguments within the established discourse. Thus they support WTO principles of free trade and transparency but criticize the developed world's hypocrisy in this regard. If one could divine a worldview from their statements and policies, it is support for limited global economic governance, which differentiates sharply between developed and developing countries and fosters international (with plenty of trade and FDI to be sure) rather than truly global/transnational capitalism. The motivation for this stance is easily explained in terms of state power rather than any broader vision. In neo-Gramscian terms, the rising powers have accepted the underlying common sense assumptions concerning global capitalism and global development, while querying some of the detail.

Crucial factors in their inability to provide alternative leadership are their own identities and attitudes to global governance. China and India self-identify as developing countries and as such resist offering specific and firm commitments on the global stage; rather they focus on criticizing developed countries for their lack of commitment. This is reinforced by a mistrust of strong interventionist global governance, all of which means that they are ill-equipped to engage in global debates over universal norms or public goods. The development of the BRICS as a grouping signifies an effort to form a bloc within the global system rather than to reshape the global system. Even in the case of the global AfT initiative (which could have been an opportunity for them to take a leadership role and to influence the international aid regime) they have remained on the sidelines. They, correctly, distinguish South-South cooperation from developed world aid commitments but will only make the most minimal commitments themselves. Also, it is striking that in the case of the global Post-2015 agenda they have been relatively quiescent in the ongoing debates. Their significance here stems more from what they represent than the ideas and proposals they generate. While the BRICS focus on intergovernmental processes, the pre-existing global institutions are continuing to generate ideas and proposals, based on essentially Eurocentric (for better or worse) worldviews. The relatively muted role of civil society in China (in particular) weakens its ability to engage in these kinds of global debates. In conclusion, this chapter argues that the rising powers are not presenting a radical challenge to the ideas and institutions predominant in this sphere of global governance. Of course, this comes with the caveat that it is very early to make any kind of definitive judgment on their role and impact in the long term.

Notes

1 Phillip Curtin, *Cross-Cultural Trade in World History* (Cambridge: Cambridge University Press, 1984).
2 Ian Bremner, *Every Nation for Itself: What Happens When No One Leads the World* (New York: Penguin, 2013).
3 Milton Friedman, *Capitalism and Freedom* (Chicago, Ill.: University of Chicago Press, 2002).

4 Adam Harmes, "The Rise of Neoliberal Nationalism," *Review of International Political Economy* 9, no. 1 (2012): 59–86.
5 Jagdish Bhagwati, *In Defence of Globalization* (New York: Oxford University Press, 2004).
6 Rorden Wilkinson, *The WTO, Crisis and the Governance of International Trade* (London: Routledge, 2006), 83–90.
7 Jean-Christophe Ganz, "Transnational Mercantilism and the Emerging Global Trading Order," *Review of International Political Economy* 11, no. 3 (2004): 597–617.
8 Stephen Gill, "Globalization, Market Civilization, and Disciplinary Neoliberalism," *Millennium* 24, no. 3 (1995): 399–412.
9 Robert Cox, "Gramsci, hegemony and international relations: an essay in method," *Millennium* 12, no. 2 (1983): 162–175; Adam Morton, *Unravelling Gramsci: Hegemony and Passive Revolution in the Global Political Economy* (London: Pluto, 2007).
10 Nicholas Wheeler, "Pluralist or Solidarist Conceptions of International Society: Bull and Vincent on Humanitarian Intervention," *Millennium* 21, (December 1992): 463–487.
11 Jeffrey Checkel, "Why Comply? Social Learning and European Identity Change," *International Organization* 55 (2001): 553–88; Martha Finnemore and Kathryn Sikkink, "International Norm Dynamics and Political Change," *International Organization* 52, no. 4 (1998): 887–917.
12 Wilkinson, *The WTO, Crisis and the Governance of International Trade*, 46–75.
13 Kevin Watkins and Penny Fowler, *Rigged Rules and Double Standards: Trade, Globalisation, and the Fight Against Poverty* (Oxford: Oxfam Publishing, 2002).
14 Kevin Gallagher, "Understanding developing country resistance to the Doha Round," *Review of International Political Economy* 15, no. 1 (2008): 62–85.
15 Amrita Narlikar, *International Trade and Developing Countries: Coalitions in the GATT and WTO* (London: Routledge, 2003).
16 Amrita Narlikar and Diana Tussie, "The G20 at the Cancun Ministerial: Developing Countries and their Evolving Coalitions in the WTO," *The World Economy* 27, no. 7 (2004): 947–966.
17 Aaditya Mattoo, Francis Ng and Arvind Subramanian, "The Elephant in the Green Room, China and the Doha Round," Peterson Institute for International Economics, Policy Brief Number PB11, 3 May 2011, 3–4, www.iie.com/publications/pb/pb11-03.pdf.
18 Atul Kaushik, "India's Stand in the Doha Round," Cuts International Briefing Paper 1, 2009, www.cuts-citee.org/pdf/BP09-WTO-01.pdf.
19 Ibid., 3.
20 "The Third Meeting of the BRICS Trade Ministers," Durban, 26 March 2013, www.brics5.co.za/assets/BRICS-Trade-Ministers-Communique-25-March-2013.pdf.
21 Gallagher, "Understanding developing country resistance to the Doha Round"; Robert Wade, "What strategies are available for developing countries today, the World Trade Organization and the shrinking of development space," *Review of International Political Economy* 10, no. 4 (2003): 621–644.

22 Deborah Elms and Patrick Low, eds, *Global Value Chains in a Changing World* (Geneva: WTO/Fung Global Institute/Temasek Foundation, 2013).

23 "BRICS Trade Ministers' Statement on the sidelines of the first G-20 Trade Ministerial Meeting," Mexico, 2012, www.brics5.co.za/about-brics/sectoria l-declaration/trade-ministers-meeting/brics-trade-ministers-statement-puerto-vallarta-mexico-19-april-2012.

24 "Fifth BRICS Summit, eThekwini Declaration," Durban, 27 March 2013, www.brics5.co.za/about-brics/summit-declaration/fifth-summit.

25 "BRICS Ministerial Declarations on the sidelines of the 8th WTO Ministerial Conference," 2011, www.brics5.co.za/about-brics/sectorial-declaration/trade-ministers-meeting/ministerial-declaration.

26 Bidwai Praful, "BRICS: A loosely held group with little sense of purpose," 4 April 2013, www.dnaindia.com/analysis/column-brics-a-loosely-held-grou p-with-little-sense-of-purpose-1818693. See also Matthias Vom Hau, James Scott and David Hulme, "Beyond the BRICs: Alternative Strategies of Influence in the Global Politics of Development," *European Journal of Development Research* 24, no. 2 (2012): 187–204.

27 Laurence Chandy and Kharas H. Homi, "Why Can't We All Just Get Along? The Practical Limits to International Development Cooperation," *Journal of International Development* 23, no. 5 (2011): 739–751; Simon Lightfoot and Kim Soyeun, "Does DAC-ability matter? The emergence of Non-DAC donors," *Journal of International Development* 23, no. 5 (2011): 711–21; Richard Manning, "Will 'Emerging Donors' Change the Face of International Cooperation?" *Development Policy Review* 24, no. 4 (2006): 371–85.

28 Lightfoot and Soyeun, "Does DAC-ability matter," 739–51.

29 Ngaire Woods, "China, Emerging Donors and the Silent Revolution in Development Assistance," *International Affairs* 84, no. 6 (2008): 1–18; Sebastian Paulo and Helmut Reisen, "Eastern Donors and Western Soft Law: Towards a DAC Donor Peer Review of China and India?" *Development Policy Review* 28, no. 5 (2010): 535–552.

30 Woods, "China, Emerging Donors and the Silent Revolution in Development Assistance," 1–18.

31 Christine Hackenesch and Heiner Janus, "Post-2015: How Emerging Economies Shape the Relevance of a New Agenda," German Development Institute/DIE, Briefing Paper 14/2013.

32 "Busan Partnership for Effective Development Cooperation," 2011, www. dev-practitioners.eu/fileadmin/Redaktion/Documents/Post-Busan_03_2012/ Busan_FINAL_EN.pdf.

33 OECD, *Trade-related South-South Cooperation, India* (Paris: OECD, 2012), 12.

34 OECD, *Trade-related South-South Cooperation, China* (Paris: OECD, 2012), 19.

35 "WTO Aid for Trade Taskforce, Recommendations," 27 July 2006, http://a ric.adb.org/aid-for-trade-asia/pdf/WT%20AFT%201.pdf.

36 OECD/WTO, *Aid for Trade at a Glance 2013: Connecting to Value Chains* (Paris: OECD, 2013).

37 WTO, "Fourth Global Review of Aid For Trade 2013 Connecting to Value Chains," Summary Report 93, 8–10 July 2013, www.wto.org/english/tra top_e/devel_e/a4t_e/4th_AFT_Summary_Report_side_events_E_v4.pdf.

38   Ibid., 99.
39   Chinese Government's Official Web Portal, "White Paper on Foreign Aid Activities," 2011, www.gov.cn/english/2011-04/21/content_1849764.htm.
40   OECD/WTO, *Aid for Trade at a Glance 2013: Connecting to Value Chains*, 50.
41   OECD, *Trade-related South South Cooperation, China*, 11.
42   Isobel Coleman, "Ten Questions for the New BRICS Bank," *Foreign Policy* journal website, 2013, www.foreignpolicy.com/articles/2013/04/09/ten_questions_for_the_new_brics_bank.
43   OECD/WTO, *Aid for Trade at a Glance 2013: Connecting to Value Chains*, 50.
44   OECD, *Questionnaire for South-South Cooperation: China* 5, 2009, www.oecd.org/aidfortrade/self-assessments.htm.
45   OECD, *Questionnaire for South-South Cooperation: China*, 5; OECD, *Questionnaire for South-South Cooperation: India*, 2011, www.oecd.org/aidfortrade/self-assessments.htm.
46   United Nations System Task Team, "Realising the Future We Want for All," Report to the Secretary General (New York: UN, 2012).
47   United Nations System Task Team, "A Renewed Global Partnership for Development," (New York: UN, 2013), 5–6.
48   Ibid.
49   Ibid., 13.
50   Ibid.
51   Yingfan Wang, Chinese Diplomat and Member of the Secretary-General's MDG Advocacy Group, Izabella Teixeira, Minister for the Environment of Brazil, Abhijit Banerjee, Professor of Economics (India) and Elvira Nabiullina, Economic Advisor to the Russian President.
52   High Level Panel of Eminent Persons on the Post-2015 Development Agenda, "A New Global Partnership: Eradicate Poverty and Transform Economies through Sustainable Development," May 2013, www.post2015hlp.org/the-report/.
53   Justin Yifu Lin and Yan Wang, "Beyond the Marshall Plan: A Global Structural Transformation Fund," Background research paper submitted to the High Level Panel on the post-2015 Development Agenda, May 2013. www.post2015hlp.org/wp-content/uploads/2013/05/Lin-Wang_Beyond-the-Marshall-Plan-A-Global-Structural-Transformation-Fund.pdf.
54   High Level Panel, "A New Global Partnership."

6 China in East Asia

Confusion on the horizon?

Catherine Jones and Shaun Breslin

- **China and the region**
- **Locating the region**
- **China and Southeast Asia**
- **China and North Korea**
- **China and Northeast Asia**
- **Conclusion**

The academic debate as to whether China has a grand strategy rumbles on.[1] However, despite continuing disagreements and the rise of a new element to this debate concerning China's assertiveness,[2] discussion has begun to coalesce around a few key points: (1) China's approach varies according to both the audience and the speaker;[3] (2) China's normative contribution is an absence of an ideologically derived normative position.[4] Instead, it has some core interests that may guide key decisions;[5] (3) China's foreign policy tends to be incremental, gradual, practical, and responsive.[6]

This debate concerns the region China inhabits as much as—or perhaps even more than—the global context. Predictions about the emergence of a Chinese world order have greater resonance for, and therefore tap into the fears of, China's neighbors more than they do the world at large. As a result, this chapter takes the coalescence that has emerged regarding China as a global player as the basis for discussion of China in the East Asian region. But in doing so it points to the potential problems that are appearing for the continuation of this approach. As we will show, at present China is speaking to a number of different regional audiences without clear coherence between the different messages it is trying to present to each one: in Southeast Asia we see China taking a multilateral turn; in relation to the democratic states in Northeast Asia, bilateral and autonomously confident actions are adopted; whereas in the case of North Korea, there seem to be a number of voices feeding into the situation resulting in contradictory actions and approaches. In consequence, China appears to be reacting to events rather than pursuing a coherent strategy in its regional engagements.

A key thrust in Chinese policy since the mid-1990s has been to present the country as a reconciliatory as well as responsible regional power. This is done through rhetoric (for example, repeatedly assuring others that it will never seek hegemony) and action (for example, by increasingly engaging with regional and global multilateral institutions). But China has been perceived to have adopted an increasingly assertive stance in the region, particularly since the global financial crisis. As a result, the more positive images of China that took a number of years to establish have been rather quickly overturned in some parts of East Asia.

For strategic studies scholars, it is exactly such a mixed presentation of a country and lack of a clear grand strategy—what it stands for, what it wants, and how it plans to get it—that increases the risk of misperception and therefore the danger of conflict.[7] Meanwhile, Constructivist approaches also point to the way in which China is perceived and understood as a great power, and how it is consequently predicted to behave in the future, being more important in generating policy responses from others than actual and existing material changes to China's behavior.[8] Somewhat ironically then, these two groups of scholars—not usually seen to hold the same fears—share concerns about the persistence of China's reactive foreign policy. Adding to this problem is that some actors within the policy arena are increasingly confident in the posture they represent to the outside world, but continue to react to events rather than being seen to have a clear plan that enables a determination of the structure and context of interactions, thus, intensifying the tensions that are present. As a result, rather than gradually responding to international problems with reserve, China has (in response to a number of triggers) jumped to more notable and significant activities.

The bottom line is that China may have changed its foreign policy by adopting a more decisive and active response to the actions of others; but, at the same time there is an altered level of concern from other regional players which is also of significance. In addition, the lack of a clear normative agenda to China's external policymaking, one that might enable other states to predict how they will react in a given situation, could be said to increase concerns and tensions in the region.

In reaching this conclusion, this chapter discusses China in East Asia with reference to three groupings in the region, namely: Northeast Asia, Southeast Asia, and North Korea. North Korea is separated from Northeast Asia as it presents distinctive and divergent problems and in many ways does not fit with China's diplomacy towards South Korea and Japan on other issues. In each section we discuss the different actors and approaches that are apparent in China's regional engagements in order to present an overall view of the highly charged confusion that pervades these issues. What we find is the absence of a clear image of China in the regional order as well as a lack of coherence in China's approaches to sub-regional groupings.

China and the region

As noted above, there is a substantial body of literature on China's approach to international order. Within this literature, a point of broad agreement is that China has a non-normative approach. By this we mean that there has been a clear state-led effort to present an idea of China as being different from other great powers (past and present). These other powers have attempted to impose their own ideational and organization preferences on weaker states and to establish a global order that builds in power asymmetries and biases in their favor. As a global power, China will not only refrain from doing the same, but also attempt to work on behalf of other developing and rising powers to democratize the global order and undermine the power of the West. The official promotion of this supposedly anti-normative global agenda thus becomes, in a strange way, a normative agenda in its own right.

In assessing the literature on China's regional role and strategy, we can identify an evolving narrative that suggests a three stage process: China's approach has moved from being skeptical and conservative in its relations with the region,[9] towards active engagement in the regional multilateral forums,[10] and on to the current lack of consistency that seems to lead to a perception (at least) that China is becoming more assertive.[11] Although this narrative is presented here as a linear evolution of China's regional engagement, we argue that these three different approaches actually operate simultaneously over time, and across different actors and different situations. Rather, than seeking simplicity and discrete historical epochs, it is the contradictions and complexities that need to be highlighted in order to provide a useful analysis for understanding China's regional engagements.

If the two enduring elements of these discussions are put side by side—China's non-normative approach and the perception of a more assertive regional stance—then it is possible to tentatively suggest that China has remained responsive to regional challenges and situations but has—in the public arena—become less guarded and more active in responding to them. Yet, these active responses still lack an internal coherence, and there is a question over whether China, or actors within China's foreign policy machinery, are creating this more active perception; or whether, because China is globally more visible, any response is likely to be perceived and portrayed as being more assertive. Is it China that has changed or is China being placed under closer scrutiny by observers with preconceived and fixed ideas about how China will behave as a great power?

The perceived danger then arises because misjudgments, misperceptions, and miscalculations are more likely. Put another way, the construction of the other may be as likely to be a misconstruction. As responses become more active and decisive there is less room for traditional face-saving activities to take place, but there is also an absence of clear logic and an ability to predict what those responses will be. Even across core interests there are inconsistencies in actions because of the range of actors involved. It is important to remember that core interests do not prescribe the actions that are necessary in order to protect these interests but rather indicate the final extent that China is willing to reach in their protection.

Locating the region

Identifying the region that China is either a part of or engaging with (or both), is not a simple task. When it comes to Southeast Asia, its membership of ASEAN provides a clear starting point—although even here there is the question of which states dominate the organization and whose interests matter most.[12] Not least as a response to the growing influence of China in this region, and potentially on an ASEAN plus three understanding of its horizons, Japanese elites have favored a broader conception of the region that includes the Australasian states and India to provide a counterweight to China. This understanding was most clearly manifest in the original proposals for an East Asia Summit, before the inclusion of Russia and the United States in 2011 expanded its membership and diluted its ability to evolve into a coherent and effective institution of regional governance. A similar preference for an understanding of the region defined in terms of the Indo-Pacific has also gained salience in Australia. This not only places Australia firmly as part of the region rather than as an outsider, but also gives Australia a privileged position as the gateway to the region for other Western powers (most notably the United States). An even broader concept of the region is found in the notion of the Asia Pacific, which, in the form of APEC, has not only established a key role for the United States, but also for the promotion of (Western) neoliberal forms of economic governance.[13]

The result has been a "noodle bowl"[14] of regional institutions with different memberships and competencies often predicated on different understandings of what the region is, could be or should be, which in turn is usually predicated on how different state elites perceive the best way of securing their own interests (and blocking those of others). This is before we bring in the importance of bilateral relations, which still remain the most significant loci of activity when it comes to competing territorial claims and questions of sovereignty in particular.[15]

China and Southeast Asia

China's relations with Southeast Asian states (specifically the ASEAN states of Indonesia, Laos, Cambodia, Malaysia, Thailand, Myanmar, Philippines, Vietnam, Singapore, and Brunei) have evolved over the past two decades. In this evolution and extension, contradictions and tensions in understanding China's foreign policies have increased, adding to the complexity of comprehending China's approach to the region. Broadly speaking, China's regional engagements straddle two approaches: multilateral and bilateral.

Since the early 1990s, as China's presence in Southeast Asia steadily increased,[16] China has normalized relations with each of the states in the region (the last being Vietnam in 1991), developed economic relations (the height of which was the creation of a China–ASEAN Free trade area), and become increasingly involved in multilateral forums.[17] This has been described by some authors as China taking a "multilateral turn"[18] in order to reassure the region that it will not seek regional hegemony. It is also seen as a reflection in China that its own economic fortunes have become inextricably intertwined with those of its neighbors—an issue that became abundantly clear during the Asian financial crisis of 1997, resulting in a renewed focus in China on the importance of assuring its own economic security through greater regional cooperation.

In this approach, and deviating from major expectations for rising or great powers and regional engagement,[19] a key characteristic of China's engagement has been the extent to which it has done so with ASEAN states on their terms. To date China has become enmeshed in a number of ASEAN-centered forums including ASEAN plus three (ASEAN plus China, Japan, and South Korea), the ASEAN Regional Forum, and the ASEAN–China Free Trade Agreement. These forums are noteworthy as it is argued that they have "ASEAN in the driving seat."[20] Even when proposals and suggestions emanate from China, these proposals do not get off the ground without significant ASEAN support. In the past this has resulted in China having to make concessions to ensure that its proposals are accepted.

In moving to look at the range of China's foreign policy actors involved in ASEAN relations, these extend far beyond the Foreign Ministry to include the Ministries of Commerce and Finance, Transport, Science and Technology and the Leadership.[21] In addition to focusing on the diplomatic side and the power relations between states, it is important to recognize that commercial interests and actors are important. These business actors have been both a positive and negative force in the creation of a free trade area. For example, in the discussions surrounding the implementation of the China–ASEAN free trade agreement (CAFTA or ACFTA), ASEAN states were concerned their markets would be swamped by Chinese goods and companies. As a result, the Chinese government had to play an instrumental role in reassuring states.[22]

Considering that ASEAN is a collection of weakly coordinated small and medium powers, it is perhaps surprising that China is willing to continue to develop its engagement with this organization. It is even more surprising that China has chosen to make so many concessions to ASEAN. But, this approach may be more easily understood by considering the other that Chinese action is identified against. The alternative is the United States hub and spokes approach of the Cold War and the subsequent United States inspired APEC. The United States is also the major proponent of the Trans-Pacific Partnership (TPP), which, if successful, would divide the region and send a crack through the framework of ASEAN. Thus, China's engagement in the region offers an opportunity not only to be seen as distinct and different from the United States, but also for China to be seen to be operating on a more level playing field with smaller powers (thus suggesting that it will not dominate the region).

In contrast to this multilateral compliant image of China in Southeast Asia there is another very different narrative that focuses on China's bilateralism in maritime disputes. Commentators on these disputes argue that their ongoing nature demonstrates that China is not fully embedded in these regional institutions, and therefore indicates the limits to which China's rise can be mitigated through regional arrangements.[23] In dealing with these disputes China has been seen to prefer bilateral engagement over multilateral institutions (either global or regional).

In the South China Sea there are overlapping claims from China, Vietnam, the Philippines, Brunei, Malaysia, and Indonesia, to a number of islands and corresponding surrounding areas and resources. These disputed territories have led to a number of tense and volatile situations between the claimants. In the past decade there have been disputes over the Scarborough Shoal, the Spratly Islands, and the Paracel Islands. In seeking to resolve these disputes, it is noted by some commentators, that ASEAN has not played a significant role;[24] however, there is an argument to be made that as these disputes do not involve all ASEAN states, it is not the most relevant body to deal with these disputes. So rather than using the ASEAN forums, the Philippines has sought resolution through the UN Convention on the Law of the Sea II.[25] In stark contrast to China's "multilateral turn" outlined above, China has not acknowledged the authority of this approach and instead has consistently sought to deal with each of the claimants bilaterally. To add to this confusion, China is a signatory to the Code of Conduct of the parties which was an ASEAN document and is so far the only multilateral agreement that China has endorsed on this issue.[26] So, in these disputes we see three images: China preferring bilateralism; China signing an unenforceable regional multilateral code; and China disputing the authority of broader international forums for dispute resolution.

In these bilateral relations, it is evident that the main players within China influencing their position in each case are different. In bilateral issues that concern sovereignty and territory, especially where the security of the state is concerned, the politburo and military are both key actors. Whereas, in the multilateral forums in the region a wider collection of actors are present, including the Ministry of Commerce and State Owned Enterprises. In consequence, as noted increasingly in works on Chinese foreign policy, the approaches and aims of China's actions in its engagement in this region are not necessarily consistent or coherent across different issues, contexts, or between different actors.

China and North Korea

On the surface the relationship and exchanges between China and the Democratic People's Republic of Korea (DPRK) are simple and obvious. This relationship is commonly presented as these two states being "as close as lips and teeth" and enduring because it has been a "militant friendship sealed in blood."[27] Yet, in one flippant but indicative commentary in China, North Korea was stated as being "a hundred times more of a headache than the Diaoyu/Senkaku islands."[28] Indeed after the testing of nuclear materials in 2006, China was vehement in its condemnation of North Korea's actions. Moreover in subsequent tests of missiles and nuclear materials China has vocally condemned the DPRK in statements by the Foreign Ministry[29] and in the UNSC.[30] In consequence, in this relationship we have (at least) two conflicting images which make understanding or predicting China's overall approach problematic.

These apparent contradictions, however, begin to make sense by adopting a more fine grained analysis of this relationship. This section demonstrates that it is possible to discern and then disaggregate a number of different actors and issues in which China and North Korea engage with each other, and in each of these interactions both the audience and the actors are different. This approach then contributes to comprehending the complexity of the engagements that are present in this relationship.

The most common and striking images of North Korea, and public assumptions of the relationship with China, erupt at times of nuclear or missile tests that have prompted UN Security Council actions. The first of these was in 2006 which resulted in the imposition of sanctions in resolution 1718.[31] Subsequently these sanctions have been extended in further UNSC resolutions.[32] In an attempt to make these sanctions more effective, in 2009 a Panel of Experts was instituted to investigate and report to the Sanctions Committee. China has voted in favor of all of these resolutions and has a member on the Panel of Experts. Ostensibly, on the global stage—where China is increasingly challenged to act as a responsible power—this suggests that China's relationship with DPRK is shifting and it is becoming increasingly critical and concerned with its weapons developments. In this interaction, the statements of criticism come from the Foreign Ministry or from the representative on the Security Council.

In looking in more detail at the enforcement of sanctions against North Korea, the image of China becomes increasingly distorted and confused. For example, in implementation of these resolutions, China made it evident that it does not support the "practice of inspecting cargo to and from the DPRK."[33] Furthermore, in the Panel of Experts reports of 2012 and 2013 there are incidents noted that highlight the semi-permeable nature of flows of goods between these countries. In their investigations, the Panel found that China (including Taiwan and Hong Kong) is the most frequently used final port of call for goods heading to the DPRK, including goods that seem to contravene the sanctions.[34]

At the very least this brings into question either the determination or ability (or both) of China to fully implement these resolutions and stop the shipment of prohibited goods (or goods that could violate the spirit of resolutions). But on this stage, and at this moment in the story, the implementation activities of China are viewed by a narrow audience. Although the Panel of Experts reports are openly accessible, they are not generally picked up for casual reading by a wide general audience. As Committee meetings are generally closed, and the Panel members are not free to discuss their activities, any activities by individual members within these forums that either promote or stymie the effectiveness of these sanctions are difficult to pin-point, thus outcome documents and reports assume great importance, but must be used with some care. In these documents there are a number of detailed incidents where seemingly sanctioned goods have been able to enter North Korea, although these reports also painstakingly suggest that for the most part it is the spirit rather than the letter of the sanctions that may actually have been violated.[35] An interesting aside to this narrative can be found in the briefings of the Chair of the Committee to the Security Council. Here, it is noted that China is "continuing to advocate for a cautious approach, seemingly arguing that any further Council or Committee action would only increase tensions and lead to an escalation of the situation [of a potential fourth nuclear test]."[36] Later in this document, China is noted for using bilateral meetings to try and prevent a fourth nuclear test and that any form of UN action may undermine this approach.

In summary, with regards to sanctions against North Korea there are a number of different actors and audiences that are important in the presentation of China's position. As a result, the degree to which China supports the regime in Pyongyang or the sanctions regime becomes very confusing. On the one hand, in public forums like the Security Council or after nuclear or missile tests when the world is watching China's actions, China has clearly made statements that condemn Pyongyang. Yet, behind the scenes in the Committee or the Panel concerned with the implementation of sanctions against the regime in Pyongyang, China's crucial role in implementation remains obscured; although there are suggestions in the documents that China has not fully implemented these sanctions to ensure a halt to North Korea's nuclear ambitions. Thus, we can see at least two images of China here, represented by two different groupings within China's foreign policy apparatus. On the one hand, we see public displays of China acting as a responsible power according to the West's definition. On the other hand, we also see some evidence to suggest that this responsible activity is not fully followed through in private arenas.

One final place of interaction that should be acknowledged in the discussions between China and the DPRK is in the borderlands and final ports of call;[37] that is the places of implementation. As briefly indicated above, these play an important role in the implementation of sanctions, but the reality that actors in these places have their own interests and procedures is almost always overlooked. An excellent study on China–DPRK border relations from SAIS highlights the different level of importance that cross-border trade has for the Chinese province compared with the rest of China and the heightened concerns of their province concerning any potential collapse of the DPRK.[38] Their research and analysis indicates that although North Korean trade is of negligible importance to China's national economy, it is of significance to the provincial economy.[39] As a result of this trade dynamic, Freeman and Thompson argue that "in many sectors, 'China' means firms from Jilin."[40] In addition, these border areas are more vulnerable to flows of refugees from DPRK and as a result the government in the province has greater need to maintain the border. In consequence, the return of defectors back to the DPRK despite humanitarian concerns is of great importance to the provinces in China that they enter or traverse, notwithstanding the implications this may have for the image of Beijing as a responsible power.[41] At the same time there is the potential to see disharmony between activities in the public and private arenas. We also see an image of China as being fragmented and potentially unable to fully enforce these sanctions; either because of a lack of control of individual companies, or the importance of the Chinese provincial government.

Adding to these contradictory images of China's DPRK relations is the regional picture incorporating a multilateral dimension in the form of the 6-Party Talks (6PT). In this situation China is credited with hosting and brokering the talks and, after the failure of the last set of talks, with trying to bring North Korea back to the table. Furthermore, China has affirmed (in different forums and via different actors) the importance and appropriateness of the 6PT as the means to achieve a peaceful resolution to the North Korean issue.[42]

This last image of China suggests one thing about China's approach to North Korea: that its short-term goal is the resumption of the 6PT. But, as noted above, this objective doesn't prescribe or proscribe the types of international behavior or statements that are appropriate to achieve this possible objective. Nor does it specify the long-term goal: what outcomes are sought from the 6PT?

In relation to North Korea then, there are a number of different voices that contribute to how China deals with its neighbor, as well as incongruities between actions that are in the public domain and those that remain private. As a consequence of these differences there are also a number of questions that need to be raised concerning China's interests regarding North Korea and whether these interests can be considered to be consistent across the range of actors involved. For example, the interests of the provincial government on the border and the central government in the short term, particularly regarding commercial considerations, appear to diverge. Whether this divergence is likely to remain in the long term may depend not only on the commercial interests at play, but also the security considerations regarding refugees.

China and Northeast Asia

In 2013 and 2014 security relations between China and Japan hit the headlines with China's declaration of an Air Defense Identification Zone (ADIZ) over a significant section of the East China Sea.[43] The Chinese initiative, and Japan's defiant response to it, resulted in tensions between the two countries reaching their lowest point for many decades. Much less noticed (outside the region at least) Japan–South Korea relations have also been seriously tested. For a year the elected leaders of South Korea and Japan did not meet bilaterally, and it took the intervention of the United States to try to force better relations between these two states. At the crux of these disputes are a number of islands in the East China Sea. Although, these islands historically have fallen within the territories of each of the claimant states, because of the vagaries of international agreements (in particular the 1951 San Francisco Treaty to which the People's Republic of China was not a signatory)[44] and the manner of international engagements since the end of the Second World War, disputes surrounding the current ownership of these islands are assuming increasing significance.

In this context, it is rather prosaic to suggest that China, Japan, and South Korea have complicated relations. The more interesting point in this medley of hostilities is that the security concerns of these relations relate back to different views of history and also conflicting interpretations of international agreements. More significantly, in these competing narratives it is not China that is the perceived sole provocateur, but (at least by South Korea) concern is also expressed regarding Japan. In particular, there are a number of press releases by the South Korean Ministry of Foreign Affairs (MOFA) that express concerns over Japan's stance towards the Dokdo/Takashima islands as well as visits to the Yasukuni Shrine by members of the Japanese government.[45] Moreover, comments by each country's political elite have served to highlight the increasing tensions between these states. The most notable of these comments was made by Prime Minister Abe to a group of journalists on the side of the Davos World Economic forum in January 2014, who reportedly compared China and Japan with Britain and Germany prior to the First World War. However, the translation of these remarks is disputed by the Japanese ministry of Foreign Affairs (MOFA).[46] In addition to these elite level statements, there have also been comments made in defense papers and by the foreign ministries. One such example is the 2013 Japanese Defense White Paper, which made an explicit claim that territories disputed between Japan and South Korea are an "inherent part of Japanese territory."[47]

Furthermore, adding to these public formal exchanges there have been public information flows from the foreign ministries that present each claimant's case for authority and sovereignty over these islands.[48] There have also been actions in the East China Sea, including the buying of islands by Japan and the extended use of the People's Liberation Army Navy in patrolling the area. All of these tension points are accompanied by contradictory rumors as to which side acted aggressively and which in a more reconciliatory manner.

In addition to these high-level territorial disputes, there have also been legal challenges. China has authorized the legal pursuit of damages for Chinese sent to work in Japan during the Second World War against Japanese companies.[49] Moreover, at the individual level, at points of intense disagreement Japanese companies have been boycotted or vandalized. All of these images of China, Japan, and (to a lesser extent) South Korea's engagements with each other suggest increasingly confident, even aggressive exchanges that seem to permeate through many speakers in each of the states concerned.

In contrast to this bleak security picture in Northeast Asia, economic relations between these states are very dynamic. Trade between China and Japan has increased steadily in the past two decades. At the time of writing, China was Japan's largest trading partner.[50] This picture posits a number of questions regarding the importance of economic ties and whether they can mitigate security concerns. According to some leading scholars and commentators, the economic risks are too great to allow hostilities to seriously impact on trade. As a result, economics should act as a glass ceiling to increasing hostilities.[51] In looking in more detail at this argument it becomes increasingly compelling.

Nonetheless, it is not just the material security concerns that need to be mitigated but also the contingent identity issues that are at stake. Japan, China, and South Korea all have political leaderships that are concerned with reputation and national identity.[52] For each of the states involved, domestic legitimacy and national identity are increasingly based on sovereignty and territorial claims as well as economic success.

Conclusion

This chapter set out with a very modest goal: to establish the complexity of relations between China and East Asia. In doing so it has asserted that debates over whether China has a grand strategy, in East Asia or elsewhere, neutralize and hide this complexity in ways that obscure the most interesting questions about how China engages with its neighbors. The argument does not suggest that China is unique in displaying this level of international intricacy and contradiction. After all, most states around the world arguably act inconsistently according to perceived changes in their interest or domestic politics. Nonetheless, this is compounded in China's case by its non-normative approach to foreign policy engagements. As has been demonstrated across these three groups of relations, China presents different faces to different audiences. The potentially troubling element here is in the increasingly rapid response to new situations, which contributes to the construction of these events as demonstrative of China's increasing assertiveness. In some situations, for example in South East Asia, this undermines over a decade of commitment to multilateralism and responsibility.

Yet it is perhaps worth pondering whether a lack of a normative agenda, or a clear grand strategy, actually reduces the risk of hostilities rather than promoting them. Moving away from any theoretical prediction of the risks of misperception, there is the natural logic that if you have a strategy and normative agenda you actually have a plan that you may seek to fulfill. This brings with it the danger that, knowing your plan, other powers may pursue counter-measures—leading to conflict.

In returning to the three elements of discussions on Chinese foreign policy set out in this chapter, the region offers a petri-dish to explore how these elements may evolve. The non-normative approach of China contributes to a lack of trust between China and its neighbors. More significantly the expression of China's core interests, its red lines on which it will not compromise, focuses attention on areas of East Asia, but does not offer clarity as to the actions that China will see as a threat to these interests, nor does it set out the responses that China will adopt. Emphasizing the importance of these interests, which include Taiwan and various disputed territories, coupled with an incremental approach to responding to foreign policy issues, creates an increasing impression of uncertainty. Finally, although it is readily acknowledged that China utilizes different domestic actors in different settings to speak to different audiences, it has been less readily noted that in some instances these actors may also have different (if not divergent) interests.

The problems created by these multilayered, multifaceted, and multifunctional engagements in East Asia suggest—or even demand—the development of a less bifurcated discussion of individual events. There is a need to pause and consider a greater context as well as ponder the diversity of actors and forms of governance in operation. Doing so may shed more light on current situations than a focus on immediate responses or reactions which might tend to obscure the bigger picture.

Notes

1　Shaun Breslin, "China and the Global Order: Signaling Threat or Friendship?" *International Affairs* 89, no. 3 (2013): 615–634; Jisi Wang, "China's Search for a Grand Strategy," *Foreign Affairs* 90, no. 2 (2011): 68–79; Feng Zhang, "Rethinking China's Grand Strategy: Beijing's Evolving National Interests and Strategic Ideas in the Reform Era," *International Politics* 49 (2012): 318–45.

2　Thomas J. Christensen, "The Advantages of an Assertive China: Responding to Beijing's Abrasive Diplomacy," *Foreign Affairs* 90, no. 2 (2011): 54–67; Kai He and Huiyan Feng, "Debating China's Assertiveness: Taking China's Power and Interests seriously," *International Politics* 49, (2012): 633–644; Andrew Scobell and Scott W. Harold, "An 'Assertive' China? Insights from Interviews," *Asian Security* 9, no. 2 (2013): 111–131.

3　For an outline of China's foreign policy actors see: Linda Jakobson and Dean Knox, *New foreign policy actors in China*, SIPRI Policy Paper, no. 26 (Stockholm, 2010). For discussions of China's foreign policy see: Thomas J. Christensen, "More actors, Less Coordination? New Challenges for the Leaders of a Rising China," in *China's Foreign Policy: Who makes it, and how is it made?* Gilbert Rozman, ed. (New York: Palgrave Macmillan, 2013); Alastair Iain Johnston, "Chapter 3: International Structures and Chinese Foreign Policy," in *China and the World: Chinese Foreign Policy Faces the New Millennium*, Samuel S. Kim, ed. (Boulder, Colo.: Westview Press, 1998); Michael D. Swaine, "Chinese Leadership and Elite Responses to the U.S. Pacific Pivot," *China Leadership Monitor* 38.

4　One key feature of these discussions centers on whether China has what Andrew Hurrell has described as a "project and purpose" for global order, Andrew Hurrell, "Hegemony, Liberalism and Global Order: What Space for Would-Be Great Powers?" *International Affairs* 82 no. 1 (2006): 2. See also Gregory Chin and Ramesh Thakur, "Will China Change the Rules of Global Order," *The Washington Quarterly* 33, no. 4 (October 2010): 119–138; Barry Buzan "The Inaugural Kenneth N. Waltz Annual Lecture A World Order Without Superpowers: Decentred Globalism," *International Relations* 25, no. 3 (2011): 1–12.

5　This phrase was first seen to be used in a statement by Dai Bingguo on 28 July 2009. The statement and a translation are available in "Dai Bingguo:

The Core Interests of the People's Republic of China," *China Digital Times*, http://chinadigitaltimes.net/2009/08/dai-bingguo-%E6%88%B4%E7%A7%8 9%E5%9B%BD-the-core-interests-of-the-prc/. See also Michael D. Swaine, "China's assertive behaviour Part One: On 'Core Interests,'" http://carne gieendowment.org/files/Swaine_CLM_34_1114101.pdf.

6 Ivan Campbell, Thomas Wheeler, Larry Attree, Dell Marie Butler, and Bernardo Mariani, *China and Conflict-affected States: Between Principle and Pragmatism*(London: Saferworld, 2012).

7 Colin S. Gray, *Another Bloody Century* (London: Weidenfeld and Nicolson, 2005), 168–211. In addition, Aaron Friedberg argues that scholars asserting that China's elites are becoming socialized to global norms (and are therefore becoming more predictable), are "self-congratulatory" even going on to suggest they may be "self-delusional", Aaron Friedberg, *A Contest for Supremacy: China, America, and the Struggle for Mastery in Asia* (New York: W.W. Norton and Company, 2011). Underpinning these predictions are problems of misperception that are perceived to be a significant cause of conflict/competition. See, Jack Levy, "Misperception and the Causes of War: Theoretical Linkages and Analytical Problems," *World Politics* 36, no. 1 (1983): 76–99.

8 Alistair Iain Johnston, *Social States: China in International Institutions, 1980–2000* (Princeton, N.J.: Princeton University Press, 2007).

9 According to Ian Storey, in 1967, 10 days after the Bangkok declaration that created ASEAN, China spelled out its "disdain for the new organization," Ian Storey, *Southeast Asia and the Rise of China* (London: Routledge, 2011), 26; Shaun Breslin, "Understanding China's Regional Rise: Interpretations, Identities and Implications," *International Affairs* 85, no. 4 (2009): 817–835; Lai Foon Wong, "China-ASEAN and Japan-ASEAN Relations during the Post-Cold War Era," *Chinese Journal of International Politics* 1 (2007): 373–404.

10 Alice Ba, "China and ASEAN: Renavigating relations for a 21st Century Asia," *Asian Survey* 43, no. 4 (2003): 349–647; Breslin, "Understanding China's Regional Rise"; Wong, "China-ASEAN and Japan-ASEAN"; Ian Storey, *Southeast Asia and the Rise of China*; Guogang Wu and Helen Lansdowne, *China turns to Multilateralism: Foreign Policy and Regional Security* (London, Routledge: 2008).

11 Incidents including disputes over the Scarborough Shoal, Paracel, and Spratly Islands have encouraged some regional states to seek greater engagement with the United States—for example, Vietnam's joint military exercises with the US in the South China Sea.

12 See Ralf Emmers, "Indonesia's Role in ASEAN: A case of incomplete and sectorial leadership," *The Pacific Review* 27, no. 4 (2014): 543–562.

13 For a more detailed discussion see: Il Hyun Cho and Seo-Hyun Park, "Domestic legitimacy politics and varieties of regionalism in East Asia," *Review of International Studies* 40, no. 3 (2014): 583–606.

14 This phrase is commonly used in reference to Asia's institutions; see Seng Tan "Introduction," in *Do Institutions Matter? Regional Institutions and Regionalism in East Asia*, See Seng Tan, ed. (Singapore: RSIS, 2008), 2.

15 Jim Thomas, Zack Cooper and Iskander Rehman, *Gateway to the Indo-Pacific: Australian Defense Strategy and the Future of the Australia-US*

Alliance (Washington, DC: Centre for Strategic and Budgetary Assessments, 2013).

16   According to Lai Foon Wong, China-ASEAN leadership exchanges have more than doubled in the years 1990–2005, Wong, "China-ASEAN and Japan-ASEAN," 378.

17   China was the first outside power to sign the Treaty of Amity and Cooperation in 1991; it became a consultative partner in the same year and finally a full dialogue partner in 1996. In 1997 the first China-ASEAN summit was held.

18   Wu and Lansdowne, *China turns to Multilateralism*.

19   Andrew Hurrell, "One World? Many Worlds? The Place of Regions in the Study of International Society," *International Affairs* 83, no. 1 (2007): 103.

20   The extent and nature to which ASEAN does control the region remains disputed. See Lee Jones, "Still in the driver's seat, but for how long? ASEAN's capacity for leadership in East-Asian International Relations," *Journal of Current Southeast Asian Affairs* 29, no. 3 (2010): 95–113.

21   Wong, "China-ASEAN and Japan-ASEAN," 379. Since this publication this web of connections has increased.

22   Such as, the staggered entry of ASEAN members and the start of the "Early Harvest Programme" see Raul L. Cordenillo, "The Economic Benefits to ASEAN of the ASEAN-China Free Trade Area (ACFTA)," Studies Unit Bureau for Economic Integration ASEAN Secretariat, 18 January 2005, www.asean.org/news/item/the-economic-benefits-to-asean-of-the-asean-china-free-trade-area-acfta-1-by-raul-l-cordenillo-2.

23   Some commentators have suggested that ASEAN embraced China in regional frameworks, see Alice Ba, "China and ASEAN: Renavigating relations for a 21st Century Asia," *Asian Survey* 43, no. 4 (2003): 622–647. Others have remained skeptical of the role ASEAN can play in mitigating the dangers of China's rise, see Hugh White, "ASEAN won't help US manage China," CogitASIA, 3 August 2012, http://cogitasia.com/asean-wont-help-us-to-manage-china/.

24   In the 2012 East Asia Summit the problem of the South China Sea dispute was raised at the regional security forum and was widely cited as being the reason for an absence of joint statement after the meeting. Since then it has been difficult to hold an ASEAN meeting that concerns the dispute and also produce a statement from the forum.

25   Christopher Ward, "South China Sea on the Rocks: Philippines arbitration request," East Asia Forum, 21 April 2014, www.eastasiaforum.org/2014/04/21/south-china-sea-on-the-rocks-the-philippines-arbitration-request/.

26   ASEAN, *Declaration on the Code of Conduct in the South China Sea*, signed 4 November 2002, www.asean.org/asean/external-relations/china/item/declaration-on-the-conduct-of-parties-in-the-south-china-sea.

27   These phrases are commonly used in discussions of China and North Korea see: Chen Ping, "China's (North) Korea Policy: Misperception and Reality (an independent Chinese perspective on Sino-Korean Relations)," in *China's Foreign Policy: Who Makes it, and how is it made?* Gilbert Rozman ed. (New York: Palgrave Macmillan, 2012), 252–274, 256; Carla Freeman and Drew Thompson, *China on the Edge: China's Border Provinces and Chinese Security Policy* (Baltimore, Md.: The Centre for the National Interest and John Hopkins SAIS, 2011).

28 "So, speaking for China, the North Korean problem is a headache a hundred times greater than the Diaoyu Islands dispute," "因此⊠对于中国来说⊠朝核威胁其实是比钓鱼岛争端头疼百倍," "Yinci, duiyu zohongguo lai shou, chaohe weixie qishi shi bi diaoyudao touteng bai bei" from Sanjun, "朝鲜核试验后⊠中国一个集团军调往鸭绿江." 19 February 2013, www.sanjun.com/zhongguo/20130219/3547.html.

29 FMPRC Statement 9 October 2006; also "China resolutely opposes DPRK nuclear test," *Xinhua*, 9 October 2006, http://news.xinhuanet.com/english/2006-10/09/content_5180203.htm.

30 Security Council verbatim record S.PV5551, October 2006.

31 Security Council resolution 1718, 14 October 2006.

32 Security Council resolution 1874, 12 June 2009; Security Council resolution 2087, 22 January 2013; Security Council resolution 2094, 7 March 2013.

33 *UN Yearbook 2006*, Chapter 4, 446; Security Council verbatim report, S/PV.5551, October 2006, 4.

34 The most notable of these incidents was the movement of missiles at a Birthday parade in Pyongyang where the lumber transporter used to transport missiles was found to have come from China, see Security Council report by the Panel of Experts, S/2012/422, 14 June 2012, 19; Security Council report by the Panel of Experts S/2013/337, 26.

35 See Panel Reports: Security Council report by the Panel of Experts, S/2012/422, 14 June 2012; Security Council report by the Panel of Experts S/2013/337.

36 "Briefing by the Chair of the 1718 DPRK Sanctions Committee," *What's in Blue: Insights on the work of the UN Security Council*, 19 May 2014, www.whatsinblue.org/2014/05/briefing-by-the-chair-of-the-1718-dprk-sanctions-committee.php.

37 According to the 2010 Panel of Experts report, China accounted for the highest number of exports to North Korea and this has steadily increased from 2000 to 2009, Security Council report by the Panel of Experts, S/2010/571, 5 November 2010, 19.

38 Freeman and Thompson, *China on the Edge*.

39 Freeman and Thompson, *China on the Edge*, 40.

40 Freeman and Thompson, *China on the Edge*, 39.

41 China has been criticized for returning North Korean defectors, which it considers to be "illegal border crossers", see "China Arrests North Korean Refugees: Reports," *Radio Free Asia*, 18 November 2013, www.rfa.org/english/news/korea/arrest-11182013171205.html.

42 MOFA, "Wang Yi: China always upholds impartial and objective position on Korean Peninsula Issue," 26 May 2014, www.fmprc.gov.cn/mfa_eng/zxxx_662805/t1160324.shtml; Security Council verbatim meeting, S/PV.6141, 12 June 2009.

43 Ministry of National Defense People's Republic of China, "Announcement of the Aircraft Identification Rules for the East China Sea Air Defense Identification Zone of the P.R.C.," 23 November 2013, http://eng.mod.gov.cn/Press/2013-11/23/content_4476143.htm.

44 According to the 1951 San Francisco Treaty Chapter II, articles 2 and 3, Japan was obligated to return and renounce the rights to a series of territories; however, the agreement is unclear about precisely which islands must be renounced. Whereas some islands are specifically identified such as Dagelet and Taiwan (Formosa), other territories and rights refer back to

older treaties (notably the Boxer protocol of 7 September 1901) Chapter IV article 10, resulting in a lack of clarity over ownership of sectors now disputed in the East China Sea. See Treaty No. 1832 "Treaty of Peace with Japan (with two declarations), signed in San Francisco 8 September 1951," *UN Treaty Series*, https://treaties.un.org/doc/Publication/.../volume-136-I-1 832-English.pdf; for commentaries on these disputes see Seokwoo Lee, "The 1951 San Francisco Peace Treaty with Japan and the Territorial disputes in East Asia," *Pacific Rim Law and Policy Journal* 11, no. 1 (2002): 63–146; Seokwoo Lee and Jon M. Van Dyke, "The 1951 San Francisco Peace Treaty and its relevance to the Sovereignty over Dokdo," *Chinese Journal of International Law* 9, no. 4 (2010): 741–762.

45 South Korean MOFA, "MOFA Spokesperson's Commentary on the Japanese Prime Minister's Offering to the Yasukuni Shrine," 21 April 2014; South Korea MOFA, "MOFA Spokesperson's Commentary on Japan's Provocation over Dokdo through a Tokyo Rally," 5 June 2014, press release 476, www.mofa.go.kr/ENG/press/pressreleases/index.jsp?menu=m_10_20.

46 Robert Peston, "Davos: What Abe Said," *BBC News*, 22 January 2014, www.bbc.co.uk/news/business-25847276. See also Asahi Shimbun, "Analysis: Fallout Lingering from Abe's World War I reference" *Asahi Shimbun*, published 25 January 2014, http://ajw.asahi.com/article/behind_news/politics/AJ201401250056.

47 Japanese Ministry of Defense, "Defense of Japan 2013," http://www.mod.go.jp/e/publ/w_paper/2013.html; South Korean MOFA, "MOFA Spokesperson's Commentary on the Japanese Prime Minister's Offering to the Yasukuni Shrine," 21 April 2014, press release number 4890, www.mofa.go.kr/ENG/press/pressreleases/index.jsp?menu=m_10_20; South Korea MOFA, "Foreign Ministry Spokesperson's Statement on Defense of Japan 2013 (Annual White Paper)," 9 July 2013, press release number 4399, www.mofa.go.kr/ENG/press/pressreleases/index.jsp?menu=m_10_20.

48 See MOFA Channel (youtube), "Senkaku Islands seeking maritime peace based on the rule of law not force or coercion," www.youtube.com/watch?v=aC9gyVeCAp0;CCTV, "Diaoyu Islands: China's Inherent territory," http://english.cntv.cn/special/diaoyuchina/homepage/index.shtml.

49 In 2014 Chinese courts allowed a petition that enabled Chinese victims of forced labor during the Second World War to sue the two Japanese companies involved (now owned by Nippon and Mitsubishi).

50 WTO country profile, March 2014, http://stat.wto.org/CountryProfile/WSDBCountryPFView.aspx?Language=E&Country=CN%2cJP.

51 Amy King, "Japan and China: warm trade ties temper political tensions," *East Asia Forum*, October 2012, www.eastasiaforum.org/2012/10/22/japan-and-china-warm-trade-ties-temper-political-tensions/.

52 Il Hyun Cho and Seo-Hyun Park, "Domestic legitimacy politics and varieties of regionalism in East Asia," *Review of International Studies* 40, no. 3 (2014): 583–606.

7 Rising powers and regional organization in the Middle East

Louise Fawcett

- **Which powers might rise to regional leadership?**
- **What is the state of regional organization?**
- **Conclusion**

The potential ordering properties of regional or global hegemons, of which rising powers may be considered a category, are widely acknowledged. So is their role in international organization. Not all regional organizations have been driven by hegemons and not all regional powers seek to enhance their power in this way; but in many cases they have played a role in their start-up, consolidation, or development. Regional organizations provide aspiring powers a platform to demonstrate muscle and provide a gateway to global power and influence, both normative and material.

Although the roles of regional powers have been gathering more attention—a reflection of their enhanced status in a post-bipolar international system—the relationship between rising powers, a relatively new category of analysis, and regional organizations is under-researched.[1] This is particularly true for the Middle East given the widely perceived absence of influential powers and the weaknesses of regional organizations.[2] The region has been loosely referred to as a site of rising powers or leaders like Egypt, Saudi Arabia, Iran, or Turkey. Indeed, the CIVETS include Egypt and Turkey, and MIST includes Turkey. However, in general, the rising power phenomenon is mostly identified outside the region, resting with countries like Brazil, China, India, or South Africa. Recent evidence from the region in the light of economic developments and the Arab Spring uprisings suggests some alternative scenarios that deserve exploration, particularly given the instability of the region and the high demand for leadership.

This chapter aims to explore the relationships between regional powers, regional organizations, and order in the Middle East. First, it discusses the rising phenomenon as it relates to the region; then it considers Middle East regional organizations and their capabilities and how these have developed over time; third, it links the roles of regional powers to the activities of regional organization, offering a critical evaluation of their potential roles in regional and global governance and norms.

The intention is to show that, despite some evidence to the contrary, the hitherto limited capabilities of regional powers have impeded the development of cooperation and the promotion of regional order in the Middle East and, by extension, the ability of the region to contribute to wider global order. The aspirations of such powers have been blocked by regional rivalries, external intervention, and concerns about regime survival, all of which trump leadership initiatives. Although regional leadership may not be a sufficient condition for effective organization, the two are closely correlated and the absence of leadership is detrimental to institutional and normative developments, and therefore regional order.

Which powers might rise to regional leadership?

Historically there have been various contenders for regional leadership in the Middle East and some have shared attributes with the rising power category: states that can potentially influence and reshape the global system and its norms.[3] This observation thus qualifies the notion that "the concept of regional power is not useful for analyzing the Middle East."[4] As discussed below, there have been important episodes where regional powers have sought to influence regional, even global outcomes. From another perspective the very *absence* of regional powers is, in itself, important. It is true, however, that in terms of durable leadership credentials, the contemporary region, despite its relative economic weight, looks weak.

Egypt, Turkey, Iraq, Saudi Arabia, Iran, and Syria (perhaps also Israel) are all states that have aspired to regional leadership, although their ambitions, and even their idea of what constitutes their region, have diverged. Indeed, different conceptions of region may be part of the problem. At least three of these states—Turkey, Iran, and Saudi Arabia—may today be considered as aspiring regional powers. Yet it also remains true that, in contrast to other regions, the Middle East has demonstrated an absence of consistent leadership patterns. The interest of states in leadership tends to be rhetorical and self-serving rather than reflective of any deep commitment to cooperation. Institutional design and policy reflect this. Under the present conditions of external interference, internal rivalry, and regime insecurity, which all inhibit autonomy of action, this pattern is likely to continue.

Egypt, for its size, location and history, has often been regarded as the natural leader of the Arab world, and at times displayed the characteristics of a hegemon, particularly during the charismatic presidency of Nasser (and briefly following the Arab uprisings when President Morsi sought to promote Egypt as a new regional fulcrum). Egypt under President Nasser (1956–1970), given its leading roles in regional politics and in the global Non-Aligned Movement, was an exemplary case of a potential rising power with the possibility to influence both regional and global norms.[5] Yet, for all its ideological attraction, under the banner of anti-colonialism and Arab nationalism (as revealed in the Suez crisis and the formation of the United Arab Republic), its economic, military, and even cultural power was not robust enough, particularly when faced with the determined opposition of external, and some regional actors. Above all, the competitive international environment of the Cold War proved detrimental to the projection of rising power of the form sought by Egypt. Under President Sadat, the country moved away from reformism and closer to the prevailing norms of Western international society: embarking on economic liberalization and engaging with the Arab–Israel peace process brokered by the United States in the late 1970s. This policy, however, resulted in a loss of legitimacy in the wider Arab world.[6]

As Egypt's position declined, speeded by the signature of a bilateral treaty with Israel and comparative economic weakness, particularly in the light of the challenge from the new rentier states, states like Iraq and Syria made bids for regional dominance, using military and nationalist tools to some effect in regional conflicts and debates. Tellingly, despite their common Ba'athist ideology, both sought independently to establish regional leadership credentials: Iraq in the context of the Iran–Iraq War, in which it wooed the West, but also much of the Arab world, by demonstrating its anti-Iranian stance. In the Gulf War of 1991 Iraq reversed course, attempting to lead an anti-Western alliance by appealing to Arab support through its rhetoric of anti-imperialism. In the absence of Egyptian leadership, Syria too flexed its regional muscle, supporting radical and anti-Western policies, demonstrated in relations with Iran, dominance in Lebanon, and in its opposition to Israel.[7] Regime change in Iraq in 2003 and closer relations with Iran, resulting in the so-called Shi'i axis, also placed Syria in a stronger regional position, at least until the start of the Syrian uprising. Neither state, however, enjoyed widespread regional legitimacy, nor did their power base significantly expand extra-regionally. Apart from promoting the Nasserite idea of support for a broad Arab coalition—against the West, against Israel, or in the case of Iraq, against Iran—and with considerably less success than Nasser, few other leadership qualities or regional public goods were offered such as to make either state qualify for rising power status—an argument that may be extended to their roles in regional institutions as discussed below. It was not just that their foreign policies (despite some appeal to a rejectionist and radical constituency vis-à-vis the West and Israel) failed to attract a wide public; their domestic arrangements did not command legitimacy and were unattractive as models for the region and wider world.

Among the wealthy Arab Gulf monarchies, Saudi Arabia is another state with evident leadership credentials. Its independent history, relative longevity, wealth and size support this claim. Its power base—resting on a union of the Al Saud tribe and the Wahhabi religious movement—is stable, supported by claims to religious legitimacy, extensive patronage networks, and the economic advantages conferred by significant oil reserves. Yet, despite its regional outreach through the provision of development aid and assistance, management of the *hajj*, initiatives within the wider pan-Islamic, Organization of Islamic Cooperation (OIC) framework, or the sub-regional Gulf Cooperation Council (GCC) context, the Saudis have been historically cautious and modest in their leadership aspirations, above all avoiding foreign policy postures that might lose them friends at home and abroad.[8] This was evident in their positioning on the oil embargo of the early 1970s, which, despite its immediate impact and challenge to prevailing international norms, proved ephemeral. Saudi Arabia defected from the embargo—as did other core states—following pressure from Western consumers. Despite the accolades that the Arab Organization of the Petroleum Exporting Countries (OPEC) group received from the wider developing world—it was inspirational in the actions of the G77—the Saudis themselves suffered reputational damage, while the opportunity further to lead the Arab oil producers, and thereby produce significant changes to regional, even global order, was not taken. Saudi leaders then, as now, must tread delicately within the region, given their role as guardian of Islam's most holy sites, and outside, where their power base, indeed the very survival of the monarchy has been, and remains, linked historically to the United States, without whose longstanding support the kingdom would arguably have been unstable.

It is true that after the invasion of Iraq in 2003 and the Arab Spring we have seen the rise of a more regionally assertive Saudi Arabia,[9] as further discussed below. However, its leadership capabilities are contested and arguably under-utilized. Like other Gulf monarchies, survival and avoidance of sectarian fall out has been a primary response to the Arab uprisings.[10] Qualified support for international intervention in Libya and Syria should be seen in this light rather than as the sign of a new normative turn towards R2P, as the counter-example of support for GCC intervention to quash uprisings in Bahrain showed. Declining a non-permanent seat on the UN Security Council (in October 2013) as a sign of frustration at UN and Western policy did not generate a wave of regional solidarity and Jordan quickly took Saudi Arabia's place. Furthermore, even its predominance in the Arab Gulf sub-region is contested, as shown by differing stances taken by a state like Qatar—a small but highly significant power in its own right—in regard to positioning towards Iran or Egypt.[11]

Iran itself presents a different profile as aspiring regional leader. Iran has long been a powerful regional state, whether under the last Shah, Mohammed Reza Pahlavi—when relations with the United States were particularly close[12]—or the Islamic Republic. Its region, however, lies on a different axis to much of the Arab world, embracing parts of Central and South Asia, and, through Shi'ism, it reaches a distinctive Islamic constituency. It is partly this reason, and Iran's unique racial and cultural make up, that makes it neither an obvious, nor widely accepted regional leader. Despite the strengthening of Iran's position since the early years of the revolution and conclusion of the Iran–Iraq War—reflected in its influence among more radical Islamic groups, its ongoing nuclear program, or in the growth of Shi'i influence since 2003—Iran does not command a significant regional following. It has soft power resources, manifested in Iran's Islamic and Third World links (with Venezuela for example).[13] It also provides public goods, including assistance to victims of natural disasters and wars, as well as educational and cultural activities in the region. Iran has also supported groups like Hezbollah and Hamas. Such influence attempts may worry Israel, the Gulf States, and their Western allies, but they have arguably not made Iran a leader state. The more moderate Khatami presidency with its dialogue of civilizations approach could be seen as a partial exception (as could the current presidency of Rouhani), but rising power would not seem to be the right category to employ here, not least since Khatami was replaced by the conservative Ahmadinejad. Despite attempts at regional outreach, Iran's domestic structure and politics, and frequently bellicose international posture, have not always been easy to reconcile with a wider regional, to say nothing of a global constituency.

The Turkish case has recently received more attention, as indicated by its presence in the two rising power groups above. For a long time it was seen as a relative regional outlier with a more pro-European than Middle Eastern orientation. Its distinctive modern history, including being a founder member of the Baghdad Pact and membership of NATO, discredited it in the eyes of many Arabs. Yet, Turkey emerged from the regional shadows in the 1980s, as an impressive economic power and potential mediator in regional conflicts. It sought new foreign policy alignments, reaching out to Middle Eastern regimes and publics as peace-broker, and later advocate of democratization and moderate Islamism after the victory of the Justice and Development Party (AKP) in 2002. It has been spoken of as a bridge, or anchor state.[14] As such, it has sought more important roles in regional and international organizations, not only through existing links to the North Atlantic and Western Europe, but also in Central Asia, the Middle East, and Islamic world, as shown by its closer involvement with the OIC.

An opportunity to test its regional stature was provided by the Arab uprisings, where Turkey sought to portray itself as an exemplary regional state and model of good governance.[15] Showing leadership on the Tunisian and Egyptian question was relatively easy because less was invested. Despite vacillation over the Libyan intervention and removal of Gadhafi, Turkey was for a time viewed rather positively in the region as the state that had "best handled" the Arab Spring.[16] Things became harder after the Syrian crisis when Turkey's initial hesitation over how to retreat from its previous friendship with President Assad suggested vulnerability and the limits of its normative power.[17] Although it had aspirations to become an honest broker, and a power that the West hoped might balance out the dangers of regional extremism, it has not secured a deep regional following. It too remains domestically vulnerable (as Istanbul uprisings of 2013 and subsequent public protest over the curtailment of freedom of expression showed). By late 2013, some claimed that Turkey's idealistic foreign policy had failed and Turkey had lost its chance to lead.[18] This may be overstated, but there are good reasons to agree that, beyond its evident economic weight, Turkey will remain an aspiring hegemon.

An exception and outlier to the above is Israel. In some senses, Israel is an obvious regional great power in military and economic terms;[19] yet it is one that has not aspired to leadership. Israel is regionally isolated, and aligns with the United States and Europe. Israel possesses the military capacity to influence outcomes and has frequently exercised it. Its domestic arrangements, although seen as discriminatory to Arabs, are more immediately attractive than those of many regional states. It has twice been involved in greater regional engagement:

following the Camp David accords of 1979 and the Oslo process of the early 1990s, but in both cases the opportunity for regional leadership was not taken.[20] Israel is not a regional hegemon in the sense of providing leadership, public goods, or regional institutions. With its very existence still contested by regional radicals and its territory contested by UN resolutions, Israel's support base is internal and extra-regional, linked to the very external influences that other regional powers challenge. As a fierce and often hostile regional state, it can also act as veto-player to block other aspirants to leadership.

As noted, changes to the regional balance of power since the Arab Spring have elevated the prospects of some states while temporarily eliminating others. These changes are ongoing and their effects hard to measure. Clearly, the Arab Gulf monarchies, headed by Saudi Arabia and Qatar (not always in unison), with their control of important media outlets and evident economic weight, have assumed greater importance, leading new regional initiatives to contain unrest and preserve regional order. Turkey and Iran also display leadership credentials in attempts to reposition themselves to their own advantage amid the prevailing regional instability. But these are not coherent or durable leadership initiatives. None of these states are immune to internal, or indeed international, pressures—consider Iran's earlier Green Revolution and Turkey's subsequent unrest. Leadership claims are thus reflective of the regional balance of power and attempts to manage this in favor of individual states. There is no *obvious* regional leader, and multiple and contradictory leadership claims prevent regional consensus on core issues.

Considering the above changes, it is noteworthy how an external power, the United States, as Jeffry Legro persuasively argues, has provided many of the elements of leadership that have been lacking among regional powers. Notwithstanding a relative decline in United States influence and the increased significance of China and Russia in the region, this is surely the exemplary case where we cannot begin to discuss leadership and regional order "without reference to the role of the United States."[21] Prior to the 2003 invasion of Iraq, consider how every major peace initiative in the Arab-Israeli conflict has been in large part initiated by the United States. The United States has similarly been involved at some level in every Gulf War. No other region, even Latin America, in the very shadow of the United States, has been so constrained in its leadership options.

In short, for the different reasons described above, none of the major regional states have succeeded in rising to durable leadership status or translating their power to effective collective action. If power in

International Relations is demonstrated in the ability to influence outcomes, or to persuade others to change their behavior, it is clear that most Middle Eastern states have failed to acquire it.[22] This regional pattern may be extended to the wider global arena. Middle East states have a long history of interaction with, and at times hostility towards the West but have not hitherto seriously challenged the institutions of international society.[23] This is not to say that individual states (or indeed non-state actors) do not have global influence in certain issue areas; but this remains aspirational or transient, and does not confer rising power status. The reasons, as elaborated here, include high and continuing levels of external interference, longstanding inter-regional tensions and rivalries, compounded by challenges to the very legitimacy of states. Above all, the contrary and persistent effect of external penetration cannot be ignored. Outside powers have repeatedly attempted to impose their order and leadership agendas on the Middle East. France and Britain did so before, and even after the Second World War; the United States and USSR during the Cold War; and the United States, and to a lesser extent both Russia and China, since. Although these efforts have not, so far, resulted in regional stability, they have nonetheless obstructed aspiring leaders.

Despite the lack of a dominant regional power, the Middle East has seen attempts at hegemony: the case of Nasser's Egypt, OPEC's brief successes, and the recent actions of the Gulf states are all relevant here and illustrate the possible opportunities for rising powers. However, their relative weakness and lack of global reach does constitute a useful explanatory variable and link to current regional (dis)order. It also contributes to explaining the region's failure to develop more effective institutions, another potential source of order and global impact, which is the subject of the next section.

What is the state of regional organization?

In this section I consider different regional organizations and their roles. Which are the relevant institutions in the Middle East framework and what is their sphere of activity? How do these institutions interact with assumptions about order, power, and questions of regional leadership? Like other regions of the world, the Middle East since 1945 has seen the growth and functional expansion of regional institutions.[24] Although the region has not been short of regional initiatives, its record is comparatively weak by most measures. Regional states, individually or collectively, have demonstrated little sustained interest in the design and maintenance of efficient institutions.[25] Is institutional failure then a way of understanding the current disorder in the Middle East, and if so to which causes might such failure be ascribed?[26] I focus on the main regional organization, the League of Arab States (LAS), but also consider other sub-regional and cross-regional organizations like the GCC and OIC.[27]

Regionalism in the Middle East, as in other parts of the world, may be crudely but usefully divided into two waves, covering the Cold War and post-Cold War periods. In the former period, both pan-Arab and more modest projects aimed at union and federation were tried alongside attempts at economic integration on the European model. In the latter, there were further efforts at economic and political and security cooperation. In this respect, the Middle East differs from other regions, not in terms of institutional start up and numbers, but in terms of the failure of institutions to evolve. Indeed, it might be argued that Middle East regionalism reached a plateau from which it has failed to advance and improve institutional capacity.[28] Conflict has played a role here, as has regime type and the nature of the regional economy. Notable has been the proliferation of initiatives by external actors, mainly Europe and the United States, to promote regional cooperation in different contexts, even to redefine the region itself, as the *Greater Middle East* and Mediterranean concepts suggest.

Any consideration of Middle East regionalism must start with the pan-Arab question and the LAS.[29] The LAS was one of the first formal regional organizations outside the Americas and one that played a role in discussions about the relationship between the United Nations and regional bodies. As such it was a highly statist organization, and this suited the agendas of many members. One could argue that the League has mostly sought to complement rather than overturn the prevailing norms of international society. Yet, it also embodied a more revisionist, pan-Arab idea in which Arabs rejected aspects of the colonial settlement and aspired to greater unity among the Arab territories of the former Ottoman Empire. The discourse of pan-Arabism has remained popular, as witnessed in regional wars and the Arab Spring. However, the tension between state centrism and the rhetoric of unity remained a complicating factor in the development of the institution. As Barnett comments: "if the institution of sovereignty instructed the newly independent Arab states to recognize each other's borders and authority over its population, the institution of pan-Arabism sanctioned just the opposite."[30]

The League enjoyed some successes in conflict mediation as envisaged by its Charter.[31] Its annex on Palestine, following the creation of Israel in 1948, was an important document, establishing a common position of non-recognition. The League's first summit in 1964 welcomed the PLO. Subsequent summits showed a level of regional solidarity on core issues. Still, it remained a weak institution when measured in terms of attempts to promote economic, political, or security cooperation.[32] For example, efforts to emulate the EC model to create an Arab Common Market produced few lasting results, although this attempt was later revived. Such early failure, however, was unremarkable in a Third World context where state building took priority and the necessary demand-supply conditions for integration did not exist. Amid multiple regional disputes, not least the protracted Arab–Israel conflict, the region's security record was also disappointing. The League, which expanded from a core of six to include all 22 Arab countries, was a large and diverse institution, despite linguistic, geographic, and religious ties, making it hard to establish common policy frameworks. It excludes the three non-Arab powers of the region, Iran, Turkey, and Israel, all of whom carry veto-player capabilities.

Outside the League, other attempts at inter-state cooperation and federation were responses to the colonial legacy and the Cold War. The Baghdad Pact, later the Central Eastern Treaty Organization (CENTO), was an undisguised instrument of colonial influence and United States containment. Including the pro-Western states of Turkey and Iran, it earned the odium of most Arab states. In response there were coalitions of Arab states like the United Arab Republic (1958–61) and the Federation of Arab Republics (1971–73). Such unions, or the different military alliances constructed for the purpose of fighting regional wars, were, however, short-lived and did not survive in any institutionalized form.

Some new dynamics came into play with the creation, in 1969, of the OIC, reflecting an attempt to craft an Islamic version of the Arab League, embodying another pan- (and in this case cross-)regional idea, again with a strictly statist orientation. In addition, the formation of the United Arab Emirates (1971) as a federation of the small Gulf emirates and the GCC (1981), a response not to the Cold War, but to Gulf insecurity after Britain's departure and the Iranian revolution of 1979, heralded more lasting forms of regional governance. In turn, the Islamic Republic of Iran, demonstrating its regional muscle, was instrumental in the founding and later expansion of the Economic Conference Organization (1985), placing its own economic and security interests on a different axis following failed attempts to win sympathy from, and spread revolution to, the wider Arab world.

With the exception of the GCC, none of the above formulas enjoyed significant success from either an ideological or material perspective. Wars, regime insecurity, external interference, and the complicating factor of oil rents, introduced new regional divides among regional haves and have-nots, blocking further moves at integration. Peacemaking efforts also proved highly controversial as the Arab League rejected the Camp David accords and banished Egypt, yet subsequently proved unable to broker any alternative Arab–Israel settlement. In some respects, again, this lack of progress was unremarkable from a comparative perspective. Outside Europe, regionalism had not taken off, giving rise to questions about the usefulness of that model when applied to newer and weaker states.[33] Only with the end of the Cold War did this picture change as the multiple studies of new regionalism attest.[34] However, the setting free of regions and the accompanying institutional and normative changes identified by scholars,[35] did not occur in the Middle East. The region's tensions and rivalries were not of the Cold War type; superpower overlay was not removed, regional states did not enjoy greater autonomy, nor did the incentive for regime change—an important push factor for regionalist efforts—significantly materialize. In this regard, the persistence of external intervention (as in the wars of 1991 and 2003), the absence of regional leadership, and weakness of regional organization went hand in hand.

There were some trickle-down effects of the new regionalism. The 1980s saw the establishment of the Arab Maghreb Union and the Arab Cooperation Council, although the latter soon collapsed with Iraq's invasion of Kuwait. Yemeni unification and the Middle East Peace Process were also products of the Cold War's ending. However the first post-Cold War decade ended without significant institutional progress. More remarkable perhaps was the high level of external involvement in efforts to remake Middle East politics, economics, and society. Even the very boundaries of the Middle East were the subject of continuing Western attempts at refashioning as suggested by concepts like the Euro-Mediterranean, or the Greater Middle East, both of which crossed over existing regional divides.[36]

Until the Arab Spring, the contemporary regional scene was extraordinary in demonstrating the relative absence of internal agency and norm production and a predominance of external initiatives. Although there is, arguably, a discernible Asian Way and African Way of regionalism, incorporating distinctive ideas and policies, there is no Middle Eastern way. This observation would no doubt be objected to by some regional states. There are regular high-level meetings among *Arab* foreign ministers under the auspices of the Arab League. The League has revived earlier common market proposals via the Greater Arab Free Trade Area project. It has endorsed a 2002 Saudi peace plan in respect of Palestine-Israel relations. Turkey now has League observer status. The GCC, in turn, has moved towards a customs union and plans a more effective security structure making it a more serious economic and political actor on the regional and even the global stage.[37] The OIC offers a platform for the discussion of issues of common concern to Islamic states and incorporates Iran and Turkey, both active members. However, effective regional organization is still lacking as reflected in three indicative security areas: non-proliferation, anti-terrorist measures, and peace-operations. In respect of the latter, it is notable that despite high levels of regional conflict Middle Eastern, as opposed to UN peace operations, in contrast to a region like Africa, are virtually non-existent.[38] Rather than new projects, the region has seen continuing initiatives by Western powers, notably the European Union and the United States to promote alternative visions of regional order, of which democracy promotion is one, hitherto not particularly successful, example.[39]

In sum, despite new opportunities since the end of the Cold War the regionalist experiments in the Middle East have failed significantly to contribute to conflict management and cooperation, and thus to guide regional transformation or promote regional order. This is in contrast to other world regions. Until the Arab Spring, the single perhaps most important development in the region to have taken place was the externally facilitated Middle East Peace Process initiated by the Oslo Accords in 1993.[40] In this process, as in former peace processes, the League was conspicuously absent. Its failure was followed by a period of greater instability in which regional actors and institutions struggled to adjust to new realities and sustain a united stand on economic, political, or security issues, when confronted with the continuing crises in Iraq, Lebanon, Israel-Palestine relations, and finally the Arab Spring uprisings. The 2003 Iraq invasion was opposed by all Arab states except Kuwait; yet despite its impact no major new institutional initiative emerged. Rather it was the United States and Western institutions that continued to operate an effective security hierarchy in the region.[41]

Events since 2003, particularly following the Arab Spring, have adjusted this picture, generating expectations about a wave of new regionalism in the Middle East.[42] Following the short Israel-Lebanon War of 2006, the LAS, which had registered successes in earlier Lebanese settlements, was supportive of UN resolutions and helped to broker the subsequent Doha agreement of 2008.[43] In the Arab uprisings, the LAS, GCC, and OIC all showed new activism in the wake of widespread social unrest and repressive regime responses, particularly in Libya and Syria. The Arab Spring had profound implications for regional order, posing a huge challenge for an institution like the Arab

League. Under the leadership of emerging regional leaders like Qatar and Saudi Arabia, the League took an uncharacteristically strong stand over the Libyan crisis, suspending Libyan membership, supporting UN resolutions and international intervention contributing to the fall of Libya's long-term president, Gadhafi. It played mediating roles in the crisis in Yemen where the former president stood down, and in Syria, where early League attempts at mediation and collaboration with the United Nations led to a suspension of Syria's membership and support for regime change. League members provided support to Syrian rebel groups and the Arab League in 2012 formally recognized the major Syrian opposition bloc, the Syrian National Council. This apparent embrace by the Arab League, alongside that of other regional organizations like the GCC and OIC, of UN resolution 1973 on Libya and the implicit endorsement thereby of the R2P principle, led to widespread speculation about the revival of the League and the possibility of its playing a more activist role in a regional and wider multilateral security framework.[44] In particular the notion that Middle Eastern states might be taking the initiative to mediate regional conflicts seemed to gain ground.

If the changed regional climate following Arab Spring events has led to new activism by the League and sub-regional institutions like the GCC, the enthusiasm expressed about the League's new roles needs to be qualified. What were the motivations for action and what do these reveal about the possibilities and limits of its cooperative potential? Does this represent a new normative turn in terms of contemporary Arab views of and participation in international society or is this more geopolitics as usual? On this point, there are certainly pressures, external and internal, on the League to function more effectively as a security institution within a wider multilateral framework. These, however, have been driven by core regional states, like Saudi Arabia and Qatar, and outside powers, notably the United States, meaning that it may be premature to believe that the organization is set on a more liberal path or poised to undertake new security roles in the short term.[45] On the other hand, it might be argued that the League, like ASEAN for example, which adopted a Charter in 2008, is gradually incorporating new international norms and practices. In this regard an earlier relevant development was the adoption, in 1994, of an Arab Charter on Human Rights (an amended version of which entered into force in 2008), although less than half of the League's members are signatories and aspects of the charter remain inconsistent with the international human rights regime.[46] It may, however, signal the advent of further normative changes.

However, other reforms and additions to the League which have long been mooted, including the establishment of an Arab Court of Justice, have failed to materialize.[47] So if there is evidence of normative change, we should be cautious. Serious obstacles remain in the path of further developments in regional organization. Significantly, the Arab League, while containing some elements of a regional security regime, has failed permanently to secure peaceful relations between its members or to serve as an effective vehicle for the promotion of a wider regional security order including non-Arab states. Some regard League actions as mere damage limitation, reflecting the unrivalled power of the GCC monarchies and the triumph of geopolitics.[48]

Just as during the Cold War, regional conditions remain broadly hostile to the development of regionalism and regional initiatives. Then, an arrangement like the Baghdad Pact merely encouraged local resistance and counter alliances. Today, direct and continuing Western regional involvement has proved to be highly divisive, impeding the conditions for regime change and institutional growth and generating confused and contradictory reactions to Western inspired projects. Rather than generating a rallying effect, Middle East crises remain subject to superpower overlay. There is little talk of Middle Eastern solutions to Middle Eastern problems. In one sense, the Middle East is still a region within what Peter Katzenstein has aptly called the "American imperium," and this reality conditions regional outcomes.[49] This is not to ignore the role of the EU, or the recent growth of Russian or Chinese involvement in the region. In the Syrian crisis, Russia was a game changer in averting intervention, but no other outside power comes close to the United States in terms of regional influence.

Conclusion

The above two sections considered the possibilities and limitations of regional states and institutions in the fashioning of regional order in the Middle East. What are the linkages between the two, or to what degree has regional order depended on leader states and the creation of effective institutions? Regional leadership of the kind that might be supplied by rising powers could evidently be key to the development of regional organization and to normative spillovers. This has arguably been the case in Africa, Latin America, and Asia, where states have sought to adapt to or contest international norms in regional institutions; for example, in respect of financial crisis or humanitarian intervention. The fact that leadership and regional institutions are weak in the Middle East suggests a correlation between rising powers and order: their absence does matter.[50]

If we analyze this correlation, drawing on the two sections above, we find that periods of relative activism in regional organization were related to the leadership and perceived legitimacy of regional powers. Attempts at such leadership include the Nasser period, during which the Arab League undoubtedly carried more weight under Egyptian leadership. Its demise after 1979 was a serious blow and subsequent efforts by Iraq and Syria to assert their hegemony (notably in Kuwait and Lebanon) failed. Similarly, the coordination of the oil embargo by leading Arab states, notably Saudi Arabia, from 1973–4, was also critical in the success of that short-lived regime.

Since the Iraq Wars of 1991 and 2003, low points for Middle East regionalism which revealed the absence of coherent regional initiatives and reliance on external actors, there have been shifts in the regional balance of power to favor the stable oil-rich Gulf monarchies led by Saudi Arabia and Qatar. The GCC group, which since 2013 has been discussing a security pact to reinforce cooperation, is partly responsible for the new consensus. That Gulf leadership has been significant in driving the League itself, also points to a possible harmony between sub-regional and pan-Arab groupings. The Arab Spring has also seen a tentative understanding between these stronger regional players and Western powers in respect of the desired regional order. But the picture is a fragile and contested one. Gulf leadership has been made possible by the relative weakness of other states and even within the GCC there is disagreement between Saudi Arabia and Qatar. New norms, for example, that of support for humanitarian intervention, have been inconsistently applied and regime stability prioritized. Whether this understanding can survive and contribute to a new regional order embracing new post-Arab Spring regimes remains an open question. GCC intervention in Bahrain points away from this conclusion, as does the unraveling of the conflicts in Syria and Iraq, which both suggest regional fragmentation rather than unity.

This chapter has sought to highlight different ways of thinking about how regional actors can impact on order and norms at the local and global level. Lurking behind these ideas is the question as to whether or not regional states, aspiring rising powers, are leaders, followers, or outliers as regards prevailing international norms. The analysis here suggests that in the post-independence period there was greater assertiveness by Middle Eastern states in a Third World, Cold War setting, as the Arab nationalist and OPEC moments showed. Arabs then attempted to influence the prevailing norms of international society, acting as entrepreneurs. The OPEC action, although short lived, was widely viewed as an important signpost for developing countries seeking to assert themselves in a hostile international system. After the 1970s however, and particularly since the Cold War ended, the emergence of new powers and regional institutions, have either led to short-lived acts of defiance (as in Iraq's attempt to annex Kuwait) or convergence with international norms as suggested by the experience of the Gulf states and major regional organizations during the Libyan uprising and Arab Spring events. There are two caveats. On the one hand, attempts to impose distinctive *Arab* norms, visible for example in opposition to Western intervention in 2003, over the Palestine-Israel questions, or the Saudi refusal to take up its Security Council seat, show some of the old assertiveness. Perhaps the defense of Arab Gulf monarchies against the current disorder is another such norm. On the other hand, core states, like Iran, alongside a host of new societal actors (like the radical groups in Iraq and Syria seeking to establish an Islamic state) continue to challenge some of the foundational norms and institutions of international society.[51]

In the Middle East, regional powers and new patterns and practices of regional governance have left their mark, from the very foundations of the Arab League which closely coincided with that of the United Nations, through the Nasserite period, to the recent activities of the Gulf States. Expectations of any radical change in regional governance and norms should be moderated, however. These would require regime change, a downgrading of regional tensions, institutional reform and a gradual decoupling of external actors from regional affairs. Only then might it be possible to discern the emergence of a more stable and influential regional regime, although whether it will tend towards convergence with the West or become part of a more radical global south is open to question. Former Secretary General Amr Moussa's description of the League and the UN as "historical twins" was factually correct in terms of their establishment, but the Arab League has yet to prove itself as a durable and reliable partner in any more effective multilateral system.[52]

Notes

1 Dirk Nabers, "Power, Leadership and Hegemony in International Politics," in *Regional Leadership in the Global System*, Daniel Flemes, ed. (Farnham: Ashgate, 2010), 51.
2 Ian Lustick, "The Absence of Middle Eastern Great Powers: Political Backwardness in Historical Perspective," *International Organization* 51, no. 4 (1997): 653–683.

3 Daniel Flemes and Andrew Cooper "Foreign Policy Strategies of Emerging Powers in a Multipolar World," *Third World Quarterly* 34, no. 6 (2013): 943–962.

4 Martin Beck, "Israel: Regional Politics in a Highly Fragmented Region," in *Regional Leadership*, Daniel Flemes, ed., 147.

5 Ian Lustick, "The Absence of Middle Eastern Great Powers," 667–670.

6 Raymond Baker, *Sadat and After. The Struggle for Egypt's Political Soul* (Harvard, Mass.: Harvard University Press, 1990), xii.

7 Patrick Seale, *Asad of Syria: The Struggle for the Middle East* (Berkeley: University of California Press, 1989).

8 F. Gregory Gause III, *Saudi Arabia in the New Middle East* (Washington, DC: Council on Foreign Relations, 2011).

9 Louise Fawcett, "The Iran War ten years on: assessing the fall-out," *International Affairs* 89, no. 2 (2013): 333–334.

10 Crystal A. Ennis and Bessma Momani, "Shaping the Middle East in the Midst of the Arab Uprisings: Turkish and Saudi Foreign Policy Strategies," *Third World Quarterly* 34, no. 6 (2013), 1127–1144.

11 Steven Wright, "Qatar," in *Power and Politics in the Persian Gulf Monarchies*, Christopher M. Davidson, ed. (London: Hurst and Co., 2011), 113–134.

12 Roham Alvandi, *Nixon, Kissinger and the Shah* (Oxford: Oxford University Press, 2014).

13 Anoush Ehteshami and Mahjoob Zweiri, *Iran's Foreign Policy from Khatami to Ahmadinejad* (Ithaca, N.Y.: Cornell University Press, 2008), p. xiv.

14 Philip Robins, "Turkey's Double Gravity predicament: The foreign policy of a newly activist power," *International Affairs* 89, no. 2 (2013): 381–383.

15 Ennis and Momani, "Shaping the Middle East," 1128–1130.

16 Shibley Telhami, "The 2011 Arab Public Opinion Poll," Brookings Institution, www.brookings.edu/research/reports/2011/11/21-arab-public-opinion-telhami.

17 Philip Robins, "Turkey and R2P," in *The International Politics of Human Rights*, Monica Serrano and Thomas G. Weiss, eds (London: Routledge, 2014), 200–204.

18 Ennis and Momani, "Turkish and Saudi Foreign Policy," 1137.

19 Beck, "Israel," 136.

20 Avi Shlaim, "The Rise and Fall of the Oslo Peace Process," in *International Relations of the Middle East*, Louise Fawcett, ed. (Oxford: Oxford University Press, 2013), 13.

21 Jeffrey Legro, "The Omni-power: the United States and regional orders," in *Regional Powers and Regional Orders*, Nadine Godehardt and Dirk Nabers eds. (London: Routledge, 2011), 175–192.

22 Joseph Nye, "US Power and Strategy after Iraq," *Foreign Affairs* 82, no. 4 (2003): 67.

23 Fred Halliday, "The Middle East and Conceptions of 'International Society,'" in *International Society and the Middle East*, Barry Buzan and Ana Gonzalez-Pelaez, eds (London: Palgrave, 2009), 1.

24 Louise Fawcett, "Alliances and Regionalism in the Middle East," in *International Relations of the Middle East*, Louise Fawcett, ed.

25 Paul Aarts, "The Middle East: A Region without Regionalism or the end of Exceptionalism?", *Third World Quarterly* 20, no. 5 (1999): 911–925.

26 Michael Barnett and Etel Solingen, "Designed to Fail or Failure of Design? The origins and legacy of the Arab League," in *Crafting Cooperation. Regional International Institutions in Comparative Perspective*, Amitav Acharya and Alastair Iain Johnston, eds (Cambridge: Cambridge University Press, 2007).

27 Louise Fawcett, "The League of Arab States," in *Handbook of Governance and Security*, James Sperling, ed. (Cheltenham: Edward Elgar, 2014).

28 Karl Deutsch *et al.*, *Political Community in the North Atlantic Area* (Princeton, N.J.: Princeton University Press, 1957).

29 Ahmed M. Gomaa, *The Foundations of the League of Arab States* (London: Longman, 1977).

30 Michael Barnett, "Institutions, roles, and disorder: the case of the Arab state system," *International Studies Quarterly* 37 (1993), 283.

31 Marco Pinfari, "Nothing but failure? The Arab League and the Gulf Cooperation Council as mediators in international conflicts," CSRC Working Paper 45 (London: London School of Economics, 2009).

32 Michael C. Hudson, *Middle East Dilemma: The Politics and Economics of Arab Integration* (London: IB Tauris, 1999), 10–11.

33 Louise Fawcett, "Regionalism from an historical perspective," in *Global Politics of Regionalism*, Mary Farrell, Bjorn Hettne, and Luk Langenhove, eds (London: Pluto Press, 2004).

34 Peter Robson "The New Regionalism and Developing Countries," *Journal of Common Market Studies* 31, no. 3 (1993): 329–348.

35 Etel Solingen, *Regional Orders at Century's Dawn. Global and Domestic Influences on Grand Strategy* (Princeton, N.J.: Princeton University Press, 1998).

36 Fawcett, "Alliances and Regionalism," 199.

37 Matteo Legrenzi, *The GCC and International Relations of the Gulf* (London: IB Tauris, 2011).

38 www.unmissions.org/.

39 Larbi Sadiki, *Rethinking Arab Democratization: Elections without Democracy* (Oxford: Oxford University Press, 2009).

40 Bahgat Korany and Ali E. Hillal Dessouki, *The Foreign Policies of Arab States* (Boulder, Colo.: Westview, 2009).

41 David A. Lake, *Hierarchy in International Relations* (Ithaca, N.Y.: Cornell University Press, 2009).

42 Fawcett, "Alliances and Regionalism," 201.

43 Farah Dakhlallah, "The Arab League in Lebanon 2005–2008," *Cambridge Review of International Studies* 25 (2012): 53–74.

44 Prince El Hassan bin Talal and Rolf Shwarz, "The Responsibility to Protect and the Arab World. An Emerging International Norm?" *Contemporary Security Policy* 34 (2013): 1–15.

45 Louise Fawcett, "Alliances and Regionalism," 334.

46 Mervat Rishmawi, "The Arab Charter on Human Rights and the League of Arab States," *Human Rights Law Review* 10 (2010): 169–178.

47 Michelle Burgis, *Boundaries of discourse in the International Court of Justice: Mapping arguments in Arab territorial disputes* (Boston, Mass.: Martinus Nijhoff Publishers, 2009), 91–92.

48 Bassel F. Salloukh, "The Arab Spring and Geopolitics," *The International Spectator* 48, no. 2 (2013), 32–46.

49 Peter Katzenstein, *A World of Regions. Asia and Europe in the American Imperium* (Ithaca, NY: Cornell University Press, 2005).
50 Louise Fawcett, "Regional Leadership? Understanding Power and Transformation in the Middle East," in *Regional Powers and Regional Order*, Nadine Godehardt and Dirk Nabers, eds (Abingdon: Routledge, 2011), 155–172.
51 Buzan and Gonzalez-Pelaez, *International Society and the Middle East*.
52 Amre Moussa, "The UN and the League of Arab States," in *The UN and the Regions: Third World Report on Regional Integration*, Philippe De Lombaerde, Francis Baert, and Tânia Felíci, eds (New York: Springer, 2012), 107; Jochen Prantl, ed., *Effective Multilateralism* (London: Palgrave, 2013).

8 "Africa Rising" and the rising powers

Rebecca Davies and Ian Taylor

- **An alternative?**
- **Institutions, Africa, and the BRICS**
- **Towards an African century?**
- **"A hopeful continent"?**
- **Conclusion**

Africa is currently said to be rising, turning a definitive page in its history. African per capita growth figures (if taken at face value) are relatively high and have now been sustained for a decade or so. This has been constructed on the back of "a commodity price boom that was unprecedented in its magnitude and duration [where the] real prices of energy and metals more than doubled in five years from 2003 to 2008, while the real price of food commodities increased 75%."[1] The commodity price hike of the first decade of the twenty-first century has been credited to the robust growth performance of emerging economies, particularly China.[2] High growth rates and the increase in activities by emerging economies across Africa are said to be in the process of reshaping the continent's international relations. Analyses thus far have had a strong evangelical aspect to them, suggesting that Africa has turned a corner.

Barely a week passes without some new official report, media article, or conference eulogizing the continent and its growth figures. Africa is now the "rising star."[3] We are living in "Africa's moment,"[4] where it is "Africa's turn."[5] In this new world, "Africa emerges,"[6] moving from "darkness to destiny,"[7] where it is "leading the way."[8] In fact, we are told, "The Next Asia Is Africa,"[9] based on an "African Growth Miracle."[10] We are even told "Why Africa will rule the 21st century"[11] and "Business conferences are filled with frothy talk of African lions overtaking Asian tigers."[12] Previous studies on the political economy of Africa are dismissed as "Afro-pessimism," to be swept away by "The Ultimate Frontier Market."[13] A recent book on "the story behind Africa's economic revolution" has a quasi-Superman springing from Africa on its front cover.[14] In short, "It's time for Africa."[15] More sober analyses that "the present growth is socially unsustainable"[16] are generally crowded out.

In the context of stagnating or slowly growing economies in the West, at face value Africa's growth *does* look comparatively healthy, setting aside for one moment the flattening out of over 50 variable countries into one entity known as "Africa." However, beyond the growth figures, ongoing dynamics are entrenching Africa's dependent position in the global economy. Indeed, the current process "deepens and intensifies Africa's inveterate and deleterious terms of (mal)integration within the global political economy—terms which continue to be characterized by external dominance and socially damaging and extraverted forms of accumulation."[17] This is why the Kenyan writer and investigative journalist, Parselelo Kantai, refers to the Africa Rising trope as an "insidious little fiction manufactured by global corporate finance,"[18] while *Africa Confidential* notes that "Much of the [Africa]-boosting, local and international, will serve [only] political and financial interests."[19]

Although this vast and growing body of literature examines the different activities of these rising powers and new trading geographies, there has been much less focus on whether or not the supposed reshaping or diversification of Africa's international relations, characterized largely by this increased engagement with emerging economies, belies genuine structural change. For all the rhetoric, the continent remains predominantly an exporter of primary commodities and there is little hint of these dynamics undoing Africa's subordinate position in the global economy. Despite renewed economic growth, the governance of poverty, inequality, and (under)development on the African continent thus remains one of the most fundamental ethical issues confronting scholars and practitioners of global governance today. As this chapter will demonstrate by focusing on China's relations with Africa, whether or not the approach of the BRICS powers, with their different interests and strategies, portend structural transformation in the hegemonic order can only be explored contextually. By focusing on the broader global context, as well as the neo-patrimonial nature of local political economies, it brings into view the possibilities of changing governance and development outcomes on the continent.

An alternative?

Since around 2000, there has been greater engagement between Africa and the global North, reflected in various initiatives largely focused on the issue of poverty with a strong emphasis on "good governance."[20] With this, conditionalities have been applied, often in a fairly static and dogmatic fashion—a continuation of a longstanding pattern. This has oftentimes been bitterly resented by African elites, even though Africa's own New Partnership for African Development (NEPAD) placed standard liberal definitions of governance at the centre of its project.[21] What is interesting with regard to the BRICS is that they provide options without the traditional North-South axis. An emphasis on developing infrastructure has been notable in this new set of relations, something that has at times been neglected by traditional actors.[22] Politically, this has also introduced new competitive dynamics into Africa's international relations: Africa has "never been in such a strong bargaining position" than at the present, with numerous "suitors."[23] The growing diversity of partners potentially offers a "tremendous opportunity ... as each country brings with it an array of capital goods, developmental experience, products and technology as well as new opportunities to trade goods, knowledge and models."[24] Trade with—and investment from—emerging economies potentially reduces the North's political leverage and economic dominance in Africa,[25] which may "increase the negotiating power enjoyed by [African] governments seeking to maximise local benefits."[26]

These developments may be interpreted in alternative ways. It may be put forward that these new actors now emerging are merely exploitative and self-interested; overall just as damaging to Africa as the extant and well-established set of relations with the traditional powers. Alternatively, these new relationships may be seen as somehow reflecting South-South values (whatever that may mean) and contributing to Africa's developmental goals. This appears to be what many African elites believe. Yet it seems obvious that Africa is the weaker partner in these new relationships. Specifically regarding the BRICS, actors from those states are in Africa not because of some notional love of Africa or Africans, but for reasons based on capitalist logics. Interest in gaining access to natural resources in Africa is often central.[27] As Kimenyi and Lewis put it, the attention of emerging economies towards Africa "is not based on an altruistic goal to improve the economic well-being of Africans" but rather, *just like most other external actors*, actors from emerging economies are "trying to maximise their own strategic economic and political interests by engaging with African countries."[28] Their relationships with Sub-Saharan Africa (SSA) do not exhibit any notable "exceptionalism," but rather display patterns that are "broadly similar to those of SSA 'traditional' partners and mostly reinforce existing commodity-based export structures."[29] This contrasts with the diplomatic claims made by the emerging economies that their engagement with Africa is qualitatively different—and *better*—than that of the North, with relentless incantations about "South-South" ties, "solidarity," "mutual benefits," "win-win relations," and "partnerships."

Given the "growing expectations among the citizens in countries targeted by the emerging economies of the immediate upswings in their livelihoods and improvements in quality of life,"[30] the solidarity rhetoric may backfire. It is obvious that the quality of a country's governance institutions is a crucial determinant in development and growth and although there have been *some* improvements in governance in Africa of late, incidents of corruption and general pathologies of maldevelopment remain a regular occurrence. Possibly compounding this situation is the "non-interference" practiced by some of the new partners. What this means in practical terms is that until and unless the elites in Africa themselves promote pro-development policies, no such standards will be adopted. In such a milieu, the perpetual question will then be: how might Africa engage with and exploit the increased engagement by new partners in order to benefit ordinary people and promote development?

Institutions, Africa, and the BRICS

Recently, a revitalized diplomacy has been initiated towards Africa. With regards to the emerging economies specifically, various summits, institutions, and agreements have been established which have witnessed an outpouring of enthusiasm for the continent: the Korea–Africa Forum, the Turkey–Africa Partnership, the Africa–Singapore Business Forum, the Malaysia–Africa Business Forum, the Taiwan–Africa Summit, Brazil–Africa Forum, and so on. All of these have (consciously or not) replicated the Chinese example set by the Forum on China-Africa Cooperation (FOCAC), established in 2000.

The background to FOCAC can be traced to the visit by Chinese Premier Jiang Zemin to Africa in 1996, when he publicly unveiled a new Chinese approach to Africa. According to a Chinese report, "The guiding principle that China follows in developing relations with African countries in the new situation is: to treat each other as equals, develop sincere friendship, strengthen solidarity and cooperation, and seek common development."[31] During a keynote speech to the Organization of African Unity (OAU), entitled "Toward a New Historical Milestone of Sino–African Friendship," Jiang advanced a five-point proposal for a new relationship between China and Africa:

vii fostering a sincere friendship between China and Africa and both sides becoming each other's reliable "all-weather friends";
viii treating each other as equals and respecting each other's sovereignty and not interfering in each other's internal affairs;
  ix seeking common development on the basis of mutual benefit;
   x enhancing consultation and cooperation in international affairs; and
  xi looking into the future and create a better world.[32]

Jiang's proposal was warmly received by the OAU and may be seen as laying the foundation for current Sino–African relations. FOCAC has subsequently been the official vehicle to realize these ambitions.

In October 2000 a Forum on China–Africa Cooperation Ministerial Conference in Beijing was held that culminated in the formation of FOCAC. Previously, in October 1999, President Jiang Zemin had written to all heads of African states, as well as the Secretary-General of the OAU, to propose the convening of a Sino–Africa forum. When this was greeted with a favorable reception, the Chinese established a preparatory committee comprising 18 ministries, with the Ministry of Foreign Affairs and Ministry of Foreign Trade and Economic Cooperation (MOFTEC) assigned the roles of anchormen. Interestingly, Chinese sources claim that it was African leaders who initiated and asked for a summit. He Wenping asserts that:

> At the end of the 1990s, some African countries proposed that as the United States, Britain, France, Japan and Europe had established mechanisms for contact with Africa, it was necessary for China and Africa to establish a similar mechanism to fit in with the need to strengthen relations. After earnest study, China decided to echo the suggestions of African countries, and proposed to hold the Forum in 2000.[33]

Whether or not it was Beijing or African states that called for and initiated the summit, FOCAC has quickly proved to be a major feature in Africa's international relations.

The meeting in October 2000 was attended by 80 ministers charged with foreign affairs and international trade and economic development, from 45 African states. Representatives of international and regional organizations also attended, as did delegates from two African countries that did not then have diplomatic ties with China (Liberia and Malawi). Discussions were organized into four separate sessions: trade; economic reform (with China's program being showcased as a possible model);

poverty eradication and sustainable development; and, cooperation in education, science technology, and health care.

At the meeting, Jiang Zemin gave the keynote speech, starting off with the implicit claim that China was the leader of the developing world, and the oft-reported refrain that "China is the largest developing country in the world and Africa is the continent with the largest number of developing countries."[34] This Third Worldism was then made explicit by Jiang's claim that the meeting was a tangible example of South-South linkages: "closer South-South co-operation and the establishment of an equitable and just new international political and economic order" was needed.[35] Notably, Jiang cast Sino–African relations within an international context that "is moving towards multipolarity and [where] the international situation is on the whole easing off."[36] This was seen as providing new opportunities for trade and cooperation. These favorable conditions, however, were potentially threatened as "Hegemonism and power politics still exist."[37] Conflict and instability in the developing world was squarely blamed on the "many irrational and inequitable factors in the current international political and economic order [which] are detrimental not only to world peace and development, but also to the stability and development of the vast number of developing countries."[38]

Jiang then went on to outline four key ways that China and Africa could, working together, help establish a new global order:

1   "strengthen solidarity and promote South-South cooperation." South-South cooperation was seen as the main way developing countries could "give full play to their advantages in natural and human resources, tap to the full their respective productive and technological potential, take advantage of the others' strengths to make up for their own weaknesses, and achieve common improvement"[39];

2   "Enhance dialogue and improve North-South relations." According to Jiang, "Developed countries should take full account and care of the interests of the less privileged developing countries and increase financial investment and technology transfer to them to help build up their capacity for development." Intrinsic to this point was the assertion by Jiang that "A smaller development gap and better political and economic relations between the North and the South is an important foundation for a just and equitable new international political and economic order"[40];

3   "Take part in international affairs on the basis of equality and in an enterprising spirit." According to Jiang, China and Africa

needed to increase consultation and cooperation on both "the bilateral and multilateral fronts" and vigorously participate in international affairs and the formulation of international rules. Central to this was the promotion of reform of the international economic system to ensure that "a fair international environment will be created and the legitimate rights and interests of developing countries will be effectively safeguarded"[41]; and

4   "Look forward into the future and establish a new long-term stable partnership of equality and mutual benefit." Jiang stated that increased exchanges, "especially direct contacts between top leaders of both China and African countries" would be pursued as central to this goal.

FOCAC now meets every three years (alternately in Africa and China) and is a formalization of China's engagement with Africa. Its model has been copied by others. India, for example, instigated the India–Africa Forum Summit in 2008, which "marked the culmination of India's renewed focus on Africa."[42] Fourteen African countries attended the summit, which gave rise to two declaratory documents: the *India–Africa Framework for Cooperation Forum* and the *Delhi Declaration*. Both documents stressed South-South cooperation, capacity building, and mutual interests. A plan of action was launched, a clear replication of FOCAC's own institutional framework.[43] Subsequent to the summit, New Delhi committed a $5.4 billion credit line over the next five years (rising from $2.15 billion in the past five years), grants worth $500 million and a unilateral opening of the Indian domestic economy to exports from all LDCs. Similarly, in April 2012 the first "Brazil–Africa Forum 2012" met in Johannesburg in September 2012.

This growing interest in Africa has arguably also been reflected by a changing attitude towards a greater inclusion of African voices in international financial institutions. Although ultimately unsuccessful, the very fact that the Nigerian economist Ngozi Okonjo-Iweala led a credible campaign to become president of the World Bank speaks volumes. Setting aside her decidedly orthodox neoliberal position and status as a World Bank insider, along with former Colombian finance minister Jose Antonio Ocampo, Okonjo-Iweala helped create the bank's first-ever competitive race for the presidency. That an African was one of the candidates—*and was taken seriously*—is noteworthy. Previously, the World Bank Group's Annual Meeting in 2008 agreed on reforms that created an additional Chair at the World Bank Board for Africa. The continent has become "increasingly assertive in international forums and aware of its influence" as a region, making up nearly 25 percent of the world's countries, and thus is a potentially significant bloc.[44]

For its part, the IMF has been discussing reforming its voting structure in order to better reflect the contemporary world, rather than the world as it was when the organization was founded. As part of this process, it was suggested that emerging economies would be granted increasing voting weight. Interestingly, African countries "reacted furiously" to such proposals and argued that this would give undue priority to emerging countries "while delaying action to give the world's poorest countries greater influence over the body that often dictates their economic policies."[45] Rather than endorse the proposal in the spirit of South-South solidarity, African elites argued that such plans would leave them in an even weaker and more dependent position than ever. Although they ultimately stalled (the United States Congress refused to ratify the quota increase), such discussions do reflect a changing global reality. The plan is to make China the third-largest voting member and revise the IMF's board to reduce Europe's dominance as "part of a broader plan by the IMF to recognize within the organization the growing economic clout of emerging economies."[46]

However, the reforms, supposed to be introduced in late 2012, were, at the time of writing, held up by interminable wrangling over the formula used to decide voting weight. What such developments indicate is that emerging economies' elites are more and more pressing for some reform of global relations, albeit in problem-solving terms. Africa's support in such questions is actively sought, although there remains no common African position and the African Union (AU) continues to have no serious strategy for managing the continent's burgeoning relationships.

Towards an African century?

As noted, Africa's generalized robust economic performance (in terms of growth) has coincided with increasing engagement with emerging economies. The diversification of Africa's international relations has been increasingly influenced by the shift in relative capabilities to those states. The financial crisis of 2008 had potentially significant repercussions for the international system in that a shift in material capabilities from traditional to emerging powers appeared evident, not least in the absolute need by the guardians of the global liberal order to incorporate new partners from the South to legitimize the overall system. The debate over IMF quota shares and a reliance on emerging actors to provide capital injections in order to stabilize the global economy reflect this.[47] The very decision to expand the G8 to the G20 as the key international institution to discuss future economic global governance was a further manifestation of these processes.

Until the turn of the century, it would be fair to say that many African economies were dependent on the Northern-based international financial institutions (IFIs) for establishing key ideas and approaches to their development models *and* for access to capital and policy advice. This has now changed somewhat. The emerging economies' rise in material capabilities, and their incorporation into the key global governance architecture, has given rise to the notion that Africa's international relations are in a process of change, perhaps away from the North and towards the South, with attendant debates over the possibility of alternative models of development. Certainly, the potential ability to access different methodologies and new ideas concerning developmental thinking could possibly lessen Africa's dependence on the IFIs and their conditionalities.[48] Although conditionalities can be seen as reflecting neocolonial impulses—and the policy advice has been rigidly doctrinaire in its application of neoliberal prescriptions—it is uncertain that shifting to *no* conditions is better, given the governance modalities of many African states. Equally, the environmental and social models on which the emerging economies base their rise (intensified labor and environmental exploitation and a free rein to capital) hardly add up to a superior alternative.

As Africa is routinely ranked the most corrupt region of the world, a hands-off approach by the BRICS over matters related to governance is unhelpful, not least because such an approach discounts new means of dealing with the ethical challenges raised by processes of underdevelopment. Indeed, by not practicing political conditionality at the same time as broadly advocating a policy of non-interference in domestic affairs, the BRICS risk undermining even the most tentative transformation of contemporary practices of global governance. Furthermore, a set of new relationships based on the intensification of natural resource extraction will be equally problematic. One of the key lessons for Africa from the financial crisis was that those countries that were more diversified generally tended to be more resilient than those that were highly dependent on a few primary commodities.[49] Re-inscribing African dependence on commodities hardly offers a novel framework to emerging relationships with Africa and undermines the BRICS' claims to be somehow "different." Even if the emphasis placed by some of the BRICS on addressing structural bottlenecks in Africa has been beneficial for the continent, new roads and railways in the absence of serious reforms are unlikely to make a sustainable and long-term contribution.

This returns us to the question as to whether emerging economies' increasing engagement with Africa is exploitative or benign. This question can only be answered in a contextual manner, dependent on which actor from which emerging economy and in which sector of which country in Africa is being discussed. But it is important to remember that actors such as the BRICS have increased engagement with Africa as a means to achieve their own economic and political goals and that, overall, Africa remains the weaker partner. This weakness is usually ascribed to the continent's dependent relationship in the international system and Africa's historic insertion into the global capitalist economy. However, dependence is "a historical process, a matrix of action," that permits the prospect of alteration stemming from changes in the dynamics, processes, and organization of the international system and the fundamental tendencies within Africa's political economy.[50] Current emergent trends, such as robust economic growth and an increasing diversification of the continent's international relations may play important roles in this regard, yet massive challenges remain. Africa's world market share in processing industries is extraordinarily low: SSA exports just 0.9 and 0.3 percent of world light and heavy manufacturing exports, respectively.[51] The bulk of the growth in African exports in the last decade or more has been heavily underpinned by mining-related commodities, deeply problematic in terms of development. After all, the export growth that the Asian economies used to leapfrog development was based on an increasing list of manufactures. Africa is nowhere near that position.

This closer engagement does present the prospect of greater autonomy for African elites. However, the dynamics of this agency are conditioned both by the practices and nature of external partners, as well as by the different histories, sovereignty regimes, properties, and capacities of African states. In more successful states such as Ethiopia, Ghana, and Rwanda, it would appear that neo-patrimonialism "is a 'good enough' form of governance for economic development."[52] Although Africa has possibly never been in a stronger bargaining position than at present, the key question remains: how can African leaders take advantage for the benefit of the ordinary citizen? Currently, this does not seem to be happening. A recent Afrobarometer survey revealed that despite a decade of strong GDP growth and the incessant narrative of an "Africa Rising," there is "a wide gap in perceptions between ordinary Africans and the global economic community," where "a majority (53%) rate the current condition of their national economy as 'fairly' or 'very bad,'" and only "one in three Africans (31%) think the condition of their national economies has improved in the past year, compared to 38% who say things have gotten worse." Notably, when it came to their own elites, "Africans give their governments failing marks for economic management (56% say they are doing 'fairly' or 'very badly'), improving the living standards of the poor (69% fairly/very badly), creating jobs (71% fairly/very badly), and narrowing income gaps (76% fairly/very badly)."[53] As Hofmeyr notes, "popular opinion is thus increasingly out of sync with the 'Africa Rising' narrative that has been gaining traction among government officials and international investors."[54]

"A hopeful continent"?

As mentioned, the trope around Africa has shifted from one extreme to another. Now, it is "A hopeful continent."[55] The mood swing about Africa is "due, directly or indirectly, to the increasing global demand for the continent's resources: notably for oil, but also for gas, minerals, and other energy sources. This was driven, above all, by the sudden appearance of China as a world economic actor, whose dramatic burst of late industrialization fuelled a global upswing."[56] This has been missed by the Africa Rising mantra, which prefers to construct endogenous factors as drivers. Yet as Bond notes:

> Ongoing resource extraction by Western firms was joined, and in some cases overtaken, by China [and others] … Still, Africa's subordinate position did not change, and aside from greater amounts of overseas development aid flowing into fewer than 15 "fragile states", the North-South flows were not to Africans' advantage. One would not know this from reading reports by the elite multilateral institutions in 2011, which celebrated the continent's national economies as among the world's leading cases of post-meltdown economic recovery.[57]

The flip-flop regarding the continent has, to a certain extent, refuted the familiar media images of fly-blown children that so dominate much discussion of Africa. This *is* a good thing. Yet equally, the narrative has swung almost entirely in the opposite direction, with little critical reflection. Growths in GDP and opportunities for investors are the new intonations in a crude binary construction of Africa that has shifted almost overnight from basket case to bonanza.

The Africa Rising discourse neglects a most fundamental context: "only for nine of the forty three [Sub-Saharan] countries were growth rates during 1980–2008 high enough to double per capita income in less than thirty years, and only sixteen in less than one hundred years.

Performance would have been considerably worse had it not been for the brief years of relatively rapid growth in the mid-2000s."[58] Africa needs to grow at least 7 percent a year for the next 20 or 30 years if any serious tackling of continental poverty is to be realized. However, growth induced by commodity prices increases, new discoveries of natural resources, or increases in sources of foreign capital "is simply not sustainable."[59]

What GDP growth that has occurred is overwhelmingly characterized by the deployment and inflow of capital-intensive investment for the extraction and exportation of natural resources. There is a conspicuous lack of value added on the African side. Indeed, "The principal focus of this activity is in oil, which not only offers limited opportunities for local employment, but also deliberately and actively seeks to avoid the hiring of African labor for fear of encountering resistance and the costs of appeasing affected local communities."[60] Problematically:

> while the hope of the development literature has been that higher rates of inflow of capital investment will have downstream effects on African employment (through increased government revenues and spending alongside an injection of consumer wealth into local economies), there is little evidence that this will take place on a substantial scale. The fundamental reason for this is that the [growth] rests heavily on the engagements of foreign governments and corporations with African elites.[61]

In *most* neopatrimonial administrations, of which Africa has many, sustainable and broad-based development is unlikely to occur.[62]

In late 2012, the Deputy Executive Secretary of the Economic Commission for Africa noted that the relatively good economic growth performance over the past decade had been driven mostly by non-renewable natural resources and high commodity prices. Alongside this, he noted, deindustrialization had been a key feature, with the share of manufacturing in Africa's GDP falling from 15 percent in 1990 to 10 percent in 2008, going hand-in-hand with an increase in unemployment.[63] McMillan and Rodrik[64] in fact show that, since 1990, Africa has experienced a relative shift in the composition of employment toward sectors that create too few high productivity jobs. Manufacturing growth has been near the bottom in 12 growth sectors—only public administration lagged behind.

This of course is not to write off the recent growth as devoid of any value at all. At the minimum, improved fiscal space is being generated. Retail sectors are growing, with revenue increasing by around 4 percent per year, and there is growing investment in infrastructure.[65] Given that there is a correlation "between infrastructure and export diversification, and the current low levels and distorted composition of exports from SSA are partly due to poor trade infrastructure," it can be stated that the improvement in infrastructure "has *per se* a positive impact on SSA growth and trade capacity."[66] Africa's debts have fallen, partly thanks to the Heavily Indebted Poor Countries Initiative (HIPC) and the Multilateral Debt Relief Initiative (MDRI), and partly because of improved management (although it should be noted that "in spite of the HIPC initiative, only half of SSA countries have witnessed a temporary reduction of their annual debt service").[67] In social sectors, performance is varied but increases in the years of schooling are reported across the continent, albeit unevenly. Health outcomes, particularly life expectancy at birth, have also generally improved, in some countries substantially. These are all obviously to be welcomed.

However, it is a contention of this chapter that there is a desperate need to convert natural resources and high commodity prices into structural change, "defined as an increase in the share of industry or services in the economy, or as the diversification and sophistication of exports...or as the shift of workers from sectors with low labor productivity to those with high labor productivity."[68] This is not happening. Instead, with the arrival of emerging economies in Africa alongside traditional trade associates, historical processes of underdevelopment are in danger of being further entrenched. There has been a huge rise in commodity prices and this has contributed in a big way to Africa Rising, if taken as an increase in GDP per capita, but the benefit to African economies in terms of providing a sustained platform for development is far more muted.

Indeed, the drivers of Africa's "recovery" during the second half of the 2000s appear to have been a commodity price boom, debt relief, and a decline in domestic conflicts.[69] World Bank figures with regard to the annual percentage growth rate of GDP at market prices, based on constant local currency (for all income levels, rounded up), compared with the movement of the Commodity Price Index (CPI) reveals this intimate link (Table 8.1).

The years when SSA's growth figures surpassed 1996 levels (2004–08) can be demonstrably linked to the period when emerging economies began to hugely demand commodities, as reflected in the CPI. In the energy realm, concern over predicted declines in petroleum reserves, apprehensions over the so-called peak oil scenario, instability in the Middle East and oil price speculation, placed further upward pressure on prices, peaking in 2008. This reality is qualitatively different from

Table 8.1 Correlation between GDP growth for SSA and the Commodity Price Index (CPI)

	1990	1991	1992	1993	1994	1995	1996	1997	1998	1999
GDP growth	1.3	0.9	-0.9	0.4	1.8	3.7	4.9	3.7	2.3	2.4
CPI			52.6	52.5	50.06	58.6	58.7	64.6	51.0	43.3

	2000	2001	2002	2003	2004	2005	2006	2007	2008	2009
GDP growth	3.7	3.7	3.5	4.4	6.4	5.8	6.1	6.9	5.0	1.9
CPI	59.4	61.9	50.1	66.3	69.1	86.7	113.1	112.9	162.4	102.4

	2010	2011	2012
GDP growth	4.9	4.5	4.2
CPI	146.1	182.1	188.4

Sources: World Bank, IMF data.

the picture of Africa Rising, where "spectacularly right" policies have driven growth. Official reports from international organizations have at times bolstered this latter interpretation, postulating Africa's "economic resurgence" as being hinged on the ability of the continent to recover from the global crisis relatively quicker than other areas of the world.[70] While true in and of itself, Africa's growth record over the last 10 years or so has occurred within the context of *overall* global growth. In this regard, Africa's growth has only been around 1 percent higher than the world average: credible, but not fantastic.[71]

Despite the celebration of improved governance across the continent and the attempts to link this to Africa's recent growth spurt, there is little evidence that overall the quality of Africa's democracies is improving or that governance is dramatically on the up and up across the continent. The composite Mo Ibrahim Index of African Governance had a continental average of 47/100 in 2000—by 2013 it had increased to 51.6/100—hardly seismic and in fact, less than half (43 percent) of people living in Africa live in a country which has shown overall governance improvement since 2010.[72] This makes nonsense of strident claims that:

> What took the UK centuries can now be a matter of decades, even years … Today Africa has the greatest room to boom on the back of two centuries of global progress … In other words, Africa is ideally poised to leapfrog centuries of industrial development … It has an added advantage in that it does not have to carry baggage from the past.[73]

In this analysis, (yet another) commodity-driven boom in Africa, this time in part propelled by emerging economies, wipes the historical slate clean, makes dependent relationships and unequal terms of trade vanish instantaneously, and positions the continent to reach OECD status virtually overnight. Of course, not all emerging economies' involvement in Africa revolves around commodities; that would be a crude caricature. But commodities certainly dominate BRICS–Africa trade (Table 8.2).

Such a situation further reinforces and helps underpin the overall structure of Africa's insertion into the global economy. The BRICS certainly did not create this milieu, but their current trade profile with the continent promotes the reification of existing and ongoing developments. Regardless of the nuances of these relations, it is true that actors from both the global North and South are now actively pursuing closer engagement with Africa. This provides the elites of the continent opportunities to extract leverage in return for access; which may

Table 8.2 Key product composition of BRICS imports from Africa (percentage share, 2010)

	Brazil	Russia	India	China	South Africa
Mineral fuels, oil, etc.	85		71	65	76
Ores, slag, ash		3	2	14	
Precious stones, metals	1		13	4	6
Copper				6	3
Fertilizers	5		1		
Edible fruit and nuts		29	2		
Cocoa		16			
Tobacco		9			
Inorganic chemicals	1	8	4	1	

or may not be a good thing, depending on the conjectural circumstances in each state formation and the nature of their external partners. It cannot be taken for granted that actors from the emerging economies, or African elites themselves, are genuinely interested in furthering Africa's developmental priorities.

Conclusion

This chapter has examined whether or not Africa's economic revival, led by rising global commodity prices and the dramatically increased engagement of the BRICS, in particular China, with the continent over the last decade, has or will lead to any kind of wider structural transformation. The role of the BRICS in Africa has received an enormous amount of attention, largely because of its implications for the nature of politics, development, and governance on the continent. Indeed, it has been suggested that the rise of the BRICS is not only significantly reshaping global governance, but so too the outlook for African development. Needless to say, their influence is nuanced and deeply contextual, as each of these powers has been "anxious to maintain open access for its investments and access to resources and markets," while being "less prescriptive and intrusive about the precise content of economic policy outside of these parameters."[74] Africa's international relations might have diversified considerably, but what are striking are the continuities which mark the governance matrix. Growth on the continent remains dependent on international commodity prices, investment in its extractive sectors, and continued foreign aid inflows. Against this backdrop, the limitations of the BRICS as states increasingly central to the functioning and shaping of patterns of global governance, and thus the ethical challenges of global poverty and insecurity, can be better understood.

As long as resource-based commodities continue to form the bulk of African exports, even if they have led to an increase in income for some African countries (or their elites), "By diverting resources from non-raw material sectors and contributing to real exchange-rate appreciation, a price boom runs the risk of locking developing-country commodity exporters into what Leamer called the 'raw-material corner', with little scope for industrial progress or skills advancement."[75] Given Africa's factor endowments being concentrated in commodities and its export profile and sector concentration being in the same, the raw material corner has been the continent's broad fate. As Afari-Gyan suggests:

> During colonisation and the period immediately after, the structure of external trade of African countries were mainly determined by the needs of the colonial masters. African countries mainly exported natural resources such as timber and minerals and imported manufactured goods. About six decades later, this structure of trade has not been significantly altered. Invariably, African countries have continually and consistently not managed to diversify trade into manufactured products.[76]

The result has been what Shivji terms "structural disarticulation," whereby Africa exhibits a "disarticulation between the structure of production and the structure of consumption. What is produced is not consumed and what is consumed is not produced."[77]

There is no doubt that the exponential growth of the emerging economies has helped stimulate the global commodity booms of the past decade.[78] This is important given that labor-intensive agricultural and manufactured goods do not feature significantly in the exports of African countries to these economies. This dependence is a two-edged sword. Countries with the highest economic integration with the BRICS generally managed to sustain growth during the global downturn, compared with a contraction observed in countries with the least ties. Interestingly, the risk analysis company Maplecroft released in 2011 its *Emerging Powers Integration Index Series*, assessing the economic integration of 180 countries with each of the BRICS.[79] According to

Maplecroft, the countries most integrated with the BRICS are resource-rich developing economies, which provide the raw materials to fuel economic growth back in the BRICS' domestic economies. Of these, many are located in Africa. Zimbabwe was ranked joint 1st, Liberia 5th, Guinea-Bissau 6th, Zambia 7th, DR Congo 10th, Mozambique 12th, Mauritania 15th, Congo 18th, and Sudan 20th. While the data showed which countries stood to gain most from the economic rise of the BRICS, it also revealed just how vulnerable some countries were if the BRICS' rise encountered difficulties. As Alyson Warhurst, CEO of Maplecroft noted, "should growth in the BRICs economies falter or lead to internal unrest and repression, we could see contagion spread to those countries that are most highly integrated with the emerging powers."[80] A similar point is made in the following commentary:

> [T]he positive effect of the world business cycle suggests that the economic performance of African countries is sensitive to world markets. Specifically, this result provides strong support for the hypothesis of the dependence of African countries' economic growth on the economic growth of industrialised nations. This implies that a relatively high degree of integration of African countries with the world economy carries some benefits in as far as the industrialised countries continue to grow. However, should industrialised countries suffer economic setbacks, this could have adverse impacts on the African economies.[81]

Exports from Africa to both traditional and non-traditional trading partners exhibit a very clear and continuous pattern in terms of commodity structure with extractive commodities dominating. In short, such processes are simply the diversification of dependency, with Africa being further trapped into low value-added production structures. This is hardly congruent with the idea of Africa Rising; nor, given the neo-patrimonial nature of local political economies, does it imply any substantive change in development outcomes for the majority of Africans.

Notes

1 Bilge Erten and José Antonio Ocampo, "Super Cycles of Commodity Prices Since the Mid-Nineteenth Century," *World Development* 44 (2013): 14.
2 Yilmaz Akyüz, *The Staggering Rise of The South?* (Geneva: South Centre, 2012).
3 *The Economist*, 3 December 2011.
4 Jean-Michel Sévérino and Olivier Ray, *Africa's Moment* (Cambridge: Polity Press, 2001).

5   Edward Miguel, *Africa's Turn?* (Cambridge, Mass.: MIT Press, 2009).
6   Robert Rotberg, *Africa Emerges* (Cambridge: Polity Press, 2013).
7   Duncan Clarke, *Africa's Future: Darkness to Destiny: How the Past Is Shaping Africa's Economic Evolution* (New York: Profile Books, 2012).
8   Steven C. Radelet, *Emerging Africa: How 17 Countries are Leading the Way* (Washington DC: Centre for Global Development, 2010).
9   Howard W. French, "The Next Asia is Africa: Inside the Continent's Rapid Economic Growth," *Atlantic Monthly*, 21 May 2012, 3.
10 Alwyn Young, "The African Growth Miracle," *Journal of Political Economy* 120, no. 4 (August 2012): 696–739.
11 *African Business*, 7 January 2013: 16, http://africanbusinessmagazine.com/profiles-and-interviews/profile/why-africa-will-rule-the-21st-century/.
12 "Africa Rising—A Hopeful Continent," *The Economist*, 2 March 2013.
13 David Matean, *Africa: The Ultimate Frontier Market: A Guide to the Business and Investment Opportunities in Emerging Africa* (Petersfield: Harriman House Publishing, 2012).
14 Charles Robertson, *The Fastest Billion: The Story Behind Africa's Economic Revolution* (London: Renaissance Capital, 2012).
15 Ernst and Young, *It's Time for Africa: Ernst and Young's 2011 Africa Attractiveness Survey* (London: Ernst and Young, 2011).
16 Africa Progress Panel, *Africa Progress Report 2012: Jobs, Justice and Equity: Seizing Opportunity in Times of Global Change* (Geneva: Africa Progress Panel Foundation, 2012), 8.
17 Sarah Bracking and Graham Harrison, "Africa, Imperialism, and New Forms of Accumulation," *Review of African Political Economy* 30, no. 95 (2003): 9.
18 Oscar Rickett, "Is This the Century of Africa's Rise?" 22 January 2013, www.vice.com.
19 Africa Confidential, "*Making the Best of the Boom*," 55, no. 2 (24 January 2014), www.africa-confidential.com/article/id/5184/Making_the_best_of_the_boom.
20 Tom Cargill, *Our Common Strategic Interests: Africa's Role in the Post-G-8 World* (London: Royal Institute of International Affairs, 2011).
21 Ian Taylor, *NEPAD: Towards Africa's Development or Another False Start?* (Boulder, Colo.: Lynne Rienner, 2005).
22 World Economic Forum, World Bank and African Development Bank, *The African Competitiveness Report 2011* (Geneva: World Economic Forum, 2011), 108.
23 Cargill, *Our Common Strategic Interests*, viii.
24 World Economic Forum *et al.*, *The African Competitiveness Report 2011*, 105.
25 Roger Southall, "Scrambling for Africa? Continuities and Discontinuities with Formal Imperialism" in *A New Scramble for Africa? Imperialism, Investment and Development*, Roger Southall and Melber Henning, eds (Scottsville: University of KwaZulu-Natal Press, 2009), 31.
26 Wilson Prichard, "The Mining Boom in Sub-Saharan Africa: Continuity, Change and Policy Implications" in ibid., 254.
27 Sanusha Naidu, Lucy Corkin, and Hayley Herman, "Introduction," *Politikon* 36, no. 1 (2009): 3.
28 Mwangi S. Kimenyi and Zenia A. Lewis, "The BRICs and the New Scramble for Africa" in *Foresight Africa: The Continent's Greatest*

Challenges and Opportunities for 2011, Brookings Institute (New York: Brookings Institute, 2011), 20.

29 Alice N. Sindzingre, "The Ambivalent Impact of Commodities: Structural Change or Status Quo in Sub-Saharan Africa?" *South African Journal of International Affairs* 20, no. 1 (2013): 45.

30 Ernest Aryeetey and Emmanuel Asmah, "Africa's New Oil Economies: Managing Expectations," in *Foresight Africa: The Continent's Greatest Challenges and Opportunities for 2011*, Brookings Institute (New York: Brookings Institute, 2011), 22.

31 *Xinhua*, 22 May 1996.

32 Ibid.

33 He Wenping, "China's Perspective on Contemporary China-Africa Relations," in *China Returns to Africa: A Rising Power and a Continent Embrace*, Chris Alden, Daniel Large, and Ricardo Soares de Oliveira, eds (Cambridge: Cambridge University Press, 2007), 147.

34 *Peoples' Daily*, 11 October 2000.

35 Ibid.

36 Ibid.

37 Ibid.

38 Ibid.

39 Ibid.

40 Ibid.

41 Ibid.

42 Peter Kragelund, "Back to BASICs? The Rejuvenation of Non-traditional Donors' Development Cooperation with Africa," *Development and Change* 42, no. 2 (2011): 596.

43 Ian Taylor, *The Forum on China-Africa Cooperation (FOCAC)* (London: Routledge, 2011).

44 Cargill, *Our Common Strategic Interests*, 43.

45 "African calls on Brown to block IMF reforms," *The Guardian*, 31 August 2006.

46 "Analysis—IMF vote reform bogged down by delays, deadlock," *Reuters*, 8 October 2012.

47 M. Ayhan Kose and Eswar S. Prasad, "Emerging markets come of age," *Finance and Development* (December 2010): 7.

48 Cargill, *Our Common Strategic Interests*, vii.

49 John Mutenyo, "Driving Africa's Growth Through Expanding Exports," in, *Foresight Africa: The Continent's Greatest Challenges and Opportunities for 2011*, Brookings Institute (New York: Brookings, 2011), 29.

50 Jean-Francois Bayart, "Africa in the World: A History of Extraversion," *African Affairs* 99, no. 395 (2000): 234.

51 World Economic Forum *et al.*, *The African Competitiveness Report 2011*, 15.

52 Tim Kelsall, *Business, Politics, and the State in Africa: Challenging the Orthodoxies of Growth and Transformation* (London: Zed Books, 2013), 47.

53 AfricaFocus Bulletin, "Africa: Whose 'Africa Rising'?", 18 October 2013.

54 Jan Hofmeyr, "'Africa Rising'? Popular Dissatisfaction with Economic Management Despite a Decade of Growth," *Afrobarometer, Policy Brief*, no. 2, October 2013: 1.

55 "Africa Rising—A Hopeful Continent," *The Economist*, 2 March 2013.

56 Ibid.

57 Patrick Bond, "Africa's 'Recovery': Economic Growth, Governance and Social Protest," *Africa Insight* 41, no. 3 (2011): 31.
58 John Weeks, "A Study for Trade and Development Report 2010: Employment, Productivity and Growth in Africa South of the Sahara," unpublished paper, Centre for Development Policy and Research, School of Oriental and African Studies, University of London, (2010): 3.
59 K. Y. Amoako, "Transforming Africa: Start Now, We Can't Wait," *African Business*, July 2011, 24.
60 Roger Southall, "The 'New Scramble' and Labour in Africa," *Labour, Capital and Society* 41, no. 2 (2008): 148.
61 Ibid., 149
62 Kelsall, *Business, Politics, and the State in Africa.*
63 *Addis Tribune*, 8 December 2012.
64 Margaret S. McMillan and Dani Rodrik, *Globalization, Structural Change and Productivity Growth*, NBER Working Paper, no. 17143, June 2011.
65 McKinsey Global Institute, *Lions on the Move: The Progress and Potential of African Economies* (London: McKinsey and Company, 2010).
66 Alice N. Sindzingre, "The Ambivalent Impact of Commodities," 44.
67 Mathieu Petithomme, "Much Ado About Nothing? The Limited Effects of Structural Adjustment Programmes and the Highly Indebted Poor Countries Initiative on the Reduction of External Debts in Sub-Saharan Africa: An Empirical Analysis," *African Journal of Political Science and International Relations* 7, no. 2 (2013): 119.
68 Sindzingre, "The Ambivalent Impact of Commodities," 26.
69 Weeks, "A Study for Trade and Development Report 2010," 10.
70 World Economic Forum *et al.*, *The African Competitiveness Report 2011*, v.
71 African Development Bank, *African Economic Outlook 2012* (Paris: OECD Publishing, 2012).
72 Mo Ibrahim Foundation, *2013 Ibrahim Index of African Governance Summary* (Swindon: Mo Ibrahim Foundation, 2013), 24, www.moibrahim foundation.org/downloads/2013/2013-IIAG-summary-report.pdf.
73 "Why Africa Will Rule the 21st Century," *African Business*, 7 January 2013, 19.
74 Pádraig Carmody, *The Rise of the BRICS in Africa: The Geopolitics of South-South Relations* (London: Zed Books 2013), 133.
75 World Economic Forum et al., *The African Competitiveness Report 2011*, 15.
76 Nana Amma Afari-Gyan, "Transforming Africa's Structure and Composition of Trade after the Global Economic Crisis," *Global Trade Alert*, no. 5, May 2010, 6.
77 Issa G. Shivji, *Accumulation in an African Periphery: A Theoretical Framework* (Dar es Salaam: Mkuki na Nyota Publishers, 2009): 59.
78 Jian-Ye Wang, *What Drives China's Growing Role in Africa?*, IMF Working Paper WP/07/211, (Washington, DC: International Monetary Fund, 2007).
79 Maplecroft, *Emerging Powers Integration Report* (Bath: Maplecroft, 2011).
80 Ibid.
81 Prosper F. Bangwayo-Skeete, "Do Common Global Economic Factors Matter for Africa's Economic Growth?" *Journal of International Development* 24 (2012): 312.

9   Russia rising? The normative renaissance of multinational organizations

P. N. Chatterje-Doody

- **Russia's role**
- **Russia's region**
- **Economic activity**
- **Political objectives**
- **Military and security cooperation**
- **Conclusion**

The period since Vladimir Putin's first accession to the Russian presidency has seen multiple attempts at institutionalizing regional and multinational cooperation. These range from those groups formed out of the ashes of the Soviet Union, in which Russia enjoys a privileged role, such as the CIS, to more recent attempts to re-define global associations, including bodies such as the BRICS, where Russia's very belonging has been questioned, and the Eurasian Union, in which Russia will be by far the dominant power—so much so that Hillary Clinton labeled it an attempt to "re-Sovietize" Russia's region.[1] This attempt to broaden Russia's multinational memberships falls within a wider strategy, aimed at advancing global multipolarity, which actually has origins in the Yeltsin period. The most significant advocate for multipolarity, and particularly strategic initiatives between the strategic triangle of Russia, India, and China, was Yevgeny Primakov, Russia's foreign minister from 1996–1998, and Prime Minister from 1998–1999. Primakov's era can be seen as one in which Russia experienced growing disillusionment with its Western partners. Western states' violations of state sovereignty in the name of humanitarian intervention were considered highly selective and hypocritical, especially given strong criticism of Russia's Chechen campaigns. This contributed to a Russian sense that the structures of global governance were increasingly oriented towards the West's new values, at the expense of Russia's longstanding interests.

More fundamentally, it fed the Russian perception, even more prevalent today, that the Western world of casual blasphemy and gay propaganda was entering a state of moral bankruptcy in which not even the most basic values were held sacred. A strategic shift was considered necessary to restore balance to Russia's foreign policy. As well as the strategic triangle, Primakov promoted closer relations with Brazil, resulting in bilateral documents outlining a formula for strategic cooperation.[2] Although the Yeltsin era did not see the full realization of Primakov's initiatives, the groundwork was nonetheless set. The concepts of multipolarity and polycentrism became common refrains in elite rhetoric, and Russia's bilateral cooperation with China and India steadily increased. Multilateral cooperation increased through the Shanghai Cooperation Organization (SCO) and from 2005 this developed into trilateral consultations between Russian, Chinese, and Indian foreign ministers, which now occur on an annual basis.

Recent years have seen further moves to diversify Russia's foreign policy. On the one hand, Russia made its failed overture to the EU in the form of the 2008 draft European Security Treaty, and participated in the short-lived reset with the United States. On the other hand, the Russian leadership has become increasingly concerned with what it sees as the relative decline of the West, and the corresponding rise of emerging powers, among whose number Russia has taken pains to identify itself, despite recurring questions over the plausibility of its belonging. As well as advocating the expansion of the SCO, Russia has been a key player in promoting the BRICS grouping. It also breathed life into what had been a stagnant Eurasian integration project, with Putin's 2011 article in *Izvestia* giving new impetus to the institutionalization of the Eurasian Customs Union (ECU).[3] As this chapter proceeds, it will become clear that there are several issues with the coherence and practical relevance of many of these initiatives, and it is by no means clear that their current format can present a long-term alternative to existing structures of global governance. However, the process of Russia's self-identification is seen to matter and has helped bring about some genuine political changes that have helped it to challenge the pro-Western norms of multinational institutions.

Traditionally, Russian foreign policy has been dominated by its bilateral relations, which often reflect specific conceptions of Russia's role within the relationship. As such role conceptions are in part created and performed within international organizations and institutions, Russia's memberships of multinational bodies can shed light on how its role and position are represented. These representations feed into foreign policy approaches, and increasingly facilitate structural changes in the international arena.

Beginning by introducing some of the insights of role theory, this chapter draws links between the dominant themes in the rhetoric of Russia's ruling elite and Russia's foreign policy activities. However, through its examination of the political elite's conceptions of Russia's role in multinational organizations, it reveals how such organizations form part of a growing normative challenge to the status quo in international relations. Through maintaining an intricate balancing act between its memberships of multiple organizations, Russia is able to play varying roles within different institutional and geographical contexts. This tactic has led to the formation of several partial normative coalitions, aimed at challenging the rationale for the pro-Western perspectives on global governance that are currently dominant. It is from this vantage point as a self-identified rising power that the Russian leadership seeks to preserve its influence, while helping to set the norms for a multipolar future. This has resulted in a normative challenge to the current state of global governance in three areas: the economy, politics, and the military/security arena. In several cases these challenges have brought about visible structural changes.

Russia's role

In a seminal study of 1970, Kalev Holsti found that the ways in which foreign policy-makers articulated their nation's international role (role conceptions) were closely linked to governments' decisions and actions on the international stage (role performance). Roles that seemed to contradict one another could nonetheless operate in tandem in different geographical, topical, or relationship contexts.[4] Thus, role conceptions can be thought of as a short-hand for the norms and expectations foreign policy-makers use to make sense of the world— they operate as a cognitive lens derived from culturally specific ideas.[5]

Several scholars have examined the Russian political elite's approach to roles and/or identity, looking at how actors across the political spectrum represent Russian identity in ways consistent with their political or ideological values, as well as how their differing political persuasions cause them to adopt specific interpretations of recurring themes.[6] In recent times, leading Russian politicians have presented a highly restrictive narrative of Russia's past. With its very limited scope of content and representation, this narrative emphasizes and naturalizes particular identity themes that support the ruling elite's approach to international relations.[7] This chapter builds on existing work by showing how the simultaneous fostering of different roles across regional organizations has enabled the formation of flexible coalitions motivated by normative convictions, which are capable of mounting a threefold challenge to dominant pro-Western perspectives on global governance. Far from being a development of purely theoretical significance, this challenge has had some visible structural implications. Before presenting a detailed analysis of these challenges and their implications across the economic, political and military/security arenas, it is useful to consider some of the recurring themes surrounding Russia's identity and its international role that appear in the discourse of Russia's ruling elite, which inform its activities within multinational organizations.

History as a guide

The importance of learning from Russia's unique past is a theme that recurs frequently in the discourse of Russia's ruling elite. All of the Russian Federation's presidents have explicitly linked Russia's future fortunes to its inheritances from the past, taking care to represent that past in ways that support their preferred policy directions.[8]

Great powerism

Leading political figures agree upon Russia's historical status as a great power.[9] Specific characterizations of this greatness variously focus on sovereignty,[10] territorial integrity,[11] or unity among the peoples of the Russian state.[12]

Instrumentalized citizenry

By comparison to this reification of the state, Russia's citizenry is frequently instrumentalized in the state's service. Ethnic or national identification is characterized as secondary to state belonging, and the citizenry is often portrayed as a resource for national development or state strength. It is recognized that such development often comes at great human cost, as the greatest advances in the country's past have occurred during periods of despotism.[13]

Russia as an international equal

As befitting its great power status, Russia is presented as worthy of equal and respectful treatment by other states.[14] There is a negative appraisal of the EU's apparent monopoly on European values, which neglects Russia's contribution to European culture and the varied traditions of values and moral norms that exist across the continent.[15] Furthermore, senior figures have vocally criticized Western states for double standards.[16]

Eurasian bridge

Much is made of Russia's strategically unique geographical position between Europe and Asia, represented as a key element in Russia's cultural contribution to Europe and the rest of the world.[17] There have even been references to a shared "northern civilization," in light of which the West's moral decline is felt particularly acutely.[18]

First among equals

The Russian political leadership views Russia as having the moral right to leadership of its geographical region, having civilized the Eurasian continent and promoted peaceful ethnic, religious, and linguistic cohabitation—a legacy only made possible by the emphasis Russians have placed on the value of tolerance.[19] This role is reinterpreted for today as the consolidation of soft power through strategic partnerships and coalitions,[20] although this obscures an approach to hard and soft power not as separate tactics for specific situations, but as two points on the same diplomatic continuum. The tendency to elide the approaches may serve to undermine Russia's efforts in this regard.

Russia's region

The CIS represents the first organization to attempt to re-institutionalize regional cooperation following the Soviet collapse. As such, it includes the greatest number of post-Soviet countries, but its value is more symbolic than practical as membership demands only loose commitments, with few coherent shared outcomes.[21] In the economic arena, the Eurasian Economic Community (EurAsEC), which was formed in 2000, is the broadest post-Soviet institution. It was granted observer status at the UN in 2003, and made the subject of a 2007 resolution on cooperation.[22] More recently, it has been the site of the most significant integrative initiative since the Soviet era—the Eurasian Customs Union (ECU), and proposed Eurasian Economic Union (EaEU) that has already formally harmonized the borders, tariffs, and trade regime between its three founder members.

In line with its predicted (and desired) multipolar world order, Russia has also invested significant diplomatic effort in promoting a number of organizations that institutionalize cooperation well beyond the post-Soviet space, and in which it cannot hope to play such a dominant role. For instance, in marketing the BRICS group of nations, recent presidencies have deliberately framed Russia's economic position as that of a resurgent power, newly rising in the global economy. The SCO, whose forerunner was created in 1995, is another forum for economic and infrastructural interaction stretching beyond Russia's immediate region, in which Russian and Chinese influence balance each other out. The organization boasts an extended membership that includes Belarus, Sri Lanka, and Turkey as dialogue partners, and Mongolia, India, Pakistan, Afghanistan, and Iran as observers. Originally conceptualized as a forum for the negotiation of common borders, the SCO remains active in regional security, although it is only the Collective Security Treaty Organization (CSTO), created in 1992, that has a legal basis for the collective use of force.

Russia's balancing act between these various institutions has caused significant tensions, most recently in its relationship with the United States and the EU following renewed commitment to the realization of the ECU (predating the Ukraine crisis). Despite the ensuing analytical complexity, this balancing act nonetheless accurately reflects Russia's preferred "multi-vector" foreign policy.[23] This enables Russia's prized bilateral relationships to be negotiated through the context of various roles across organizations, and facilitates flexible international cooperation without risk to sovereignty (Figure 9.1). The approach assists in the consolidation of a regional power base to strengthen Russia's international position, and enables Russia to take part in normative coalitions that challenge the dominant pro-Western perspective on global governance in three areas: the economy, politics, and the military/security arena.

Economic activity

Reflecting its struggle to reconcile an influential Soviet past with a current diminished economic status, Russia's activities within different institutions display a prioritization of seemingly contradictory roles. Attempts to maintain traditional great power relations contrast with vocal promotion of Russia as one of a band of newly emerging economic powers. Yet, both of these orientations are useful for reinforcing particular aspects of the Russian challenge to contemporary economic governance.

Russia clings to its leading role in the post-Soviet and Eurasian region, and Russian approaches to foreign policy[24] and national

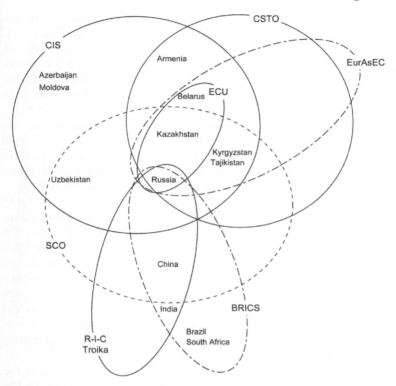

Figure 9.1 Russia in overlapping multinational organizations

security[25] have long reinforced the importance of structured economic interaction across the area, as well as reflecting the link drawn in Putin's doctoral thesis between the state of the economy, particularly in the energy sphere, and state strength.[26] These priorities are evident through the consolidation of the ECU, which had seen little tangible progress since the idea was first put forward in the mid-1990s, but benefited from a great surge following Vladimir Putin's 2011 *Izvestia* article promoting the institution. The union formally removed internal physical border controls between Russia, Belarus, and Kazakhstan, creating a common customs tariff and a regulatory body, the Eurasian Economic Commission.[27] The ECU boasts a joint population of 167 million, GDP of $2 trillion and a goods turnover of $900 billion,[28] and the fully fledged EaEU will come into force on 1 January 2015.[29]

Putin has taken pains to stress that the ECU's legal framework makes provisions for members' WTO obligations and, as such, complements the EU's economic integration projects.[30] However, despite these assertions, it is clear that the development of the ECU represents a normative challenge to the EU's former monopoly on approaches to regional economic integration, which prized democratic conditionality.[31] From the Russian perspective, economic governance should derive from economic interests, not political values. Free from democratic conditionality, the ECU's rules and procedures are nonetheless institution-led, professional, consensual and transparent, and the Commission's decisions automatically become part of the legal base of the ECU and Common Economic Space, without the need for additional ratification.[32] This alternative to EU insistence on democratic conditionality symbolizes Russia's continued push for normative influence. While Belarusian membership of the ECU is a necessity given its economic dependence on Russia, Kazakhstan is an economically strong and self-confident state in its own right, which sees the union ultimately as a route to more markets, and to Russian pipelines for exporting hydrocarbons to Europe.[33] It has voluntarily agreed to harmonize its trade norms with those of Russia, despite economic consequences that appear negative in the short term, including real losses in income, wages, returns on capital, and the commitment to two less economically liberal states.[34] In so doing, it has given Russia evidence of the attractiveness of an integration project devoid of a normative commitment to democratic standards.

Many questions have been raised over the practical relevance of the ECU. Some have charged that the union's apparent early growth figures owed more to Russia's recovery from a GDP slump than trade outcomes,[35] that Kazakhstan and Belarus have suffered economically for Russia's gain,[36] and that exclusions and exemptions to the free trade regime remain, including duties levied on Russian oil sent to Belarus that is not for domestic consumption, and as of 2014, on all oil sent from Russia to Kazakhstan.[37] Nonetheless, several other states, namely Kyrgyzstan, Tajikistan, and Armenia, have announced plans for ECU membership,[38] and Kazakh President Nazarbayev has advocated the organization's further expansion, mentioning Turkey in particular.[39] Despite domestic resistance in the light of events in Ukraine, the Tajik and Kyrgyz Presidents both moved closer to accession at the EaEU treaty signing in May 2014.[40] There is a clear practical consideration here, for leaders who recognize the necessity of good relations with Russia now more than ever. However, there is nonetheless an economic rationale. The common linguistic and educational heritage makes Russia a popular employment destination for Tajik and Kyrgyz workers, who respectively accounted for 16 percent and 7 percent of

Russia's migrant labor force in 2010.[41] With prospective member states heavily reliant on remittances from Russia, there are strong incentives to simplify labor migration.[42]

Sitting alongside such attempts to re-package Russia's longstanding regional leadership and great power status is the apparently contradictory tendency to latch onto the emerging economies in the BRICS. The founding member BRICs are all ranked in the top 10 of global economies, and together represent 15 percent of the world's GDP and more than a 50 percent share in global economic development.[43] However, recent times have seen increasingly frequent questions over the sustainability of the group's developmental model,[44] and of its rise more generally.[45] Yet such questions are blind to an important factor in the group's development, and one which is of particular interest given Russian foreign policy aspirations. The BRICS have arguably evolved from what was essentially a marketing tool to an overtly political project intimately concerned with challenging the dominant norms of global governance.

In spite of criticisms for conceptual incoherence and the unclear basis for membership (a charge that has faced Russia, Brazil, and South Africa),[46] the BRICS have presented united dissatisfaction with the pro-Western perspective on global governance. The group and its members have vocally affirmed their attachment to values of territorial integrity, sovereignty, and to the concept of global multipolarity, which they see as necessary for ensuring economic stability.[47] They have also sought to challenge globalization's inequalities by renegotiating trade and environmental regulations[48] and voting shares in global institutions. Five percent of voting shares in the IMF and three percent in the World Bank were to be re-allocated to developing and emerging economies,[49] and a BRICS development bank has been established that is anticipated to offer an alternative to the conditionality associated with existing institutions.[50]

Russia's leaders are increasingly attempting to ensure an influential role for the country in what is seen as an evolving multipolar, or polycentric global system,[51] by helping to alter the structures of global governance for the future, and by providing the missing link between a stagnant EU and a rising East Asia in the meantime.[52] With this in mind, mobilization of two apparently contradictory roles forms part of a broader strategy of challenging dominant models of multinational governance. At the same time as member states' voters signal their displeasure at the EU's integrative project, Moscow is forging ahead with its alternative model in which moral and ethical dilemmas over internal political representation and democracy are clearly separated from structures of economic governance. Similarly, within BRICS, Russia has helped to promote a more equitable treatment of emerging powers in existing multinational organizations while reiterating their right to exercise sovereignty internally. Through both of these initiatives, Russia has mounted a clear challenge to the normative content of established institutions. Given some of the teething problems and delays that have affected the consolidation of these initiatives, it remains to be seen whether the challenge to the status quo can be translated into a viable alternative system of long-term governance. Yet in the meantime, member states' treatment of the ECU and BRICS *as if* they were globally significant entities has forged outcomes that genuinely are globally significant.

Political objectives

The BRICS challenge extends well beyond international economic organization, as all of the organization's members benefit from regional "power bases and spheres of influence,"[53] and membership of BRICS enables them to cement these positions. Given a negative international reception of the Eurasian project, especially in the aftermath of events in Ukraine, BRICS membership has offered an additional outlet for the roles of leader and cultural bridge. As Russia's envoy to the UN, Vitaly Churkin, stated in the aftermath of a UN vote to declare Crimea's independence referendum invalid, "Russia is not isolated."[54] Russia once acted as a mediator between the BRICS countries and the G8,[55] making the case for greater inclusiveness in global decision-making. In the contemporary climate, Russia can emphasize continued cooperation within BRICS, just as it is being excluded from meetings of the now-G7.[56] The BRICS have so far effectively acted as a great power concert by coordinating their efforts within the G20,[57] and "noted with concern" Australian suggestions that, in light of the Ukraine crisis, President Putin may be excluded from the November 2014 G20 Summit. The statement of the BRICS foreign ministers went on to assert that "[t]he custodianship of the G20 belongs to all Member States equally and no one Member State can unilaterally determine its nature and character."[58] Thus, regardless of individual members' unease over Crimea, the BRICS have made a show of unity.

Leaders of the BRICS countries have gone to great effort to defend the group's importance, and in the case of South Africa, the strategic rationale for its inclusion.[59] Russian politicians have repeatedly and enthusiastically articulated the country's position as a new, rising power within a world that is evolving into multipolarity. This practice is significant not only for reflecting their vision of Russia's international role but also, as we have already seen, for helping to create the structures within which that role is played out. The promise of such significant global influence clearly holds considerable political attraction: Following the admittance of South Africa to the group in 2011, Turkey, Indonesia, and South Korea have all expressed their interest in membership.[60]

A similar process can be witnessed through the activities of the SCO. Although the organization has practical military and economic concerns, one element of its activities that goes under-analyzed is its issuing of statements that have no binding force. These nonetheless have an important political impact, as they serve to produce the Eurasian region as something that is politically meaningful, and so increase the claim of its members to importance on the world stage. This is particularly the case for its two leading members. China appears a regionally responsible great power, and Russia presents itself as the leader of a regional coalition in external negotiations, thus building its international influence.[61]

Aside from the discursive production of a desired world, Russia's membership of multinational organizations is also vital for its consolidation of soft power—economic and normative attractive force. The impact of shared Soviet history and the ongoing legacy of Russian language use and orthodox Christianity greatly assist in Russia's soft power project. Russia's (state-controlled) media outlets are popular in the region and there is widespread acceptance of conservative social values. As these legacy factors will gradually reduce in relevance, the ECU represents the institutionalization of Russia's soft power project for the future.

Despite the leaders of Belarus and Kazakhstan having openly rejected any grand political project, their appetite for a Russian-centered integration project is nonetheless symbolically powerful. Quite aside from its clear economic benefits to Russia, the planned expansion of the union to include Kyrgyzstan and Tajikistan would also entail significant geopolitical gains. Although Kyrgyzstan's GDP is equivalent to less than half of 1 percent of Russia's, its inclusion would extend the union's borders to Tajikistan.[62] As well as helping to bring about Putin's all-important vision of a cooperative space from the EU to the Asia-Pacific,[63] this would secure vital sources of aluminum, cotton, and labor necessary to Russian industry. Although the issue of migrant labor is particularly contentious in today's Russia, Tajik immigration is likely to be more domestically palatable than the Chinese alternative, which many Russians, wary of their own country's demographic decline, fear. Following the Ukraine crisis, a smooth expansion of the ECU is increasingly important to fulfill Moscow's soft power aspirations. However, the popular unease that has emerged in prospective member states demonstrates just one area in which the elision of soft and hard power could prove to be detrimental to Russia's long-term plans. Nonetheless, the respective elites remain engaged, and the Armenian leadership has taken the opportunity to lobby for additional Russian investment prior to its membership.[64] The Kyrgyz Prime Minister has similarly expressed a hope for significant investment from the ECU to facilitate its membership.[65]

The success, so far, of the ECU also has wider political implications, including an impact on Russia's relationships with traditional partners, such as the EU. The two parties struggled to come up with a successor to the Partnership and Cooperation Agreement (PCA) between them, which expired in 2007. Many of those difficulties originally came about because it proved difficult to move beyond the relatively straightforward principles of economic interaction that had formed the basis of the initial agreement, to more substantive agreements on political cooperation, as the disagreement over democratic conditionality showed. The EU, wary of Russia's democratic backsliding, and its increasingly geopolitically motivated foreign policy, sought to achieve a more political successor agreement. Russia, for its part, favored a treaty that would reinforce its international equality, and help to mitigate what it read as a zero-sum neo-colonial aspect to many of the EU's initiatives in the common neighborhood.[66] However, in reserving treaties for members only, the EU made it impossible for Russia to assert itself on equal terms. Thus with the maturation of the ECU, Russia sought to balance out asymmetries in the negotiating process. As well as providing the institutional challenge to the EU's focus on democratic conditionality already discussed, the Eurasian Economic Commission took on practical responsibility for members' talks in trade negotiations. However, this did not have the effect of leveling the playing field that Russia had desired. On a purely theoretical level it would have complicated negotiations by the addition of a second multinational party. Practically, however, the EU failed to recognize the ECU,[67] resulting in a vacuum for representation in the partnership talks.

In some ways, the desire of both sides to conclude a more comprehensive agreement than the PCA actually precluded the conclusion of any agreement at all. While the frozen state of negotiations allowed continued cooperation on specific matters without the need for renegotiating more substantive issues, it represented a significant qualitative retreat in

Russia–EU relations, and one which has only been exacerbated by the current crisis in Ukraine. Together with predictions of Europe's future marginalization in a changing world order, there are clear reasons why Russia seeks to fortify its normative challenge to the EU through the balancing of various other multinational relationships.

Military and security cooperation

Given Russia's inheritance of Soviet hardware, its claim to great power status is most plausible in the military arena. While Russia and the EU have multiple reasons to cooperate on security, including the various frozen conflicts in their overlapping integration space,[68] Russia's inability to defend its great power status in its security relationship with the EU has been a source of significant tension for several years. Both parties have resorted to unilateral action, including the EU's recognition of Kosovo, Russia's recognition of Abkhazia and South Ossetia, and its armed involvements in Georgia (2008) and Ukraine (2014). Importantly, Russia's disillusionment with the established mechanisms of security cooperation had been building long before the Ukraine crisis, and it has made several moves to restore the norms of international relations with which it is most comfortable.

In 2008, then-President Medvedev put forward an initiative to create a new European Security Treaty, which was intended both to demonstrate the coherence of Russia's long-term foreign policy, and to help revitalize the relationship with Europe following the tensions of Putin's first two terms. The draft document reiterated the aspects of international relations frequently invoked by the Russian side—sovereignty, territorial integrity, and criteria for the use of force—and in so doing, seemed to unnecessarily duplicate the Helsinki Final Act of 1975.[69] The initiative received little support, and Russia's great power aspirations were dealt a blow as it was obliged to deal with the very same organizations, including NATO, in which it had expressed a lack of confidence. The episode highlighted incompatibilities between Russia's desire to reorganize the structures of European security and the EU's overall satisfaction with the existing system under the auspices of OSCE and NATO.

The impossibility of any future Russian accession to NATO (and specifically the veto this would afford) is a significant barrier to Russia's great power aspirations within the current structure. In October 2011, Russia's then-envoy to NATO, Dmitry Rogozin (whose current Deputy Prime Minister's portfolio for the defense and aerospace industry earned him a place on the EU's May 2014 sanctions list) stated that the NATO–Russia Council was not performing its required function and that the new president may not be interested in attending its next summit.[70] NATO and Russia continue to view one another as key reference points for security concerns in the region and engage in regular demonstrative military exercises. Similarly, the build-up of Russian troops on Ukraine's borders in 2014 led to an increased NATO presence in Eastern Central Europe. The failure of the European Security Treaty damaged Russia's credibility as an equal European partner, worthy of international respect, and contributed to its pursuit of a multivector approach. In light of events in Ukraine, an emphasis on alternative partners has been a key part of the Russian ruling elite's counter to claims of international isolation.

Russia is the dominant party within the CSTO, an organization which conducts regular military exercises, has a legal basis for collective defense against aggression, and whose 15,000-strong rapid reaction peacekeeping force can theoretically be deployed on members' territory without the need for a UN resolution, provided that the relevant members consent.[71] In reality, the organization's focus has been on increasing foreign policy coordination and military cooperation between its members, with its most significant practical successes being in counter-trafficking operations and in the decision that members must all agree over any foreign military bases being established on its territory. In 2007, the CSTO signed a cooperation agreement with the SCO, perhaps facilitated by the "all-time high" in Russian–Chinese relations that came about during Putin's second term (2004–08) as a response to increased United States unilateralism, missile defense initiatives, and NATO expansion.[72] As attested by the exclusion of the United States from the SCO, Russia and China share an opposition to United States military and economic involvement in Central Asia,[73] and so some have represented the group as an anti-Western coalition.[74] Yet such a perspective is blind to the significant normative content of the organization, whose members share a vocal normative commitment to principles of sovereignty and non-intervention as the cornerstones of effective security. Where civil unrest within member states seems unlikely to spread to the broader region, the SCO is satisfied that it should be treated as a purely domestic matter.[75]

While the annexation of Crimea seems to most outsiders to be a clear violation of these principles, in a Russian reading, the incursion merely helped to maintain order in an area de-stabilized by external provocations. The SCO's members are all highly sensitive to the potential for external actors to foment domestic unrest, which is seen in the aftermath of the color revolutions as a likely route to further regional and regime insecurity. It is for such reasons that while the SCO refused to endorse Russia's 2008 incursions into South Ossetia and Abkhazia, its official response was nonetheless careful, complimenting Russia's active role, but urging dialogue between all parties to diffuse the situation.[76] China's own official response was deliberately late and vague, and domestic, Chinese state media represented the conflict as a justified Russian response to the provocation of an American client state.[77] Similarly, it was with reference to the phenomenon of color revolutions that China's Defense Minister, Chan Wangquan, expressed sympathy with Russia's actions in Crimea, and by contrast to the EU's sanctions, China proved happy to conclude a $400 billion gas deal with Russia in May 2014.[78] Although this might seem strange given the SCO members' emphasis on sovereignty and territorial integrity, it nonetheless reflects their shared fear of external forces destabilizing a region made predictable by studied compromise and consensus-building.

This consensus-based approach to the pursuit of security relations provides another direct contrast to the EU's preferred governance model. Originally concerned with the negotiation of common borders, the SCO has deliberately shunned legalistic approaches, preferring to focus on consensus-building and common interests over legally binding mechanisms. In expanding its remit to regional security more generally, the organization put forward a set of clear, agreed definitions that linked the "three evils" of terrorism, religious extremism, and separatism—something all members have struggled with—in order to facilitate coordinated regional responses.[79] As Stephen Aris points out, in lesser developed states, such as the SCO's Central Asian members, there is a tendency to link regional security, state building, and regime legitimacy. Coupled with the very particular regime models of China and Russia, this helps to explain why many of the SCO's activities are oriented towards regime security.[80] Members feel commonly threatened by transnational regional problems, which form the basis of the SCO's agenda. Some Central Asian analysts have cited figures from the Global Terrorism Database as evidence that the promotion of a regional anti-terrorism agenda is less closely linked to a significant threat, than to a desire to strengthen intra-regional cooperation, or to control civil insurrection.[81] Minority groups have similarly alleged that anti-terrorist initiatives have been used to stifle opposition and curb freedom of religion,[82] something that is entirely compatible with the SCO's normative stance, the broad nature of its linked definitions of the three evils,[83] and also with the prioritization of sovereignty and territorial integrity as key to security. Regardless of Western skepticism, this vision clearly has attractive potential. The organization has numerous potential new members waiting in the wings. Turkish Prime Minister Recep Tayyip Erdogan has made multiple calls for his country's full SCO membership in the context of what he sees as an unenthusiastic EU, and a spokesperson for India's Ministry for External Affairs recently hinted at similar aspirations.[84]

Conclusion

Contemporary Russian foreign policy sees multiple, apparently contradictory roles pursued across overlapping multinational organizations. This multiple-role, multiple-orientation approach has several significant outcomes. In the most basic sense, it shows support for a multipolar world system, the evolution of which Russia's political elite both anticipates and craves. It also helps to bring about changes that make the realization of such a system more plausible. For Russia, the diversification of governance structures represents the best hope for retaining significant global influence. By translating its overlapping organizational memberships into partial normative coalitions, Russia is able to contribute to the agenda for a multipolar future by challenging the dominant pro-Western perspectives on global governance in three areas: the economy, politics, and the military/security arena.

In the field of the economy, Russia has used its privileged regional role to champion the ECU, an institution which represents a clear normative challenge to the EU's model of regional economic integration, and its emphasis on shared democratic standards. At the other end of the scale, Russia's membership of BRICS has helped in the articulation of inequities in the pro-Western perspective on global governance, and is leading to structural alterations that favor newly rising powers.

Politically, also, Russia has benefited from its membership of both the BRICS group and the SCO. As these organizations appear to take on a globally significant role, they have increased the regional and international political influence of both the respective groups, and their individual members. For Russia, such gains can be seen as closely linked to its broader soft power project, for which the development of the ECU remains vital. Russia has translated some of the institutional inheritances of its past into a format of use in the present, both for demonstrating Russia's continued regional attractiveness (and thus global relevance), and creating a viable alternative to some of its more strained international relationships.

Finally, Russia has used its membership of multinational organizations to challenge the dominant mechanisms of security cooperation in Europe, and to promote a return to norms including sovereignty, territorial integrity and non-intervention—but significantly, these norms are sought beyond the military sphere. Thus, where foreign campaigning or intervention in Russia's immediate vicinity is suspected, this is interpreted by Russia as a violation of these principles, a threat to regional and regime security, and a provocation. Such an understanding can help to shed light on Russia's heavy-handed responses to perceived threats in Georgia (2008) and Ukraine (2014). The SCO's interlinked definitions of regional threats have been used by members to justify combined responses to them, often to the detriment of civil liberties. They have also helped the organization to put forward a position relatively acquiescent to Russia's actions. This corresponds with the organization's qualitatively different take on security relations— that the consensus and common interests of the organization's members should be valued above legally binding commitments.

For Western commentators, there has so far been a temptation to view these developments as the hollowing out of multinational organizations, or as the formation of loose interest-based bodies where the absence of shared normative values will impede the potential for collaboration or longevity. However, as the analysis presented in this chapter demonstrates, there are some genuine normative convictions shared between members of many of these organizations, with common concerns over the threats that the current configuration of international relations permits. They have already made various impacts on the structures of international politics that are likely to be lasting. For Russia, the balancing of different roles across multiple multinational organizations is the safest way in which it can hope to retain a globally influential voice and secure a position as one of the architects of the multipolar world order that it seeks.

Notes

1 Radio Free Europe/Radio Liberty, *Clinton Calls Eurasian Integration an Effort to 'Re-Sovietize,'* www.rferl.org/content/clinton-calls-eurasian-integration-effort-to-resovietize/24791921.html.
2 Amresh Chandra, "Strategic Triangle among Russia, China and India: Challenges and Prospects," *Journal of Peace Studies* 17, nos. 1–2 (2010): 40–60; Vladimir Davydov, "The Role of Brazil, Russia, India and China (BRIC) in the reconstruction of the international order," *Megatrend Review* 5, no. 1 (2008): 88; Andrei Tsygankov, "What is Russia to us? Westernisers and Sinophiles in Russian Foreign Policy," *Russie Nei Visions* 45 (2009).

3   S. Blockmans, H. Kostanyan, and I. Vorobiov, "Towards a Eurasian Economic Union: The challenge of integration and unity," *CEPS Special Report* 75 (December 2012).
4   Kalev J. Holsti, "National role conceptions in the study of foreign policy," *International Studies Quarterly* 14, no. 3 (1970): 233–309.
5   Lisbeth Aggestam, *Role conceptions and the politics of identity in foreign policy*, ARENA, www.deutsche-aussenpolitik.de/resources/seminars/gb/app roach/document/wp99_8.htm.
6   See Glenn Chafetz, "The struggle for a national identity in post-Soviet Russia," *Political Science Quarterly* 111, no. 4 (1996/7); Ted Hopf, "Identity, legitimacy, and the use of military force: Russia's great power identities and military intervention in Abkhazia," *Review of International Studies* 31, no. S1 (2005); N.M. Mukharyamov, "Ethnicity and the study of international relations in the post-soviet Russia," *Communist and Post-Communist Studies* 37, no. 1 (2004); Valery Tishkov, *Ethnicity, Nationalism and Conflict in and After the Soviet Union: The Mind Aflame* (London: Sage Publications Limited, 1997).
7   P.N. Chatterje-Doody, "Harnessing History: Narratives, Identity and Perceptions of Russia's Post-Soviet role," *Politics* 34, no. 2 (2014).
8   Boris Yeltsin, "Inaugural Speech," *Foreign Policy Bulletin* 2, no. 1 (1991); Vladimir Putin, "Inaugural Speech, 2000," http://archive.kremlin.ru/eng/ text/speeches/2000/05/07/0002_type82912type127286_128852.shtml; Vladimir Putin, "Inaugural Address, 2004," http://archive.kremlin.ru/eng/text/sp eeches/2004/05/07/1255_type82912type127286_64132.shtml; Dmitry Medvedev, "Inaugural Speech, 2008," http://archive.kremlin.ru/eng/speeches/ 2008/05/07/1521_type82912type127286_200295.shtml.
9   Medvedev, "Inaugural Speech"; Putin, "Inaugural Address"; Putin, "Inaugural Speech"; Yeltsin, "Inaugural Speech."
10 Yeltsin "Inaugural Speech"; Vladislav Surkov, "Natsionalizatsia budushchego," *Ekspert* 43, no. 537 (2006).
11 Putin, "Inaugural Address."
12 Yeltsin, "Inaugural Speech"; Putin, "Inaugural Speech"; Putin, "Inaugural Address"; Medvedev, "Inaugural Speech."
13 Putin, "Inaugural Address"; Yeltsin, "Inaugural Speech"; Surkov, "Natsionalizatsia budushchego (Nationalisation of the Future)"; Medvedev, "Inaugural Speech"; Dmitry Medvedev, "Rossiya Vpered!" www.kremlin. ru/transcripts/5413.
14 Yeltsin, "Inaugural Speech"; Medvedev, "Inaugural Speech"; Putin, "Inaugural Address"; Putin, "Inaugural Speech."
15 Surkov, "Natsionalizatsia budushchego."
16 Russia Today, "Russia hits back at US 'barefaced cynicism and double standards' over Ukraine," http://rt.com/news/state-department-putin-list-234/; Tom Parfitt "Vladimir Putin accuses Britain and US of double standards," *The Telegraph*, 2012, www.telegraph.co.uk/news/worldnews/vladim ir-putin/9526300/Vladimir-Putin-accuses-Britain-and-US-of-double-standa rds.html.
17 Ministry of Foreign Affairs (MFA), *National Security Concept of the Russian Federation*, Moscow, www.mid.ru/ns-osndoc.nsf/0e9272befa34209743256 c630 042d1aa/b8d88f7503bc644fc325752e0047174b?OpenDocument;   Vladimir

Putin, "Annual Address to the Federal Assembly of the Russian Federation, 2007," http://archive.kremlin.ru/text/appears/2007/04/125339.shtml.

18 Gregory P. Lannon, "Russia's New Look Army Reforms and Russian Foreign Policy," *The Journal of Slavic Military Studies* 24, no. 1 (2011): 31.

19 Vladimir Putin, "Annual Address to the Federal Assembly of the Russian Federation, 2005," http://archive.kremlin.ru/text/appears/2005/04/87049. shtml; Surkov, "Natsionalizatsia budushchego."

20 Ibid.; Medvedev, "Rossiya Vpered!".

21 Olga Shumylo-Tapiola, "The Eurasian Customs Union: Friend or Foe of the EU?" *Carnegie*, http://carnegieendowment.org/2012/10/03/eurasia n-customs-union-friend-or-foe-of-eu/dyir.

22 EurAsEC, *Osnovye Itogi funktsionirovaniia Tamozhennogo soiuza v ram-kakh EvrAzES i pervoocherednye zadachi na 2011–2012 gody*, 2011, no. 80.

23 MFA, *National Security Strategy of the Russian Federation to 2020*, www. ln.mid.ru/ns-osndoc.nsf/0e9272befa34209743256c630042d1aa/8abb3c17eb3 d2626c32575b500320ae4?OpenDocument II.9.

24 FAS, *Foreign Policy Concept of the Russian Federation, 2000*, www.fas.org/ nuke/guide/russia/doctrine/econcept.htm, 2000; Kremlin, *Foreign Policy Concept of the Russian Federation*, http://archive.kremlin.ru/eng/text/docs/2008/ 07/204750.shtml; Ministry of Foreign Affairs, *Foreign Policy Concept of the Russian Federation, 2013*, www.mid.ru/brp_4.nsf/0/76389FEC168189 ED442 57B2E0039B16D.

25 MFA, *National Security Concept*; MFA, *National Security Strategy*.

26 Kevork Oskanian, *FPC Briefing: Putin's Eurasian Union- from pre-electoral sideshow to quest for empire?*, http://fpc.org.uk/fsblob/1561.pdf.

27 Rilka Dragneva and Katarina Wolczuk, *Briefing Paper—Russia, the Eurasian Customs Union and the EU: Cooperation, Stagnation or Rivalry?* (London: Chatham House, 2012); Arkady Moshes, "Will Ukraine Join (and Save) the Eurasian Customs Union?", 247, *PONARS Policy Memo* (2013).

28 Igor Krotov, "Customs Union between the Republic of Belarus, the Republic of Kazakhstan and the Russian Federation within the framework of the Eurasian Economic Community," *World Customs Journal* 5, no. 2 (2011): 129–138.

29 Radio Free Europe/Radio Liberty, *Russia, Kazakhstan, Belarus sign treaty creating Economic Union*, www.rferl.org/content/putin-in-astana-to-in k-eurasia-economic-union/25402319.html.

30 Francisco Carneiro, "What Promises Does the Eurasian Customs Union Hold for the Future?", *World Bank Economic Premise* (2013); Iwona Wisniewska, *The Customs Union of Belarus, Kazakhstan and Russia: a way to strengthen Moscow's position in the region*, 146, *IPSI Analysis* (2012); Shumylo-Tapiola, *The Eurasian Customs Union*.

31 Dragneva and Wolczuk, *Briefing Paper—Russia, the Eurasian Customs Union and the EU*.

32 Wisniewska, *The Customs Union of Belarus, Kazakhstan and Russia: a way to strengthen Moscow's position in the region*.

33 Moshes, "Will Ukraine Join (and Save) the Eurasian Customs Union?"

34 Carneiro, "What Promises Does the Eurasian Customs Union Hold for the Future?"

35 Moshes, "Will Ukraine Join (and Save) the Eurasian Customs Union?"

36 Ibid.; Carneiro, "What Promises Does the Eurasian Customs Union Hold for the Future?"
37 Wisniewska, *The Customs Union of Belarus, Kazakhstan and Russia: a way to strengthen Moscow's position in the region.*
38 Shumylo-Tapiola, *The Eurasian Customs Union*; Radio Free Europe/Radio Liberty, *Kyrgyzstan To Join Russian-Led Customs Union, Ukraine To Observe*, www.rferl.org/content/kyrgyzstan-ukraine-russia-customs-union/25001114.html; Lukas Alpert, "Armenia to Join Russian-led Customs Union and Eurasian Economic Union," *Wall Street Journal*, http://online.wsj.com/article/BT-CO-20130903-705259.html.
39 President of Kazakhstan, *Press-briefing following the participation at the Fourth Summit of the Cooperation Council of the Turkic Speaking States*, www.akorda.kz/en/page/page_216973_.
40 Radio Free Europe/Radio Liberty, *Russia, Kazakhstan, Belarus sign treaty.*
41 Irina Sinitsina, *Economic Cooperation between Russia and Central Asian Countries: Trends and Outlook*, University of Central Asia Institute of Public Policy and Administration, www.ucentralasia.org/downloads/UCA-IPPA-WP5-RussiaInfluence-Eng.pdf.
42 Christopher Hartwell, "A Eurasian (or a Soviet) Union? Consequences of further economic integration in the Commonwealth of Independent States," *Business Horizons* 56 (2013): 411–420.
43 President of Russia, "BRIC Countries: Common Goals—Common Actions," Speech, 13 April 2010, http://archive.kremlin.ru/eng/text/speeches/2010/04/13/0911_type104017_225331.shtml; Cynthia Roberts, "Building the New World Order BRIC by BRIC," *The European Financial Review* (February–March 2011); Juan Luis Suarez de Vivero and Juan C. Rodriguez Mateos, "Ocean governance in a competitive world. The BRIC countries as emerging maritime powers—building new geopolitical scenarios," *Marine Policy* 34 (2010): 967–978.
44 Lorenzo Fioramonti, *The BRICS of collapse? Why emerging economies need a different development model*, Open Democracy, www.opendemocracy.net/lorenzo-fioramonti/brics-of-collapse-why-emerging-economies-need-different-development-model.
45 Ruchir Sharma, "The Ever-Emerging Markets: Why Economic Forecasts Fail," *Foreign Affairs*, www.foreignaffairs.com/articles/140342/ruchir-sharma/the-ever-emerging-markets; Erich Follath and Martin Hesse, "Troubled Times: Developing Economies Hit a BRICS Wall," *Der Spiegel*, www.spiegel.de/international/world/economy-slows-in-brics-countries-as-worries-mount-a-951453.html.
46 Ibid.; Sebastien Hervieu, "South Africa gains entry to Bric club," *Guardian Weekly*, 2011, www.theguardian.com/world/2011/apr/19/south-africa-joins-bric-club; Tsygankov, "What is Russia to us?"
47 Aglaya Snetkov and Stephen Aris, "Russia and the Narrative of BRIC," *Russian Analytical Digest* 91, (2011).
48 David Kerr, "Central Asian and Russian perspectives on China's strategic emergence," *International Affairs* 86, no. 1 (2010): 127–152; Suarez de Vivero and Rodriguez Mateos, "Ocean governance in a competitive world."
49 President of Russia, "BRIC Countries: Common Goals—Common Actions," Speech, 13 April 2010; Roberts, *Building the New World Order BRIC by BRIC*.

50 Daria Korsunskaya, Lidia Kelly, and Larry King, "BRICS to set up their bank within five years, progress slow—Russia," *Reuters*, http://in.reuters.com/article/2014/02/25/russia-brics-banks-idINDEEA1O0DK20140225.

51 Sergei Lavrov, *Press conference summarising the results of the activities of Russian diplomacy*, Russian Ministry of Foreign Affairs, Moscow, 21 January 2014, www.mid.ru/BDOMP/Brp_4.nsf/arh/9ECCD0C0F39435F344257C6A003247B2?OpenDocument.

52 Ministry of Foreign Affairs, *Foreign Policy Concept*; Oskanian, *FPC Briefing: Putin's Eurasian Union—from pre-electoral sideshow to quest for empire?*

53 Suarez de Vivero and Rodriguez Mateos, "Ocean governance in a competitive world."

54 RIA Novosti, *UN Vote on Crimea Proves Russia is Not Isolated—Envoy Churkin*, http://en.ria.ru/world/20140327/188817012/UN-Vote-on-Crimea-Proves-Russia-is-Not-Isolated—Envoy-Churkin.html.

55 Davydov, "The Role of BRIC in the reconstruction of the international order."

56 "Russia, China to closer coordinate foreign policy steps within UN, BRICS, APEC," *Voice of Russia*, http://voiceofrussia.com/news/2014_05_20/Russia-China-to-closer-coordinate-foreign-policy-steps-within-UN-BRICS-APEC-4195/.

57 M. Skak, "The BRIC Powers as Actors in World Affairs. Soft Balancing or … ?" paper presented to *IPSA-ECPR Joint Conference hosted by the Brazilian Political Science Association Whatever happened to North-South?*, University of Sao Paulo February, (2011).

58 Maite Nkoana-Mashabane, *Chairperson's Statement on the BRICS Foreign Ministers Meeting held on 24 March 2014 in The Hague, Netherlands*, www.dfa.gov.za/docs/2014/brics0324.html.

59 BRICS5, *South Africa in BRICS*, BRICS 2013—Fifth BRICS Summit, www.brics5.co.za/about-brics/south-africa-in-brics/.

60 Roberts, *Building the New World Order BRIC by BRIC*.

61 Derek Averre, "'Sovereign Democracy' and Russia's Relations with the European Union," *Demokratizatsiya* 15, no. 2 (2007): 173–180.

62 Eli Keene, *Growing the Eurasian Customs Union within the WTO*, http://carnegieendowment.org/2013/05/30/growing-eurasian-customs-union-within-wto/g7ee.

63 Ibid.

64 G. Lomsadze, *Customs Union: Armenia Makes Demands While the Sun Shines*, Eurasianet, www.eurasianet.org/node/68083.

65 J. Kostenko, *Kyrgyz government hopes to receive $400 mln for border equipment from CU partners*, www.eng.24.kg/parliament/170574-news24.html.

66 Arkady Moshes, "EU-Russia relations: unfortunate continuity," *European Issues*, Fondation Robert Schuman, 129, (2009).

67 Shumylo-Tapiola, *The Eurasian Customs Union*.

68 Iris Kempe and Hanna Smith, "A Decade of Partnership and Cooperation in Russia-EU relations," paper presented at *A Decade of Partnership and Cooperation Russia-EU relations: Perceptions, Perspectives and Progress—Possibilities for the Next Decade*, Helsinki (2006).

69 Fyodor Lukyanov, "Rethinking Security in 'Greater Europe,'" *Russia in Global Affairs* 3 (2009): 94–102.

70 Arkady Moshes, "Russia's European policy under Medvedev: how sustainable is a new compromise?" *International Affairs* 88, no. 1 (2012): 17–30.

71 A. Gabuev and V. Solov'ev, "SNG postavil pered paktom," in *Kommersant*, 2007, www.kommersant.ru/doc/812422.

72 Chandra, "Strategic Triangle among Russia, China and India: Challenges and Prospects."

73 Kerr, "Central Asian and Russian perspectives on China's strategic emergence."

74 Stephen Aris, "The Shanghai Cooperation Organisation: 'Tackling the Three Evils'. A Regional Response to Non-traditional Security Challenges or an Anti-Western Bloc?" *Europe-Asia Studies* 61, no. 3, (2009).

75 Ibid.; Stephen Aris, "The Response of the Shanghai Cooperation Organisation to the Crisis in Kyrgyzstan," *Civil Wars* 14, no. 3 (2012).

76 Teemu Naarajärvi, "China, Russia and the Shanghai Cooperation Organisation: blessing or curse for new regionalism in Central Asia?" *Asia Europe Journal* 10, nos. 2–3 (2012).

77 Tsygankov, "What is Russia to us?"; Susan Turner, "China and Russia After the Russian-Georgian War," *Comparative Strategy* 30, no. 1 (2011): 50–59.

78 "Russia thanks China for its understanding of Moscow's steps in regard to Ukraine situation," *Voice of Russia*, http://voiceofrussia.com/news/2014_04_01/Shoigu-thanks-China-for-its-understanding-of-Russias-steps-in-regard-to-Ukraine-situation-1366/; "China and Russia sign 'historic' gas deal," *EurActiv*, www.euractiv.com/sections/energy/china-and-russia-sign-historic-gas-deal-302295.

79 Ruslan Maksutov, "The Shanghai Cooperation Organization: A Central Asian Perspective" *Sipri Project Paper*, http://archives.sipri.org/contents/worldsec/Ruslan.SCO.pdf; Aris, "Tackling the Three Evils."

80 Ibid.

81 Kerr, "Central Asian and Russian perspectives on China's strategic emergence."

82 Maksutov, "The Shanghai Cooperation Organization: A Central Asian Perspective."

83 Aris, "Tackling the Three Evils."

84 Zachary Keck, "Turkey Renews Plea to Join Shanghai Cooperation Organization," *The Diplomat*, http://thediplomat.com/2013/12/turkey-renews-plea-to-join-shanghai-cooperation-organization/; Sanjay Kumar, "India: Drawn to the Shanghai Cooperation Organization," *The Diplomat*, http://thediplomat.com/2014/02/india-drawn-to-the-shanghai-cooperation-organization/.

10 Conclusion

Jamie Gaskarth

Although change is everywhere in world politics, what is fascinating about the phenomena of globalization and rising powers is that we are seeing potentially game-changing transformations occurring in just a few decades. The emergence of states such as China, Brazil, and India to become significant global economic and political actors is forcing policy-makers and theorists to rethink their assumptions about how global governance should operate. In this conclusion, I intend to highlight some key conceptual problems that are exposed in the previous chapters. In particular, the understanding of power, the exercise of authority, the distributive justice of the international system, the management of change, and the underlying ethos of governance are important ethical dilemmas that have arisen in the preceding discussions and need to be addressed. There are no permanent resolutions to these problems. Indeed, they are recognizable in political philosophy debates across recorded human history. However, each generation needs to consider them anew and attempt to reconcile them with the particular circumstances with which they are faced.

The definition of power that Yale Ferguson cites in his chapter, "A has power over B with respect to issue C under specified conditions D" sees power in affective terms and in a bilateral relationship. The difficulty of understanding power when it comes to global governance (as Ferguson acknowledges) is that there are multilevel games occurring, with configurations of actors forming and dispersing. Rather than A trying to get B to do something, it will often be A, N, R, and Q trying to persuade B, G, F, and Z to sign up to a particular commitment or refrain from a course of action. R and Q may suggest a compromise that A grudgingly accepts to move on to issue H which is more pressing. So who has exercised power? A, who forced the issue but failed to get their preferred result? R and Q, who drafted the compromise but who relied on the assent of the other powers to see it through? Or B, G, F, and Z, who resisted A's pressure and forced concessions?

Seeing power in relational terms has the benefit of clarity but tends to ignore what Steven Lukes once described as the third dimension of power,[1] which is the ability to shape other actors' wants and the wider milieu of politics. The United States may not win all, or even an expected average number of its disputes in forums such as the WTO;[2] however, having a regime in place that supports free trade and the liberalization of markets is clearly in the United States' interests and is a means for the United States to spread its ideology across global markets. In a complex policy environment, it may be difficult to identify when a particular actor has achieved a result such that it can be seen as having exercised power in a positive fashion. Indeed, the above scenario, in which A's influence attempt is thwarted, is a reminder that power can also be manifest in states' capacity to resist the influence attempts of others. One of the important facets of the rising powers discussion is that we are now seeing an increased number of potential veto actors, and veto coalitions, who could inhibit global governance initiatives.

While they have the potential to block global governance mechanisms, these powers will also be vital to their success. As Louise Fawcett's chapter demonstrates, regional and global governance forums are heavily reliant on certain states being willing to adopt leadership roles and bear the costs of setting up and maintaining institutions. The conscious attempts by rising powers to resist the burdens of responsibility by framing themselves as "developing states," noted in the chapters by Holden, and Davies and Taylor, undermines their own ability to influence outcomes. It also impedes the growth and effectiveness of global governance in areas that demand greater coordinated action, such as climate change.

Even if they were willing to assume responsibility, they in turn are reliant on other states, international organizations and civil society actors to recognize their legitimacy in doing so. Thus, it is also important not to forget the significance of lesser powers to the maintenance of governance institutions. Biersteker and Moret provide a detailed treatment of "pivotal powers" when it comes to non-proliferation and ably expose how they have both supported and challenged aspects of this regime according to their own norms and interests. States such as India, Brazil, and Turkey have questioned the unequal basis of the NPT regime and in the process threatened the legitimacy of acknowledged nuclear weapons states to restrict the supply of nuclear materials to other actors. Without authority, states struggle to provide leadership and achieve the necessary consent from other actors to maintain systems of governance. In short, global governance implies a more diffuse understanding of power in which multiple actors may have an impact, however limited, on political outcomes.

Global governance institutions are in a sense continually confronted with dilemmas about authority and legitimacy in world politics. Powerful states need to practice leadership and exert influence to create and maintain the institutions and organizations of global governance. Yet a primary reason for them to do so may be their very lack of power over an issue. Engaging in cooperative arrangements with other states and civil society actors can confer a greater degree of legitimacy over the agreed actions. However, these configurations of power may enshrine inequalities. Furthermore, as governance becomes broader and more global, it often moves further away from direct mechanisms of accountability, such as elections, and the ordinary people it is supposed to serve. The dangers of cartelism and policy-making devised and implemented by elites for elites become apparent.

The very complexity of a globalized policy world also arguably creates strains on the legitimacy of global governance. The rapid changes and complex interactions of our political and social lives outstrip the capacity of bureaucracies to respond. If Putin and Medvedev have failed to impose their "vertical of power" in authoritarian Russia, what chance do the looser mechanisms of global governance have of steering behavior in a timely and efficient manner? The desirability of enforced governance has been starkly brought into question with the failed interventions in Libya, Iraq, and Afghanistan in the last decade, which continue to experience high levels of insecurity. The governance failures before and after each intervention are a reminder of the extent to which current arrangements for providing international security are dysfunctional. It is easy to be wise after the fact and point out errors of judgment and planning in each case, (and there were many) but a more pessimistic interpretation might see these outcomes as inevitable; the result of the disconnection between the need to govern and the inability of any of the major actors in world politics to do so effectively. Policymakers are therefore caught in a legitimacy paradox: if they enforce solutions, they risk losing consent and thereby legitimacy. But if they do not act quickly enough, they may be ineffective and so the same result pertains. The contrasting responses to Iraq in 2003 and Syria in 2011–13 are illustrative cases.

In addition to these functional problems, global governance faces justifiable criticism because of its failure to seriously address global inequalities. The rising powers, especially the BRICS, are doing very little to address distributive justice issues in their own communities. While globalization may have expanded the global middle class and enriched elites, global governance faces a serious legitimacy deficit because of its abject performance when it comes to extending the benefits of growth to the wider citizenry. Although the number of people living on less than $1.25 per day has decreased, from "half the citizens in the developing world in 1981 to 21 percent in 2010," this still leaves some 1.2 billion people living in extreme poverty.[3] Seeing markets in national terms encourages states to compete for investment by lowering taxation and keeping wages and welfare standards low. Until governments work together to close down tax havens, agree common regulatory standards, and encourage their citizens to behave responsibly when it comes to energy use, these inequalities will continue. Furthermore, the focus of redistribution has tended to be on aid—albeit with differences of emphasis between developed states and rising powers. Governments and individuals need to be more creative about forging greater interaction between peoples across the globe, perhaps by encouraging remittances to be transferred beyond family and kinship networks.

Other difficulties arise with the immediacy of governance challenges. To respond in a timely fashion to emerging problems, governance arrangements may need to form and disperse in short periods of time. However, this could mean they do not have the time to build the requisite legitimacy and authority to gain consent to carry out their intended functions. Moreover, in this scenario, powerful elites are far more likely to be able to advocate policy in their interests than the wider populace. As such, change can be an impediment to achieving distributive justice, and legitimacy, as well as a means to secure them.

The management of change and the adaptability of existing institutions has been an important theme of a number of the chapters in this volume. Underlying these debates are questions over what changes should be advanced and which resisted as configurations of national power and social attitudes shift. How far should global governance forums be insisting on norm convergence over good governance principles like individual rights or social justice? If IOs reach out to authoritarian governments or ones that fail to support liberal values and democracy abroad, will they end up bringing about changes to their own ethics? In other words, rather than rising powers being socialized into the liberal order, will they end up changing that order to fit their own attitudes? Edmund Burke famously noted that "A state without the means of some change is without the means of its conservation."[4] The challenge highlighted by Weiss and Wilkinson is in seeking change that supports rather than undermines basic liberal values. A move away from individual rights might lead to a greater emphasis on economic inequality, something that has been neglected in the liberal order. Yet, it is not clear that a focus on collective rights is likely to lead to improvements in this area. Too often the latter are used as a cover to avoid interference in governance arrangements that serve the interests of elites.

This leads us to analyze the fundamental ethics of global governance. The emergence of rising powers, some of which have authoritarian governments, compels theorists to look again at the institutions of global governance and consider how far they are predicated on liberal norms and values. It is an important question as it goes to the heart of how sustainable they are in the long run. If these arrangements were either not founded on explicitly liberal principles, or are not reliant upon them and so can still continue to function with the help of non-liberal states, then there is no problem. But, if the current system of global governance was founded on liberal principles, and requires liberal beliefs among its participants to flourish, this presents greater difficulties. On a political level, governing norms such as sovereignty and non-intervention are not inherently liberal. In the nineteenth century, British policy-makers used them to justify both not supporting liberal revolutions on the continent and not opposing authoritarian counter-revolutionary forces. Their aristocratic European counterparts could see their use in preserving the old order and so gave them qualified support also. Similarly, master institutions of international society identified by Barry Buzan, such as diplomacy, territoriality, and the balance of power, predated the emergence of liberal political philosophy and so cannot require liberal ethics to function.[5]

Three areas that might arguably be predicated on liberal principles are multilateral institutions, open markets, and human rights. G. John Ikenberry sees the first two as distinctive of the current order and traces their emergence to different phases of liberal influence after each of the two World Wars.[6] The growth in international organizations and institutions after the First World War is associated with liberal faith in cooperation, rules, and international law to assuage tensions between states. Certainly, prominent liberal statespeople like Woodrow Wilson had a hand in lending rhetorical support to these developments. However, socialist and communist countries also promoted collective governance arrangements in the past, such as the Comintern, and so this does not seem to be an exclusively liberal activity. This is arguably borne out by the enthusiasm for collective security mechanisms and economic cooperation in the SCO and ECU among authoritarian governments in central Asia, as highlighted by P.N. Chatterje-Doody in her chapter.

Open markets are perhaps founded on liberal philosophical ideas about freedom, the moral worth of allowing individuals to profit from their own initiative and hard work, as well as the efficiencies and improvements that are seen to derive from a competitive ethos. The current WTO system is derived from the GATT regime set up after the Second World War as part of a series of economic measures to promote the United States' domestic liberal ideals. The difficulty for authoritarian governments is that liberalizing their markets means losing control over important coercive tools such as taxation, regulation, and market access. The tendency will be to liberalize only partially, allowing the government the power of patronage and limiting the number of potential challengers to the leadership—as occurred in Russia during the Yeltsin era and, arguably, in China in recent years. Alternatively, liberals and constructivists might see the likelihood of socialization to liberal norms among emerging elites. Thus, rather than leading to conflict, the merging of authoritarian governments into the liberal market system will simply result in assimilation.

More problematic is the norm of human rights. If the political and economic realms are not reliant on a liberal ethos, the legal-political sphere of individual rights, on which are predicated a number of important aspects of global governance, most definitely is. The liberal belief in the dignity of the human person was an important motivator of campaigns to regulate the conduct of war, via governance mechanisms such as the Geneva and Hague Conventions. Belief in individual rights and responsibilities is integral to the international criminal justice regime, which includes (but is not confined to) the International Criminal Court. The responsibility to protect doctrine emphasizes a government's duties to its citizens—an inherently liberal outlook, seeing government as the servant of the people rather than the obverse view common to authoritarian and monarchical societies. Nevertheless, an obvious rejoinder to the idea that such beliefs are integral to global governance per se is evident in the abysmal record liberal states have in upholding their own ideals. The United Kingdom violated human rights on a mass scale as it wound down its empire in places like Malaya, Kenya, and the Gulf. The United States at least since 2001 has engaged in a systematic attempt to circumvent the prohibition against torture as well as basic liberal principles such as habeas corpus and protection of prisoners of war via its rendition policy.

Yet, for all the negative behavior of developed states in recent years, their transgressions have been identified and vilified by a thriving civil society. By drawing attention to the human rights abuses of powerful states, NGOs and other civil society actors have ensured that these states have had to pay a political cost in legitimacy and authority for their actions. This is, in itself, an important corrective mechanism to attempts to subvert the ethics of global governance. It must therefore be a concern that a number of rising powers, especially Russia and China, but also Turkey and Egypt, have restricted the flourishing of domestic civil society groups pursuing liberal human rights norms. Civil society actors are important to global governance as they challenge prevailing assumptions, offer solutions and keep governments honest when it comes to upholding shared norms of governance. As Holden points out, unless they foster such actors in their own domestic societies, the rising powers will never be able to contribute to global public goods as effectively as their more open liberal counterparts.

That said, Jones and Breslin's chapter is a reminder that the rising powers may be more fragmented in their domestic governance arrangements, and more open to contestation over ideas and roles, than the often monolithic fashion in which they are represented in rising powers debates. China's elites may be nationalistic, but there is evidence that they seek a gradual process of greater openness and a more pluralistic society. Russia's elites too are unlikely to desire a return to Cold War forms of isolation.

In sum, while many of the predictions about rising powers' current and future economic performance, political clout, and normative influence have been exaggerated, the debate has provoked useful reflection on big questions, including: what does power mean in a globalized world? How can authority be exercised legitimately? How does change occur, and how is it managed, in international society? What is the ethical basis of global governance? How should the world be ordered? How can global actors manage normative differences without conflict? The chapters in this volume provide theoretical and practical responses to many of these while recognizing that the answers are never complete; they can only form part of a larger dialectic between theory and practice, and between the multitude of actors that go to make up global governance.

Notes

1 Steven Lukes, *Power: A Radical View*, 2nd edn (Basingstoke: Palgrave, 2004).
2 Bernard Hoekman, Henrik Horn, and Petros C. Mavroidis, *Winners and Losers in the Panel Stage of the WTO Dispute*, July 2008, www.econ-law.se/Papers/Hudec%20HHM%20July%2031%2008%20final.pdf.
3 World Bank, "Remarkable Declines in Global Poverty, But Major Challenges Remain," Press release, 17 April 2013, www.worldbank.org/en/news/press-release/2013/04/17/remarkable-declines-in-global-poverty-but-major-challenges-remain.
4 Edmund Burke, *Reflections on the Revolution in France*, J.G.A. Pocock, ed. (Cambridge: Hackett Publishing Company, 1987), 19.

5 Barry Buzan, *From International to World Society?: English School Theory and the Social Structure of Globalisation* (Cambridge: Cambridge University Press, 2004), 184.
6 G. John Ikenberry, "The Liberal International Order and its Discontents," *Millennium* 38, no. 3 (2010): 512.

Index

Routledge Global Institutions Series

6 Global Environmental Institutions (2006)
by Elizabeth R. DeSombre (Wellesley College)

5 Internal Displacement (2006)
Conceptualization and its consequences
by Thomas G. Weiss (The CUNY Graduate Center) and
David A. Korn

4 The UN General Assembly (2005)
by M. J. Peterson (University of Massachusetts, Amherst)

3 United Nations Global Conferences (2005)
by Michael G. Schechter (Michigan State University)

2 The UN Secretary-General and Secretariat (2005)
by Leon Gordenker (Princeton University)

1 The United Nations and Human Rights (2005)
A guide for a new era
by Julie A. Mertus (American University)

Books currently under contract include:

The Regional Development Banks
Lending with a regional flavor
by Jonathan R. Strand (University of Nevada)

Millennium Development Goals (MDGs)
For a people-centered development agenda?
by Sakiko Fukada-Parr (The New School)

The Bank for International Settlements
The politics of global financial supervision in the
age of high finance
by Kevin Ozgercin (SUNY College at Old Westbury)

International Migration
by Khalid Koser (Geneva Centre for Security Policy)

Human Development
by Richard Ponzio

The United Nations as a Knowledge Organization
by Nanette Svenson (Tulane University)

The International Criminal Court
The Politics and practice of prosecuting atrocity crimes
by Martin Mennecke (University of Copenhagen)

The Politics of International Organizations
Views from insiders
edited by Patrick Weller (Griffith University) and
Xu Yi-chong (Griffith University)

The African Union (2nd edition)
Challenges of globalization, security, and governance
by Samuel M. Makinda (Murdoch University),
F. Wafula Okumu (African Union), and
David Mickler (University of Western Australia)

BRICS
by João Pontes Nogueira (Catholic University, Rio de Janeiro) and
Monica Herz (Catholic University, Rio de Janeiro)

Expert Knowledge in Global Trade
edited by Erin Hannah (University of Western Ontario),
James Scott (University of Manchester), and
Silke Trommer (Murdoch University)

The European Union (2nd edition)
Clive Archer (Manchester Metropolitan University)

Governing Climate Change (2nd edition)
Peter Newell (University of East Anglia) and
Harriet A. Bulkeley (Durham University)

Contemporary Human Rights Ideas (2nd edition)
Bertrand Ramcharan (Geneva Graduate Institute of
International and Development Studies)

Protecting the Internally Displaced
Rhetoric and reality
Phil Orchard (University of Queensland)

The Arctic Council
Within the far north
Douglas C. Nord (Umea University)

For further information regarding the series, please contact:

Nicola Parkin, Editor, Politics & International Studies
Taylor & Francis
2 Park Square, Milton Park, Abingdon
Oxford OX14 4RN, UK
Nicola.parkin@tandf.co.uk
www.routledge.com